Foundations of Social Inquiry
Scott McNall and Charles Tilly
Series Editors

Criminological Controversies: A Methodological Primer
John Hagan, A. R. Gillis, and David Brownfield

Immigration in America's Future
David M. Heer

What Does Your Wife Do? Gender and the Transformation of Family Life
Leonard Beeghley

FORTHCOMING IN 1996

Social Change
Thomas D. Hall, Darrell La Lone, and Stephen K. Sanderson

Sexual Politics
Sheila Tobias

Contact Westview Press for information about additional upcoming titles.

Criminological Controversies

A Methodological Primer

John Hagan
University of North Carolina at Chapel Hill
University of Toronto

A. R. Gillis
University of Toronto

David Brownfield
University of Toronto

 WestviewPress
A Division of HarperCollins*Publishers*

Foundations of Social Inquiry

Published in 1996 in the United States of America by Westview Press, Inc., 5500 Central Avenue, Boulder, Colorado 80301-2877, and in the United Kingdom by Westview Press, 12 Hid's Copse Road, Cumnor Hill, Oxford OX2 9JJ

Library of Congress Cataloging-inPublication Data

Hagan, John, 1946–
    Criminological controversies : a methodical primer / John Hagan, A. R. Gillis, David Brownfield.
        p.   cm — (Foundations of Social Inquiry)
        Includes bibliographical references and index.
        ISBN 0–8133–1083–0 (alk. paper). — ISBN 0–8133–1084–9 (pbk.)
        1. Criminology. 2. Crime—Sociological aspects. I. Gillis, A. R.   II. Brownfield,
        David.   III. Title.   IV. Series: Foundations of Social Inquiry
HV6025.H269   1994
364—dc20   96–1110
                                                                                       CIP

10   9   8   7   6   5   4   3   2   1

"When the dung beetle moves," Hosteen Nashibitti had told him, "know that something has moved it. And know that its movement affects the flight of the sparrow, and that the raven deflects the eagle from the sky, and that the eagle's stiff wing bends the will of the Wind People, and know that all of this affects you and me, and the flea on the prairie dog and the leaf on the cottonwood." That had always been the point of the lesson. Interdependency of nature. Every cause has its effect. Every action its reaction. A reason for everything. In all things a pattern, and in this pattern, the beauty of harmony. Thus one learned to live with evil, by understanding it, by reading its cause. And thus one learned, gradually and methodically, if one was lucky, to always "go in beauty," to always look for the pattern, and to find it.

—Tony Hillerman, *Dance Hall of the Dead*

Contents

Tables and Illustrations

Tables

Figures

Prologue: The Fact of the Matter . . .

It is easy to feel besieged by crime, if only because we hear so much about it. It is an interesting exercise to simply observe how much news about crime we see on television, hear on the radio, and read in newspapers and magazines. Of course, reports about street crime are prominent. Local news stories feature reports of drug busts, assaults and murders, arson, as well as burglaries and robberies. Meanwhile, new kinds of street crime also proliferate and captivate national attention. Car jackings, drive-by shootings, stalkings, and home invasions compete with more familiar types of crime. In addition, crime penetrates areas of life that we would like to believe are immune to it. Insider trading infests our stock markets, health-care fraud infects our hospitals, violence intrudes into our schools, illegal recruiting invades our amateur sports, sexual abuse infiltrates religious institutions, and corruption may be an integral part of our politics. So much around us seems so full of criminal implications.

The impact of crime on society has caused controversy, and criminology is increasingly a part of the public debate. Since science at large often has proven so useful in solving serious problems, it seems reasonable to expect that a science of crime should better inform us about, if not solve, our crime problems. Criminology, the scientific study of crime, often seeks to do so, although the progress is painfully slow. Developing insights takes time, especially when empirical accuracy is a necessity. The first steps of this infant science have largely involved adding rigor and perspective to our understanding of crime. For example, we have begun by simply gaining some sense of what crime is and how much there is of it. Even these very basic questions bring controversy.

Thus, it has taken criminologists a considerable amount of time to establish the point that there is much more to crime than the acts of force and predation that occur on our streets. The famous criminologist Edwin Sutherland (1949) devoted much of his career to convincing his peers and the public that many of the sharp and unethical practices of businessmen were indeed criminal. Sutherland coined the term white-collar crime and helped to make it a part of our everyday vocabulary. To do so, Sutherland sought to convince his peers and the public that many of our large corporations and their executives participated in activities

that caused great social injury, that made these corporations or executives liable to legal punishment, and that these persons and organizations could, therefore, be thought of as criminal. That we now take this
once controversial assertion for granted is a major accomplishment of
an emerging science of crime. Today's controversies of white-collar
crime are more likely to involve questions of how wide and how deep are
the involvements of multinational corporations in corporate and white-
collar crime.

Yet white-collar crime is only one kind of "hidden crime" that criminologists have made the subject of controversy and public concern.
From the outset, those who would make a science of crime their goal
have noted that our official counts of crime are only the tip of a figura-
tive iceberg that constitutes the larger and unknown universe of crime.
After first helping to insist that police and courts unify and routinize
their official counts into Uniform Crime Reports, criminologists encouraged governments to invest resources in conducting surveys of victims
of crime (Biderman, 1967). Called victimization surveys, these studies
sought out first-hand citizen accounts of how often, in what ways, and
by whom the public had been victimized. The results revealed a large
number of crimes that were unreported and unrecorded in official crime
statistics. For example, these studies demonstrated that much spousal
and nonspousal abuse, assault and rape went unreported and unrecorded. These enumerations, although sometimes disputed, are now
more often conceded and are increasingly a basis for reassessing the
effects of crime deterrence and prevention efforts. The controversies
today are more likely to focus on how far victim surveys can be taken in
exposing problems like "date rape" among high school and college students, or childhood physical and sexual abuse by siblings and parents.

As we gain a better idea of how much crime there is we are in a better position to gauge how well-informed the public is in its perception of
crime problems. Crime research directed at this issue increasingly indicates that the public overestimates how much violent crime there is,
especially in proportion to property and public order crime involving
alcohol and drugs. Although America's crime problems are violent and
often disproportionate to those of other Western nations, the public
characteristically overestimates in absolute and relative terms how high
their personal risks of violent victimization are (Warr, 1991). Furthermore, some parts of the public that think of themselves as most at
risk, especially the elderly, are often less at risk than others. The media
often intensifies such fears. Telling those who are most fearful that they
are less at risk than they believe is a thankless and, therefore, potentially
controversial task. Yet, taking on this task may be an important part of
dissuading Americans from abandoning their streets and cities and
arming themselves for self-protection in ways that are more dangerous

than effective. Helping the public to reassess their impressions of criminal risk, both in amount and in kind, may also be an important part of tempering the public appetite for severe forms of punishment, including the use of imprisonment and the death penalty.

Probably the least appreciated contribution of criminologists in this century has involved the use of court and prison data on the punishment of offenders to document discrimination against African Americans in the use of imprisonment and the death penalty. The extent of this racial discrimination in the use of imprisonment is a continuing source of controversy (e.g., Zatz, 1987; Wilbanks, 1987), but there is substantial consensus in the research literature that the death penalty continues to be used in a discriminatory fashion to sentence to death black offenders convicted of crimes of violence against whites. The U.S. Supreme Court has essentially taken the position that no amount of research evidence on this issue will alter its view about the constitutionality of the death penalty (Ellsworth, 1988). The importance of this controversy is witnessed by the mounting use of capital punishment as well as imprisonment in America and the extent to which this punishment is imposed on African Americans.

So criminological controversies abound in number and importance. Progress is being made in developing evidence on a growing number of these issues. As the evidence builds, the shape of a science of crime is emerging. Still, the progress is small compared to the task at hand and especially compared to the controversies that surround some of the most basic research questions.

The result is that some of our basic questions about crime remain without clear answers and surrounded by controversy. Several of these controversies are addressed in this book, both as a means of developing answers and of contributing to the resolution of disputes and as a means of introducing and explaining basic methods of a social science of crime that can be applied more generally.

For example, in the first chapter of this book, John Hagan addresses the question of whether social class is related to crime. To some it may seem obvious that the poor would commit more criminal acts than the rich, if only because poor people are more deprived or desperate. Yet this issue is far from resolved among criminologists. This lack of resolution is partly because a long tradition of asking junior and senior high school students to self-report their delinquencies in anonymous surveys has shown uncertain evidence that parental social and economic position is related to youthful indiscretion. We explore the possibilities and pitfalls of this and other kinds of research on class and crime.

In the next chapter of this book Hagan seeks an answer to the question of why males seem so often and so much more criminal than females. Although many may believe that such sex differences are inborn, others have argued that the disparities can be explained by social structures and processes that are a part of the socialization of gender roles. Ultimately, this argument can take the form that patriarchal family structures create differences of gender that are expressed in differential involvement in delinquency and crime. Methods of exploring and testing this causal theory of gender and crime are presented in the second chapter.

Next we consider the connection between cities and crime. The American experience with the growth of cities in this century creates the impression that cities cause crime. Early sociologists at the University of Chicago, such as Louis Wirth (1938), added logic to this perception that cities cause crime. Yet there are also reasons to doubt that this is always and everywhere, or even usually, the case. In the third chapter of this book A. R. Gillis takes this issue into an entirely different context by considering the development of cities in France during the nineteenth century. The result is a much broader view of how we should study connections between cities and crime.

In the fourth chapter of this book Gillis turns to issues of policing and crime and seeks answers to questions about how and when police might increase, as well as deter, crime. Too often in the United States we simply assume that more police will automatically mean less crime. Little attention is given to which kinds of crime might be affected, when crime might be affected, and in what ways crime might be affected. By looking at crime in a much different time and place, during the period of modernization and urbanization in France, we can begin to see different possibilities that lead to increases as well as decreases in crime.

David Brownfield introduces the possibilities and problems associated with a particular explanation of crime known as subcultural theory in Chapter 5. This theory has often been associated with richly detailed descriptions of crime as it occurs within groups. However, a good description of a phenomenon is not always a very large or useful step toward explaining a phenomenon. The challenge is to extract from such accounts what is most promising for increasing our ability to explain group-linked involvements in crime. The meanings and methods of this extraction are introduced in Chapter 5.

In the last chapter in this book Brownfield examines connections between drugs and crime. The controversy is whether one is a cause of the other or whether both are simply parts of a whole that itself must be explained. There are good and plausible reasons for either believing that drugs make individuals criminal or, alternatively, believing that drug use and crime are more or less interchangeable parts of a criminal way of life. What is required is a method to distinguish between these possibilities, and Chapter 6 provides such a methodology, which can have broad application in resolving this and related issues.

In exploring these topics we introduce a variety of methods that criminologists use to study crime. However, since this is a small book, it must be partial in its coverage and selective in its emphasis. In the first chapter we draw heavily on qualitative observation and interview data from recent ethnographic field studies to introduce some of the key ideas of causal analysis. In following chapters, we further explore the logic and methods used in quantitative studies of crime. In particular, we focus on the use of quantitative methods to reach judgments about the causes and consequences of crime.

It is important to note that our focus on the logic and methods of quantitative research is itself controversial and is rejected by some criminologists. As our initial discussion of ethnographic work in Chapter 1 suggests, qualitative research often uses the same logic and reasoning as quantitative work and encounters similar problems of measurement; however, some scholars reject the attempt at numerical precision involved in quantitative studies. These scholars argue that it is not possible to define in exact terms what crime is, much less count and classify forms of crime for the purposes of studying its causes and consequences. For example, Matza (1969:11) writes that in attempts to precisely define crime, "the clear-cut yes or no will be gained only by suppressing and thus denying, the patent ambiguity of this novel phenomenon and the easily observable tentative, vacillating, and shifty responses to it." Matza's view is that the meanings of crime are too many (e.g., across state and national boundaries), too changeable (e.g., across time), and, therefore, too uncertain (e.g. across decision-makers) to allow precise definition for purposes of quantitative study.

Furthermore, it is sometimes argued that attempts at quantitative reasoning about crime impose a false sense of objectivity on a subjective and value-laden topic. The authors of *The New Criminology* assert, "For human behaviour to be studied scientifically it must be akin to the non-human world, it must be deterministically dominated by law-like regulations, it must be reified—have the quality of 'things'" (Taylor, Walton, and Young, 1973:23). Their view is that the human behavior involved in crime is too subjectively motivated and judged to allow objective study within the scientific tradition.

We disagree with that view. Like Durkheim, we believe that both attitudes and beliefs exist as social facts and are, therefore, detectible. All social scientists, and everyone else who uses language to refer to the empirical world, eventually get caught up in measurement, regardless of their attention to qualitative or quantitative sources of evidence. Measurement links ideas or concepts (such as "chair" and "comfort") to sets of concrete, observable indicators (the object you are sitting on, to level of satisfaction with it). This linking of ideas to observable indicators enables us to classify parts of the world as falling more or less inside

xviii / Prologue

or outside the categories represented by concepts. We are constantly involved in linking concepts with indicators, whether we begin at the observed empirical level and try to construct an idea to organize and describe the world that we see (an inductive approach) or whether we develop an idea (logically or intuitively) and then try to find concrete examples (a deductive approach) in the world we observe. We can be implicit or explicit, successful or unsuccessful, but ultimately we are all methodologists, busily engaged in linking concepts to measurable indicators, whether for purposes as mundane as managing our everyday physical environment or as consequential as creating a social life.

In contrast to Taylor, Walton, and Young (1973), then, our position is that problems of definition and measurement are surmountable and often even comparable in nature and difficulty, whether they confront a natural scientist searching for a new type of subatomic particle or a social scientist trying to locate and study new types of social groups, such as gangs. All are trying to link ideas to phenomena that they expect are "out there," and they are assisted in doing so by the use of logic. This linking of ideas to phenomena is not always easy or even possible, since some phenomena may not be discernible without specific devices (ever seen a subatomic particle?), and some concepts may not exist empirically (seen any unicorns lately?). Like microscopes and telescopes, some quantitative techniques help us to observe general patterns that are invisible to the naked eye. This information may or may not be consistent with unaided observation or personal experience. When such divergence of information occurs, it is tempting to commit to one approach and dismiss the other entirely. However, both qualitative and quantitative techniques tell us something, and when they produce conflicting results, further investigation is more than warranted—it is imperative.

Of course, it may often be easier to pick sides, declare oneself a humanistic or scientific criminologist, and to attack one's opponents. It is also possible, and perhaps easiest, to ignore social facts entirely. Then one can develop ideologically expedient arguments that are unconstrained by evidence and protect one's position by pointing to the imperfection of measurement. Yet knowledge is seldom, if ever, increased in this way.

Making these points does not mean, however, that the questions raised by the opponents of scientific criminology are useless. Their concerns often point to imperfections that should be taken seriously in collecting, analyzing, and interpreting data. Methodological imperfection is genuine and continues to make the scientific study of crime a challenge, though far from impossible. Numerical logic and systematic methods simply help more than they hinder our understanding of crime, inasmuch as they produce information that generates, evaluates, and moderates different arguments about crime. Quantitative logic and methods in the study of crime also force our definitions, measurements, and methods of inference to be explicit. The use of quantitative logic and methods not only requires us to be precise, it is an important step toward open debate and replication. Through replication we uncover unintentional error and scientific fraud, and the uncovering of error and fraud helps to keep most of us accurate and honest. For systematic measurement and quantitative techniques to be explicit, then, they must be understood.

Measurement involves an attempt to provide an accurate indicator or set of indicators that correspond to a concept. Ideal measurement occurs when variation on a conceptual level is accurately reflected by variation in indicators and when variation in indicators accurately signals change in the state of the phenomenon being estimated. For example, if you gain 5 or 10 pounds over your vacation, your bathroom scale should reflect this gain. If your scale fails to indicate an increase following such a binge, you may be personally satisfied; but if your scale lies, it will eventually be exposed by your tight clothing. Observations and comments of intimate friends and the fit of your clothes will give an alternative, less systematic estimate of your new-found flab. However, you also do not want a scale that indicates a weight gain that has not really occurred. Again, the fit of your clothing gives an independent check and will point to inconsistency. Logically, experience (eating and drinking), the fit of your clothing, and the change in the number shown on your scale should correspond. We look for correspondence. Divergence should be taken seriously, perhaps signaling stretched clothing, a broken scale, failing eyesight that blurs readings on bathroom scales, or even a physiological condition that prevents weight gain. This logic is behind the collection of victimization surveys that can be compared to police reports of crime.

Methodologists are obsessed with correspondence and divergence, not only between concepts and indicators and different indicators but between arguments and evidence as well. Hirschi and Selvin (1967:8) begin a classic exposition of the methods of a scientific criminology with the following methodological riddle:

> When it comes to reading the report of an empirical study, what is the difference between a layman, a researcher, and a methodologist? Answer: The layman reads the text and skips the tables; the researcher reads the tables and skips the text; and the methodologist does not care very much about either the tables or the text, as long as they agree with each other.

The truth of this riddle is that statistical tables, even the simple tables that increasingly fill our newspapers with the results of public opinion polls, are ignored by too many readers. Understanding the link between tables and text is the core of modern social science, even when the link is imperfectly formed. It is the basis of the claim that social science can inform and, it is to be hoped, guide us about crime and other topics. However, students sometimes take social science courses to avoid demands of quantitative methods, and they are sometimes encouraged to persist in social science careers by remonstrations against quantitative reasoning. In the end, we should all strive to become methodologically ambidextrous, insofar as we draw on and understand both quantitative and qualitative approaches.

This book is an invitation and an opportunity to pursue a path that promises substantial rewards. Paulos (1988) brings our argument to the level of simple self-interest when he warns of the costs of innumeracy in general and in the social sciences specifically. He notes that students often end up in lower-paying fields or jobs because they avoided a chemistry or an economics course with mathematics or statistics prerequisites. Paulos then suggests that too many bright students go into the humanities and some social sciences, seeking to avoid math and science courses whose tools could further enliven and enlighten the former fields. In the spirit that Paulos encourages, this book is an invitation to all students to explore a social science of crime that is both numerate and accessible.

If you take the time to patiently consider the logic outlined for the social scientific study of criminological controversies in this book, it can lift the curtain on a mode of thought that will not only improve your knowledge and understanding of an important set of public issues but also provide a crucial first step for those who want to contribute to this knowledge and understanding in a personally rewarding way. This book is about how to study crime, an exciting topic where the facts may be even more interesting than fiction.

1

The Class and Crime Controversy

John Hagan

At one time, there may have been consensus that adverse class conditions cause crime. If this was true once, it is true no more. Prominent criminologists now write of the "Myth of Social Class and Criminality" (Tittle et al., 1977) and ask, "What's Class Got to Do With It?" (Jensen and Thompson, 1990). The question of whether class causes crime is more complicated than it may at first seem, and simple answers are elusive. Nonetheless, we begin this book by attempting to clarify and answer this question. We begin this chapter by considering historical and ideological aspects of the class and crime controversy.

Class and Crime in Time

Riesman (1964) describes sociology as a "conversation between the classes." Although "conversations" linking class and crime predate both modern sociology and criminology, this metaphor usefully highlights the layers of meaning that often are communicated in discussions of class and crime. Popular discourse of earlier eras included frequent references to the "dangerous" and "criminal classes" and assumed that the poor and destitute were more criminal that those who were financially better off, while scholarly discourse today features discussions of an "underclass," which is assumed to prominently include criminals. The notion of an underclass has evoked much controversy.

Discussions of criminal or dangerous classes are traced by Silver (1967) to eighteenth- and nineteenth-century Paris and London (see also Gillis, 1989; Tombs, 1980; Ignatieff, 1978), and they were common as well in nineteenth- and twentieth-century Canada and the United States (Boritch and Hagan, 1987; Monkkonen, 1981). For example, Daniel Defoe (1730:10–11) wrote of eighteenth-century London, "The streets of the City are now the Places of Danger," while Charles Brace (1872:29) warned nearly a century and a half later in *The Dangerous Classes of New York*, "Let but law lift its hand from them for a season, or let the civilizing influences of American life fail to reach them, and, if the opportunity afforded, we should see an explosion from this class which might leave the city in ashes and blood."

As Silver (1967:4) makes clear, these discussions of the dangerous or criminal classes referred primarily to the unattached and unemployed and to their assumed propensity for crime.

Although historians continue to write about conceptions of the dangerous and criminal classes of earlier periods and different places, today the dangerous and criminal class concepts probably are heard infrequently because they were used in such an invidious and pejorative fashion. Both popular and scholarly discussions of contemporary affairs refer to the "underclass." Myrdal (1963) introduced discussion of the underclass to draw attention to persons driven to the margins of modern society by economic forces beyond their control. Marks (1991), however, has detailed a different direction in the contemporary development of the concept of the urban underclass, calling particular attention to the place of crime within that underclass. The current controversy surrounding the underclass conceptualization is partly that, like earlier discussions of the dangerous or criminal classes, it also can be used or interpreted in pejorative ways.

Marks (1991) noted that Auletta (1982:49) distinguished four distinct elements of the underclass: "hostile street and career criminals, skilled entrepreneurs of the underground economy, passive victims of government support and the severely traumatized," while Lemann (1986, 41) characterized this class in terms of "poverty, crime, poor education, dependency, and teenage out-of-wedlock childbearing." Often race is embedded in these characterizations, leading to debate about the extent to which the U.S. underclass is a black underclass. But what is most striking in these discussions is the extent to which the modern underclass, like its historical precedents described by Silver (1967), is defined by the association with crime of the unattached and unemployed. Marks (1991:454) asked, "Is . . . criminality the major ingredient of . . . underclass status?" Her concern was that "the underclass has been transformed from surplus and discarded labor into an exclusive group of black urban terrorists."

Declassifying Crime

There are both scientific and ideological reasons to carefully consider the modern linkage drawn between class and crime in the concept of the underclass. Gans (1990:272) argued that this new concept is itself "dangerous" because by focusing on crime and other non-normative behaviors in discussing the underclass, "researchers tend to assume that the behavior patterns they report are caused by norm violations on the part of area residents and not by the conditions under which they are living, or the behavioral choices open to them as a result of these conditions." Gans concluded that the effect is to identify and further stigmatize a group as "the undeserving poor."

However, this criticism is unfounded in its association with William Julius Wilson's (1987) discussion of the underclass in *The Truly Disadvantaged*. This book focused on concentrations of joblessness among the ghetto poor as explicit causes of crime and violence in these communities. Wilson (1991:12) is careful to make clear that his thesis is not confined to Black American ghettoes, noting that "the concept 'underclass' or 'ghetto poor' can be theoretically applied to all racial and ethnic groups, and to different societies if the conditions specified in the theory are met." Wilson's work has stimulated important new research on urban crime and poverty (e.g., Sampson, 1987; Matsueda and Heimer, 1987), and he (1991:6) worries that "any crusade to abandon the concept of underclass, however defined, could result in premature closure of ideas just as important new studies on the inner-city ghetto, including policy-oriented studies, are being generated." Wilson (1991) interchanges the term "ghetto poor" for "underclass" in his recent writing, while other authors sometimes refer to low income or distressed communities.

Nonetheless, the scientific utility of some uses of the underclass concept is open to question, at least for the purposes of theorizing about crime. Insofar as the conceptualization of the underclass includes within it the cultural (e.g., attitudes and values) and structural (e.g., joblessness) factors assumed to cause crime, as well as crime itself, it may be little more than a diffuse tautology. A tautology is a description posing as an explanation. Tautologous formulations seem to tell us more than they do, as when the famous analyst of baseball, Yogi Berra, instructed us, "You can see a lot by just watching." Seeing and watching are, of course, the same thing. Similarly, Billingsley (1989:23) noted, "If one asks how is underclass different from poverty, the answer is that it includes poverty. If it is asked how does it differ from unemployment, the answer is that it includes unemployment. . . . And now street crime has been added."

It may partly be this feature of some discussions of the underclass, like the dangerous and criminal class conceptualizations before it, that has engendered skepticism in criminology and limited our understanding of connections between class and crime.

From Class and Crime to Status and Delinquency

Prominent theories of crime also emphasize the harsh class circumstances experienced by poor and even more desperate segments of the population (see Matza, 1966; Hirschi, 1972), and these theories causally connect these adverse class conditions with serious crime (e.g., Merton, 1938; Shaw and MacKay, 1942; Cohen, 1955; Miller, 1958; Cloward and Ohlin, 1960; Colvin and Pauly, 1983). However, these theories separately identify class conditions and criminal behavior as distinct phenomena and then propose an association between the two. The association between class and crime proposed in these theories is largely taken for granted in descriptive ethnographic research (Liebow, 1967; Howell, 1973; Anderson, 1978; Rose, 1987; Hagedorn, 1988; Monroe and Goldman, 1988; Sullivan, 1989), and it also is observed in most research that uses census tracts or other measures of neighborhoods (e.g., from Chilton, 1964 to Sampson and Groves, 1989) to link class and crime. We will say more about these ethnographic and community level studies later.

Meanwhile, the association between class and crime is only weakly, if at all, reflected in self-report analyses based on surveys of individual adolescent students attending school (e.g., Tittle et al., 1977; Weis, 1987), leading to calls for the abandonment of class analyses of crime. Self-report studies are undertaken in a survey or interview format and use what some have called a "confessional" methodology in asking adolescents to reveal their delinquent behaviors. These studies sometimes find weak patterns, and often no significant tendency at all, for children of lower status parents to be more delinquent. Since these self-report studies are at variance with many theories of crime as well as ethnographic and community level studies reviewed later, there might seem grounds to simply reject the former method and its results. However, doing so risks underestimating the valuable role that self-report studies have played in the advancement of criminological theory. Self-report methodology (e.g., from Nye and Short [1957] through Hindelang et al. [1981]) has allowed researchers to gather extensive information otherwise unavailable about individuals, which can then be used to explain their reports of criminal behavior. Self-reports also have freed researchers from reliance on potentially biased official records of criminality. This methodology has underwritten classic contributions to theory testing in criminology (e.g., Hirschi [1969]; Matsueda [1982]).

In many such efforts, self-report survey researchers provide separate measures of the concepts of class and crime. In doing so they implicitly have questioned the taken-for-granted nature of associations of crime and poverty in much criminological writing. Self-report survey researchers rightly insist on distinct, independent measures of class and crime that can provide the building blocks for testing explanations of crime. Literary or statistical descriptions of crime-prone areas, the modern sociological analogues to Dickens's and Mayhew's early depictions of the dangerous and criminal classes of London, are not enough for the purposes of theory testing.

Instead of providing literary or statistical descriptions, self-report researchers moved into the schools of America (and later other countries) to collect extensive information on family, educational, community, and other experiences of adolescents. Three substitutions that we describe later characterized this process: (1) schools replaced the streets as sites for data collection; (2) delinquency replaced crime as the behavior to be explained; and (3) parents' occupational status replaced criminal actors' more immediate class conditions as the presumed causes of delinquency.

In some ways, these substitutions enhanced the scientific standing of criminological research, but they also distanced self-report studies from the conditions and activities that stimulated attention to the criminal or underclass in the first place. For example, although sampling lists can more accurately be established from schools than from the streets, it is out-of-school street youth who are more likely than school youth to be involved in delinquency and crime. Further, although adolescent self-reports of delinquency might be free from some kinds of mistakes and biases involved in official record-keeping about adolescents and adults, the more common self-reported adolescent indiscretions are also less likely to be the serious forms of delinquency and crime of more concern to citizens. Finally, parental occupational status can be indexed using established scales independent of the adolescent behaviors that researchers are seeking to explain. However, these well-developed measures assume that parents *have* occupations, although many may not have jobs and/or may be unemployed. Furthermore, note that these are measures for parents, not for the youth whose behaviors are being explained. These substitutions may make self-report survey research more systematic, but they also produce the unintended result that less theoretically relevant characteristics (i.e., parental occupational status in place of parental or youth unemployment) are used to explain the less serious behaviors (i.e., common delinquency in place of serious crime) of less criminally involved persons (i.e., school youths rather than street youths and adults).

Reclassifying Crime

Serious attempts have been made to improve on these features of self-report studies. These efforts at improvement most significantly have involved the use of parental and youth unemployment measures, which better represent class positions and conditions, instead of, or in addition to, the occupational status of parents. Wright (1985, 137) explained why this reconceptualization is important when he wrote that "all things being equal, all units within a given class should be more like each other than like units in other classes *with respect to whatever it is that class is meant to explain*" [emphasis in original]. The key to defining a class in this way is to identify the relevant linking conceptual mechanisms. For example, in economics or sociology, if income is the theoretical object of explanation, then educational attainment, whether an indicator of certification or skill transmission, is an obvious linking mechanism that must be incorporated in the measurement of class.

In criminology, our theoretical objects in need of explanation—delinquency and crime—demand their own distinct conceptual consideration. So we need to more directly conceptualize and measure our own linking causal mechanisms. These mechanisms may involve situations of deprivation, desperation, destitution, degradation, disrepute, and related conditions. Tittle and Meier (1990:294) spoke to the importance of such factors when they suggest that "it would make more sense to measure deprivation directly than to measure socioeconomic status (SES), which is a step removed from the real variable at issue."

In other words, when serious street crime is the focus of our attention, the relevant concern is with class more than status—especially as class operates through such linking mechanisms as deprivation, destitution, and disrepute. These linking mechanisms are more directly experienced when the actors themselves are, for example, hungry, unhoused, ill-educated, and unemployed, but the linking mechanisms may also operate indirectly through parental unemployment and housing problems such as those involving associated family disruption, neglect and abuse of children, and resulting difficulties at school. Youth and parental unemployment experiences are important sources of these kinds of direct and indirect class effects, and some survey researchers therefore have focused on these measures in self-report studies.

However, Brownfield (1986:429) reported that efforts of those who do school surveys to identify class circumstances in terms of parental joblessness still have considerable difficulty finding and studying the disreputable poor. Consider the few studies that are available. Hirschi (1969) studied delinquency in Richmond; he counted any spell of unemployment over three preceding years and found 16 percent of the family heads were unemployed. By oversampling multiple dwelling units and depressed neighborhoods, Hagan et al. (1985) produced a Toronto sample in which 9 percent of the family heads were unemployed. Johnson (1980:88) also focused on parental joblessness and selected three Seattle high schools "in order to obtain a sufficient number of underclass students" who constitute 8 percent of this sample.

The Research Triangle Institute (see Rachal et al., 1975) oversampled ethnic communities and produced a sample in which about 7 percent of the youth lived in a household with an unemployed head. The Arizona Community Tolerance Study (see Brownfield, 1986:428) overrepresented rural families, 3 percent of which had unemployed heads, including many "miners who were temporarily laid off."

More recently and most successfully, a panel study concentrated on high crime areas of Rochester, New York (Farnworth et al., 1994), has produced a sample in which one-third of the principal wage-earning parents were unemployed.

These are the only self-report studies we can find that report parental joblessness as a measure of underclass position. All attempt to overrepresent jobless parents, and all, with the recent exception of the Rochester study, find relatively few underclass families. It is particularly noteworthy that the Rochester study finds consistent evidence of a relationship between parental unemployment and self-reported delinquency but little indication of such a relationship when measures of occupational status are used.

The limited study of, and variance in, parental unemployment reduces the likelihood of finding stable or substantial associations between parental class positions and adolescent delinquency. And there is the further and possibly more important factor that the influence of parental class on adolescent delinquency is from a distance. For example, the parental class effect is assumed to operate over as long as a three-year-lag in the case of the Richmond study. Furthermore, the effects of parental class is also presumed to be indirect, operating through the variety of family, school, and other mediating variables. For example, Figure 1.1 presents a causal model of delinquency from a study that includes both youth in school and youth living on the streets of Toronto (see Hagan and McCarthy, 1992). Note the succession of paths through which the effect of parental class background passes to cause delinquency. It is a rule of thumb in such models that the further removed a causal variable is from the ultimate outcome, the weaker its

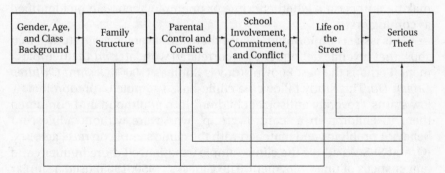

Figure 1.1 A Conceptual Model of Streetlife and Serious Theft.

Source: John Hagan and Bill McCarthy, 1992. "Streetlife and Delinquency: The Significance of a Missing Population." *British Journal of Sociology*, vol. 43, pp. 533–61.

effect will be (Blalock, 1964). This rule of thumb suggests that the impact of parental class position on delinquency *should* be weak. And it is therefore not surprising that this indirect class effect is elusive and uncertain in self-report research.

This shifts our attention to the more immediate and direct class effects of youth unemployment on crime and delinquency. Although there are many community level studies of crime and unemployment (Chiricos, 1987) that we consider later, there are again surprisingly few studies that focus on unemployment among individual adolescents. However, these individual level studies reveal higher levels of youth unemployment than is present in the studies focused on parents. Perhaps most importantly, these studies report the expected association between youth unemployment and youth involvement in delinquency and crime, even if the full nature of this association is only beginning to be understood.

For example, Farrington et al. (1986) reported that nearly half the sample of 411 London males followed in their research that tracked youths from ages 8 to 18 experienced some unemployment, and these youths self-reported more involvement in delinquency during the periods of their unemployment. This study (and further research reported later) allowed some consideration of the timing of crime and unemployment by considering the range of time when the unemployment and criminal behavior occurred. However, this study (like others) did not definitively determine the *direction* in which the causal influence between unemployment and crime flows. The problem is that the relationship between unemployment and crime may be instantaneous or simultaneous (e.g., as when an individual loses a job and immediately commits a crime), as well as lagged (e.g., as when an individual loses a job, depletes his/her savings, and then commits a crime). Farrington et al. consider the simultaneous occurrence of crime and unemployment, making it uncertain whether crime or unemployment can be identified as coming first.

This issue is important because there are several classic studies that show that juvenile delinquency is correlated with later *adult* unemployment. Perhaps the best known study is Robins's (1966) *Deviant Children Grown Up*. This study followed a clinic-based sample of predominately low status, "severely antisocial children" into adulthood and compared them to children in a "control group" who were without adolescent behavior problems and matched with the clinic sample on race, age, sex, IQ, and SES. As adults the clinic sample experienced more frequent and longer spells of unemployment. The Gluecks (1950; 1968) used a similar matched-group design to study white males from Boston who, because of their persistent delinquency, were committed to one of two correctional schools in Massachusetts. In their reanalysis of these data, Sampson and Laub (1990) found greater adult unemployment among the delinquent sample.

Two of the most systematic efforts to establish the direction of influence between youth unemployment, delinquency, and crime were by Bachman, O'Malley, and Johnston and Thornberry and Christenson. Bachman, O'Malley, and Johnston (1978) analyze self-report panel data gathered through a nationally representative sampling of 87 public high schools in the United States. They asked: "Does unemployment really heighten aggression and drug use?" They concluded: "Our findings in this area are suggestive, but not definitive. In each case an alternative path of causation is possible" (p. 218). Similarly, Thornberry and Christenson (1984) analyzed unemployment and crime among 567 subjects from a 1945 Philadelphia birth cohort; they concluded that unemployment and crime mutually influence one another over the individual's life span, with no indication of which problem occurs first.

The importance of these studies is that they both indicate that there is an association between unemployment and crime that endures over the life course. Much important work remains to be done in establishing the direction and dynamic of this relationship, as we discuss later. However, insofar as unemployment is a clear measure of class, there can be little doubt that the relationship between class and crime is a key element in criminological research.

Community- and National-Level Studies of Crime and Unemployment

We noted earlier that studies of unemployment and crime are not only done using individuals as the focus of research but also using aggregations of individuals, such as those in census tracts or neighborhoods. Studies of individuals are often referred to as micro-level research. However, studies of individuals aggregated or grouped into census tracts, city blocks, neighborhoods, or even nations and/or for year-long periods are referred to as macro-level research. Studies use different *units* and *levels of analysis*, and it is important to keep this in mind when interpreting results. What causes crime at the city block level may be different from what causes crime at the level of individuals, and when one level of research is used to draw inferences about another, the reasoning involved may be fallacious. When this kind of mistaken reasoning occurs from the macro to the micro level, it is often called the ecological fallacy (Robinson, 1950). Perhaps the most common form of this fallacy is to assume that because unemployment (or some other variable) is associated with crime at the level of neighborhoods, that the unemployment (or some other corresponding characteristic) of individuals will be associated with individual involvements in crime as well. However, it is possible that it is not the unemployed individuals who are more likely to commit the crimes in neighborhoods with high unemployment. Indeed, since so much crime is committed by adolescents who are not yet involved in the adult labor market from which unemployment data are gathered, the ecological fallacy may be a serious problem that complicates and confuses attempts to understand criminal behavior among individuals.

Meanwhile, there is also the related possibility of an "individualistic fallacy" that occurs in the reverse direction (see Sampson and Wilson, 1995). That is, even if unemployment does not directly cause individuals to commit crimes, or if it is only weakly and indirectly involved in causing crime at the level of individuals, unemployment may still breed conditions, such as weak community controls, that cause crime at the neighborhood level. The weakness of these controls might increase the influence of criminal role models. Or unemployment might establish the conditions in which individual-level factors begin to operate. For example, there is evidence that it is only in census tracts with high concentrations of unemployment that more black Americans are victims of homicide than white Americans. High unemployment may unleash widespread feelings of frustration that lower overall threshold levels at which violence occurs. Recent epidemiological studies (see Lowry et al., 1988; Centerwall, 1984; Munford et al., 1976) focusing on census tracts as units of analysis indicate that at higher socioeconomic levels, blacks and whites experience similarly low rates of homicide. Macro-level research on unemployment is therefore an important source of evidence on the class and crime relationship, but research is needed on individuals as well.

The New Ethnography of Class and Crime

We have suggested that the research reviewed to this point indicates that class, when conceived in terms of unemployment or other measures of poverty and destitution, is associated with crime. We have found this association in micro-level research focused on unemployment and crime among samples of individual adolescents and young adults, as well as in macro-level research focused on unemployment and crime over time and across aggregated levels of neighborhoods, communities, and nations. However, we have also noted that further research is needed to better establish the nature of the causal relationship between class and crime. We need, for example, to better understand how this relationship might operate among individuals as well as at higher levels of analysis. It will also be useful to know whether crime or unemployment comes first in the lives of these individuals.

Recent ethnographic studies of poverty, crime, and unemployment among individuals in community settings offer an important resource for these purposes. These community studies typically are based on extensive observation and interviewing. Although ethnographies usually do not use quantitative measurements in the way self-report and aggregate-level studies reviewed earlier do, they often employ the same logic and reasoning to establish causal relationships. This work is especially useful in developing our understanding of the relationship between unemployment and youth crime.

Although ethnographic studies often take for granted that an association exists between class and crime, recent work of this type has more systematically established ways in which this relationship might operate. Perhaps the most important of these ethnographies is Mercer Sullivan's (1989) study of three New York City neighborhoods that included an African American public housing project, a Hispanic neighborhood adjacent to a declining industrial area, and a white working-class community. This use of three communities is important because it allows Sullivan to comparatively assess how variation in the class conditions of neighborhoods can influence the lives of the individuals who live within them. Sullivan and his collaborators interviewed members of cliques within each of these neighborhoods about their life histories.

All three of the neighborhoods are seen as affected by changes in the larger world economy. These changes involve a transition to a post-industrial economy in which lower wage and less secure jobs in the information and service sectors are only partially replacing the loss of higher wage and more secure jobs in the manufacturing and industrial sectors. This is a period in which our cities and ultimately our nation have "exported" jobs and "imported" unemployment in a set of intra-national and international realignments that could prove beneficial in the long run but in the near term are producing severe economic dislocations. These dislocations concentrate conditions of poverty and isolation that disrupt community and family controls, while also encouraging the proliferation of underground activities including delinquency and crime. By studying three communities, one of which is more stable and predominantly white, Sullivan is able to examine the processes by which these changes affect individual lives.

The white working-class community serves methodologically as an essential base of comparison because although it too is confronting some of the problems of the changing economy that are eliminating higher wage and more secure jobs, it is still a community that includes access to many of these jobs through legitimate labor market networks that offer opportunities for obtaining employment through personal contacts. So in this community there are still unionized jobs in which adults have some security, and there are more two-parent stable households that are a base for viable family and community controls. As we will see later, when youth in this neighborhood get into trouble with the law, they are more likely to be reintegrated into their families and community and they are less likely to be excluded from labor market opportunities.

Access to these labor market opportunities is crucial. In the white working-class neighborhood Sullivan found personalized job referral networks that led adolescents to adult employment opportunities, with jobs circulating through friendship, family, and neighborhood-based connections that linked local residents to desirable blue-collar jobs throughout the metropolitan labor market. In contrast, the Hispanic and black neighborhoods Sullivan studied were more physically isolated from centers of employment. Many of the parents in these neighborhoods had no jobs, while those parents who were employed tended to work in government jobs that recruited by bureaucratic means rather than through personal contacts. Sullivan (1989) found that "without family connections even to low-paying jobs, these youths had to rely on more impersonal methods" (80). The net result was that for white youths, "social ties between residents and local employers reinforced physical proximity to produce a much greater supply of youth jobs than in either of the other two neighborhoods" (104).

However, Sullivan and other ethnographers do not argue that these economic problems in an immediate and direct sense lead youth to initiate lives of crime. In fact, Sullivan emphasizes that material deprivation and need per se were not what first motivated youth crime in any of these neighborhoods and that "whatever variations, . . . the income motivation during the early economic crimes appears to have been generally undeveloped" (116). Instead the argument is that economic decline in a much more indirect way creates conditions of weak family and community controls that make youthful involvement in delinquency common. This becomes more problematic as adolescents come of age to enter the labor market and experience employment difficulties that make prolonging youth crime into adulthood more likely. Indeed, it is those youth most involved in youth crime who are most likely to experience adult unemployment; and these are the individuals most likely to develop adult criminal careers. So while at the level of the community, unemployment plays a prominent role in causing juvenile delinquency and adult crime, at the level of individuals, delinquency causes adult unemployment and subsequent crime. In other words, the diminished class circumstances of communities often establish conditions in which juvenile delinquency is linked to adult problems of unemployment and crime.

Several recent ethnographies provide accounts that are consistent with this formulation of the relationship between crime, poverty, and unemployment. For example, Anderson (1990) links this kind of formulation to the expansion of the underground drug economy of a northeastern ghetto community. Here he observes that "for many young men the drug economy is an employment agency. . . . Young men who 'grew up' in the gang but now are without clear opportunities, easily become involved; they fit themselves into its structure, manning its drug houses and selling drugs on street corners" (244). In this kind of setting, the personal experience of unemployment is not the immediate source of individual involvement in delinquency, but instead, this experience creates conditions in which youth crime is common and in which there are fewer opportunities or incentives for terminating this involvement during the transition to adulthood.

Moore (1991) documented that such a process was increasingly common in distressed communities by comparing East Los Angeles gangs members from the 1950s and 1970s. The method of comparison was across time. She found that in the 1970s these gangs were more institutionalized, more salient in the lives of their members, and more involved with drugs and violence. The macro-level reasons for these gang characteristics again involve economic restructuring that in East Los Angeles as elsewhere has replaced industrial and manufacturing jobs with work that is lower paying and more unstable. However, the more immediate cause for individuals involved is that "kin-based job networks that found decent work for earlier clique members deteriorated" (133). The result is to prolong gang involvement into adulthood. Yet not all Hispanic youth in East Los Angeles are similarly affected by these changes; rather, the most affected group are the cholos, "a category of men and women who seem never to have grown out of the gang" (125). It is these youth "who are most likely to be affected by changes in the opportunities to assume meaningful adult roles" (133) and who are therefore most likely to move from juvenile delinquency to adult unemployment.

A similar pattern is found in Hagedorn's (1988) study of youth crime and gangs in Milwaukee. Moore wrote in an introduction to Hagedorn's monograph, "in both Los Angeles and Milwaukee, circumstances combine to make it increasingly difficult for young men and women to outgrow their youthful ties" (5). These youth do not move from unemployment to crime; instead their adolescent gang involvements extend into an adulthood that is characterized by unemployment. Hagedorn reports that "our data on the present circumstances of the 260 young people who founded Milwaukee's nineteen major gangs suggests a positive relationship between unemployment, lack of education, and *continued* gang involvement as adults" (114; emphasis added).

It is important to observe that all of these ethnographies emphasize the role of the police and courts in the development of these youthful criminal careers. Again, Sullivan's ethnography is particularly helpful because it includes the comparison of white and minority neighbor-hoods. Sullivan finds in the more stable white neighborhood that par-ents "sought to manipulate the system—and were often successful in doing so—by means of money and personal connections" (196).

In contrast, in both of the minority neighborhoods youths began to move farther away from home to commit violent economic crimes and encountered more serious sanctions when they did so. These crimes produced short-term gains, but they also further separated the minority youth from the legal labor market and stigmatized them in terms of job prospects. Sullivan writes of the minority youths he studied: "Their par-ticipation in regular acts of income-producing crime and the resulting involvement with the criminal justice system in turn kept them out of school and forced them to abandon their earlier occupational goals" (64). Court appearances and resulting confinements removed these youths from whatever job referral networks school might provide and placed them within prison and community-based crime networks that further isolated these youths from legitimate employment (see also Hagan and Palloni, 1990; Hagan, 1993).

Collectively, these ethnographic accounts provide a picture of dis-tressed communities in which crime is common and economic prospects are bleak. This picture is consistent with the aggregate macro-level statis-tical studies that from neighborhoods to nations report substantial asso-ciations between harsh class circumstances and increased levels of crime. At this macro-level of analysis, it seems clear that class-linked problems, including unemployment, cause crime. However, even here the causation is indirect, with the effects of unemployment operating through the dis-ruption of family and community-based processes of social control.

Meanwhile, at the micro-level of individual adolescents, the more immediate and direct causal process is often reversed. Delinquency characteristically precedes unemployment in the lives of these individu-als. Distressed communities, with their high levels of unemployment, are settings in which individuals find it difficult to terminate their youthful involvements in crime. The prolongation of youth crime into adulthood becomes more common. Thus, research on gangs, from Sullivan in New York City, to Hagedorn in Milwaukee, to Moore in East Los Angeles, increasingly finds young adults staying with their gangs and engaging in more serious forms of crime.

Conclusion

This chapter has introduced some basic ideas used in the social scien-tific study of the causes of crime. It has done so by focusing on the con-troversy surrounding the role class plays in the causation of crime. This is an ideologically charged area of debate that is further complicated by the frequent failure of scientific efforts that use self-report surveys of adolescents to find substantial associations between parental status and delinquency. However, we have argued that when appropriate class measures of unemployment are used both among individuals and at higher levels of aggregation, consistent relationships are found.

It is important to distinguish the different levels of analysis at which research on class and crime is done because the causal relationships that are observed differ by level, and it is fallacious to use research from one level of analysis to reason about processes of causation at another level. The use of research from a higher macro-level of research, such as neighborhoods, to talk about micro-level behaviors of individuals, is called the ecological fallacy. The reverse error is called the individualistic fallacy. We illustrated the problems such fallacies can produce in observing that although unemployment causes crime at the neighborhood level, crime more immediately and directly causes unemployment at the micro-level of individual adolescents. These patterns are connected in that macro-level community unemployment can create micro-level conditions for individuals in which juvenile delinquency is likely to lead to adult unemployment and associated crime.

This discussion illustrates two conditions that are commonly required to assert that causation occurs: (1) there is an association between the distinctly defined phenomena of interest; and (2) there is an established logical or temporal direction to the associated flow of causation. When these conditions are established, attention usually turns to a consideration of how other factors may influence the relationship that has been observed. Much of the chapter that follows is concerned with how we introduce and consider added factors into causal analyses, in this case, into the analysis of the association between gender and crime.

2 Testing Propositions About Gender and Crime

John Hagan

A Beginning

Criminologists who use quantitative methods in their work often begin to formulate research problems by distinguishing the independent and dependent variables they intend to study. Crime is the dependent variable criminologists usually seek to explain, although it can also be an independent variable used to explain other phenomena. To say that crime is a dependent variable is to say that it is an effect, the consequence of change in some other variable. To say that crime is an independent variable is to say that it is a cause, the source of variation in some other variable. In either case, we must be explicit as to our location of crime as a cause or an effect.

The assertion of a cause-and-effect relationship between crime and another variable is often called a proposition, and such propositions are the building blocks of criminological theories. For example, a frequently tested proposition at the core of a control theory of crime asserts that parental supervision reduces delinquent behavior. To test this primitive statement of a theory of crime we must be able to test its single proposition with distinct operational definitions (i.e., measures) of its key concepts or variables, which are parental control and delinquent behavior. These operational definitions might consist of reports on questionnaires by high school students about the extent to which their parents know where they are when they are away from home, and the extent of their involvement in behaviors (e.g., theft, vandalism, and assaults) defined by laws and by most citizens as crimes.

Once operational measures of our concepts are established, it becomes possible to answer the question of whether there is an inverse relationship, or negative covariation, as proposed in the theory, such that those adolescents who report less parental supervision also report more involvement in delinquency. If there is a negative covariance (beyond what would occur frequently by chance) observed between parental supervision and delinquency, it is possible to reject the "null hypothesis" that, counter to control theory, there is no causal relationship between parental control and delinquency. The logic of the scientific method is that we advance our theories by rejecting their alternatives.

When we cannot reject the alternative hypothesis to that put forth in our own theoretical proposition, we are encouraged to continue building our theory by adding to it further propositions that elaborate and test the implications of the theory. We describe the development of a power-control theory of gender and delinquency by this process of elaborating and testing propositions over the course of this chapter. The discussion begins simply and gradually becomes more complicated. No more than the most basic math skills are required to follow the discussion, but it will be helpful to replicate some of the procedures presented through your own hand computations. Replication of the procedures will involve interruptions in your reading of the chapter and reading some passages several times to be clear about what is being done. However, once you master the material in this chapter, you will find that you can read with understanding a great majority of the quantitative research you will encounter in criminology.

Studying Covariation

Covariation between variables can be examined in more ways than are appropriate for us to consider here. However, tabular and multiple regression analysis are two statistical techniques that have played important roles in exploring and testing propositional theories about crime. Tabular techniques played a formative role in early scientific studies of crime, and the logic of causal analysis that evolved with these techniques remains important today, for example, in the extensive use made of multiple regression analysis in contemporary journal articles and research monographs. We will introduce tabular techniques now and use them as a bridge to multiple regression techniques, which will be the focus of much of the discussion in this book.

We can continue with the same example already introduced from a control theory of delinquency, which we will then discuss as part of an elaborated power-control theory of gender and delinquency. This example proposes that as supervision of children increases, self-reported involvement in delinquency decreases. Consider Table 2.1, which is derived from a classic study of delinquency in the high schools of Richmond, California (see Hirschi, 1969); the independent variable, maternal parental supervision, is cross-tabulated with the dependent variable, self-reported delinquent behavior. *Later, we discuss how assignment of parent supervisory roles to women is part of patriarchal familism and varies.* Maternal supervision is tabulated in the three cate-

Table 2.1 Percentaged Cross-tabulation of Maternal Supervision and
Self-Reported Delinquency

Self-Reported Delinquency	% None	% One +	N
Maternal Supervision			
Low	48.92(748)	51.08(781)	1529
Moderate	62.73(1183)	37.28(703)	1886
High	77.26(6442)	22.74(1896)	8338

Source: Travis Hirschi, 1969, *Causes of Delinquency* (Berkeley: University
of California Press).

gories of low, moderate, and high, while delinquency is tabulated as
none and as one-or-more self-reported delinquent acts. Table 2.1 is
"percentaged in the causal direction." That is, the percentage of respondents who report none and one-or-more delinquent acts is calculated
within categories of the independent variable, which is maternal supervision. To establish the possible influence of an independent variable on
a dependent variable it is necessary to make sure that we percentage in
this direction. This method allows us to compare the percentages of
respondents who report delinquency within levels of supervision, which
we assume to cause delinquency. Percentaging in the alternative direction would not give us the relevant comparisons and can lead to embar-
rassingly illogical inferences. However, if we percentage in the causal
direction, we see that with each increase in the level of maternal supervision, the percentage of respondents reporting delinquent acts
decreases: from just over half (about 51 percent) reporting delinquency
under low supervision to less than a quarter (about 23 percent) reporting delinquency under high supervision.

This simple finding, that maternal supervision reduces delinquency,
gains meaning when placed in the context of patriarchal family relationships. For example, an elaborated control theory of gender and delinquency begins to emerge when it is noted that gender is related to both
maternal supervision and delinquency: boys evidence less maternal
supervision and more delinquency than girls. There is a sequence
apparent among these variables, with gender established and chan-
neled from birth and maternal supervision extending from early childhood through adolescence, when delinquency begins. From this
sequence it can be logically inferred that maternal supervision is an
"intervening" or "mediating" variable that can help "interpret" or
"account for" the relationship between gender and delinquency; that is,
lower maternal supervision helps to account for why boys are more

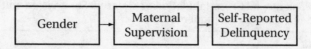

Figure 2.1   A Simplified Control Theory of Gender and Delinquency

delinquent than girls. This causal relationship is illustrated in a simple "path model" in Figure 2.1. Percentaged tables can be used to test this emergent and slightly more complex control theory of gender and delinquency.

Table 2.2 displays the relationship between gender and delinquency in Richmond high schools, as analyzed by Jensen and Eve (1976): almost 43 percent of the males reported one or more delinquent acts, compared to less than 19 percent of the girls. The 24 percentage point difference in delinquency involvement between genders is a useful measure of the strength of the relationship between these variables. So there is a substantial relationship between gender and delinquency, and we have made a logical argument that maternal supervision, which is associated with both of these variables, assumes a position in sequence between these variables. To establish that maternal supervision intervenes between gender and delinquency and in this way mediates or accounts for this relationship, we now divide the Richmond sample into three groups defined by level of maternal supervision and again crosstabulate gender and delinquency within these groupings.

If maternal supervision does indeed mediate the gender-delinquency relationship, this relationship should disappear or at least decline within each part of Table 2.3 defined by level of maternal supervision. For example, in that part of the table made up only of youth who experience low levels of maternal supervision, we should expect girls and boys to report more similar involvements in delinquency than reported in Table 2.2 where youth are combined regardless of level of

Table 2.2   Percentaged Cross-tabulation of Gender and Self-Reported Delinquency

Self-Reported Delinquency	% None	% One +	N
Male	57.11(2788)	42.89(2094)	4882
Female	81.28(5585)	18.72(1286)	6871

Source: Data from Gary F. Jensen and Raymond Eve, 1976, "Sex Differences in Delinquency," *Criminology*, vol. 13, pp. 427–48.

Table 2.3 Percentaged Cross-tabulation of Gender and Self-Reported Delinquency by Maternal Supervision

Maternal Supervision	Low		Moderate		High		N
Self-Reported Delinquency	% None	% One +	% None	% One +	% None	% One +	
Gender							
Male	44.23(487)	55.77(614)	53.99(568)	46.01(484)	63.50(1733)	36.50(996)	4882
Female	60.98(261)	39.02(167)	73.74(615)	26.26(219)	83.95(4709)	16.05(900)	6871

Source: Data from Gary F. Jensen and Raymond Eve, 1976, "Sex Differences in Delinquency," *Criminology,* vol. 13, pp. 427–48.

supervision. In particular, we should expect a substantially larger share of girls to report involvement in delinquency under low supervision, which is somewhat uncommon for girls. Note that this is exactly what we find if we compare the bottom right cell of Table 2.2 with the bottom right cell, under low maternal supervision, of Table 2.3: the percentage of girls involved in delinquency under low levels of supervision increases by more than 20 percent (from 18.72 to 39.02). Of course, the delinquency involvement of boys also increases under low levels of supervision, in this case by about 13 percent.

To get an overall measure of the extent to which maternal supervision accounts for the relationship between gender and delinquency, we can compare the percentage difference in delinquency involvement of boys and girls at each of the three levels of supervision (about 17, 20, and 20 percent) with the percentage difference we have already noted in the combined sample (24 percent). These measures indicate that the gender-delinquency relationship is reduced but by no means eliminated so that differences in maternal supervision by gender account for some, but certainly not all, of this relationship.

We have found support for a simple control theory of gender and delinquency, but a more elaborate causal theory is required to explain the gender-delinquency relationship. This is not surprising. It is often noted that behavior is the product of many small causes rather than a single all-encompassing causal force, or in other words, that most social behavior is the product of a "dense causal web" (Nettler, 1970). In addition, supervision and delinquency are measured crudely in the above tabular analysis, with only three categories of maternal supervision and delinquency indicated as some or none. Tabular techniques are limited in the numbers of variables and categories that can be considered simultaneously. Even with a very large sample, we soon run out of cases to fill the cells when more than a few variables and categories are included in the analysis. Multiple regression analysis uses more efficient statistical techniques. We describe the use of these techniques later, after we introduce an elaborated power-control theory that considers not only links between gender and delinquent acts but also links with police contacts.

Elaborating the Causal Model

Power-control theory elaborates the model we have considered by further conceptualizing the causal relationship between gender and delinquency. This elaboration notes the unique relationship that exists between mothers and daughters in patriarchal families. This relationship is illustrated in Tables 2.4 and 2.5, where we separately cross-tabulate gender and mater-

Table 2.4 Cross-tabulation of Gender and Maternal Supervision

	Maternal Supervision			
Gender	*Low*	*Moderate*	*High*	*N*
Male	22.55(1101)	21.55(1052)	55.90(2729)	4882
Female	6.23(428)	12.14(834)	81.63(5609)	6871

Table 2.5 Cross-tabulation of Gender and Paternal Supervision

	Paternal Supervision			
Gender	*Low*	*Moderate*	*High*	*N*
Male	29.56(1332)	20.86(940)	49.58(2234)	4506
Female	19.00(1129)	12.91(767)	68.10(4047)	5943

nal and paternal supervision. Table 2.4 is generated from Table 2.3 by summing cases across combined categories of delinquency within each gender and level of supervision and then repercentaging across the collapsed table. (Performing these calculations will give you a better feeling for how these tables are constructed.)

Table 2.5 is generated with a separate, analogous measure of paternal supervision. A comparison of tables 2.4 and 2.5 makes it apparent that the role of parental controls involves mothers more than fathers and the control of daughters more than the control of sons. That is, both sons and daughters are more highly controlled by their mothers than by their fathers, and the differences in levels of control imposed by mothers, with daughters more controlled than sons, are greater than levels of control imposed by fathers. The implication is that mothers and daughters are assigned distinct and unique roles as both instruments and objects of social control within the structure of the patriarchal family.

These relationships are important because they underline a patterning by gender of social control in the family. In other words, they reflect a division by gender in the social stratification of domestic social control. It is relevant to note here that while some modern statements of control theory emphasize social as well as individual aspects of the bonds or controls that constrain delinquency, other formulations of this theory deemphasize the causal force of social bonds by placing the emphasis on self-control. In other words, the emphasis in latter formulations of control theory is placed on controls that come from within the individual rather than from others. By focusing on power relationships within the family as well as on patriarchal power relationships that impinge on the family, power-control theory emphasizes socially determined links between gender and delinquency. The overarching premise of power-control theory is that these relationships play a causal role in the tendency of males to exceed females in delinquency. The patriarchal power structure of the family and the gender specific roles that it assigns to mothers and daughters in the family are important causal forces in this theory. Later we will discuss how family structures can vary.

We turn next to a condensed statement of power-control theory (see Hagan, 1989: Chap. 6 for a fuller discussion) that broadens our attention beyond delinquent behavior to include official reactions to delinquency in the form of police contacts. This elaboration of power-control theory is summarized in Figure 2.2.

The first mediating link in power-control theory asserts that it is mothers more than fathers that are held responsible for the everyday imposition of parental controls, which in turn are imposed on daughters more than on sons. This is the mother-daughter relationship observed in the earlier data and the relationship which power-control theory identifies as a cornerstone of patriarchal family relations. These parental controls can be both instrumental (as in supervision and surveillance) and relational (through processes of identification and affection), although we focus initially on instrumental controls.

The second mediating link in power-control theory proposes that these controls will have the effect of diminishing the preferences to take risks. These risk preferences are reflected in survey items that ask about liking to take chances and liking to do dangerous things. The resulting attitudes may also be linked to variations in perceptions of risk, such as in perceptions of the likelihood of getting caught and punished for delinquency. However, our emphasis for the moment is on the expectation of this theory that parental control produces an aversion to risk-taking, especially personally dangerous forms of risk-taking.

The third and fourth mediating links in this theory assert that risk aversion will reduce delinquency, and that in turn delinquent behavior will increase official police contacts. In addition to the mediating "indi-

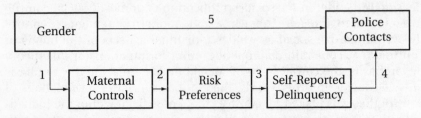

Figure 2.2 A Power-Control Model

Source: John Hagan, 1989, *Structural Criminology* (New Brunswick, NJ: Rutgers University Press).

rect" links we have identified between gender and delinquency, power-control theory also predicts that gender will have a fifth "direct" effect on official police contacts so that boys are more likely than girls to get picked up by the police, above and beyond their greater involvement in delinquent behavior. This aspect of power-control theory argues that, although mothers and daughters are more often the instruments and objects of informal social control in the private sphere of the family, male adults and sons are more often the instruments and objects of more formal social control in the public sphere that includes policing. There are important exceptions to this aspect of the theory, especially involving the punitive policing of prostitution and related status offenses involving females; nonetheless, the general tendency is for males to be more heavily policed than females. Power-control theory argues that, over time, the effect of this tendency has been to reinforce a gender division or stratification between the private and public spheres, with females having only limited and relatively recent representation in the public sphere of policing—either as police officers or as suspects. We will have more to say about the prospect of contemporary changes in the gender stratification of social control later.

We have presented a condensed and a partial statement of power-control theory. However, it is sufficient to illustrate a theory with several mediating or indirect links, as well as direct links that can be tested against actual data. This chapter provides an illustration of how such a theory can be explored using multiple regression techniques. First, however, we must introduce these multiple-regression techniques.

The Rudiments of Regression

We will explore power-control theory by using multiple regression techniques to undertake a path analysis. The paths in this analysis correspond to the direct and indirect links proposed in the theory presented earlier in this chapter. In a sense, we already have undertaken a kind of path analysis when we used percentaged tables to test the simple three variable path model summarized in Figure 2.1. We used percentaged tables to test whether gender causally influenced delinquent behavior through the mediating variable of maternal supervision. We found that gender seemed to act partially through this supervision but that gender had a substantial remaining direct effect. However, we also suggested that other mediating variables were likely involved as well, too many to be explored with percentaged tables. Later we use multiple regression equations to statistically estimate the existence and strength of additional indirect paths of influence as well as remaining direct paths of influence. This statistical estimation requires that we first develop a rudimentary working knowledge of multiple regression analysis.

As in tabular analysis, we begin multiple-regression analysis by establishing our independent and dependent variables. In multiple regression analysis the convention is to speak of regressing our dependent variable on our independent variables. We do this to estimate the significance and strength of the independent variables in predicting the dependent variable. The ultimate dependent variable in power-control theory is police contacts.

Multiple regression analysis was developed initially as a device for prediction. Imagine that in a sample of high school students we have a dependent variable or outcome which is the number of police contacts (y), and imagine that we are trying to predict this outcome on the basis of an independent variable, which is preferences for risk-taking (x). Imagine that student scores on these two dimensions can be graphed along x and y axes, as in Figure 2.3. Multiple regression analysis minimizes the scatter of scores from a line that best fits the relationship between x and y. In other words, this is a line that best allows us to predict a value of y given a value of x. A regression equation is used to establish this line.

The following is the standard form of a multiple regression equation used to estimate this line that best fits the relationship between x and y:

$$y = a + bx + u.$$

We can define the several terms in this equation:

- y is the dependent variable (e.g., police contacts) and its values;
- a is called the intercept or constant and is the value of y on the graph when x is equal to 0;
- x is the independent variable (e.g., preferences for risk-taking);
- b is the slope (also called the unstandardized regression coefficient) that the regression line takes in predicting y, indicating the amount of change that occurs in y (e.g., the number of police contacts) with each unit change in x (e.g., each unit of change in preference for risk-taking);
- u is the disturbance or error term, which represents the errors that result in attempting to predict y from x.

Several assumptions are made in using multiple regression. For immediate purposes, the most important of these assumptions is that the disturbance or error term is unrelated to the independent variable(s) used to predict the dependent variable. When this assumption is met, it is possible to say that the multiple regression equation is "properly specified." A properly specified regression equation is one in which there is no unmeasured (i.e., omitted) variable reflected in the disturbance term

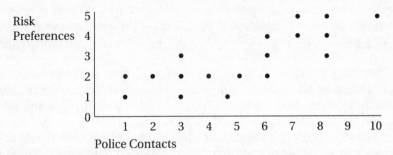

Figure 2.3 Scatterplot of Risk Preferences and Police Contacts

that is related to the independent variable(s) in the equation. In the regression equation specified above, number of self-reported delinquent acts is one obvious omitted variable. Inclusion of the term "multiple" in discussions of regression analysis reflects the fact that there are almost always a number of independent variables to be included in the prediction equation. When these variables are omitted and the regression equation is therefore misspecified, the results of a regression analysis will misrepresent the independent direct effects of the predictor variables.

Multiple independent variables are introduced into a regression analysis by expanding the form of the standard equation so that

$$y = a + b_1x_1 + b_2x_2 + \ldots b_kx_k + u.$$

In this equation b_1x_1 to b_kx_k represent the respective slopes or regression coefficients and values of the range of independent variables included in the regression analysis.

In a properly specified regression equation, which includes measures of all relevant independent variables, the slopes indicate the "net" effects of each independent variable on the dependent variable with the effects of the other independent variables statistically controlled. In other words, these regression coefficients represent the relationship between the dependent variable and each independent variable with the effects of other known variables of influence removed and in this sense, held constant.

It can be argued that controlled randomized experiments can establish causal effects of independent variables even more securely than multiple regression analysis. However, because it is ethically problematic to assign subjects randomly to conditions we expect to cause crime, experiments are rarely possible in criminology. Multiple regression analysis therefore provides one of our most important tools for establishing causal influences of explanatory variables and models in criminology.

We have noted that in their raw form slopes or regression coefficients indicate how much change in a dependent variable results from each unit change in an independent variable. For example, when solved (either through laborious hand calculations or more easily and efficiently by computer), an equation with number of police contacts as the dependent variable and number of self-reported delinquent acts as the independent variable will produce an unstandardized regression coefficient that indicates how many police contacts on average result from each self-reported delinquent act. If all acts of delinquency were known to the police through contacts, we might expect this coefficient to assume a value of one, reflecting a one-to-one relationship between acts and contacts. However, since most delinquency goes undiscovered or is of little significance, it probably will take more than a single act to produce the average police contact.

Standard multiple regression computer programs produce several other statistics that are useful in evaluating the results of these analyses. These statistics usually include a t-test for each independent variable that is the ratio of the unstandardized regression coefficient to its standard error (a measure of the reliability of the coefficient). This t-test, a test of statistical significance, indicates the likelihood that the coefficient estimated could have occurred as a result of chance fluctuations in sampling.

A measure called R^2 is also provided, which indicates how much of the variation in the dependent variable has been "accounted" for by the independent variable(s). Meanwhile, $1-R^2$ constitutes the error term, or the variance left unexplained by the independent variables.

Finally, most computer programs will standardize regression coefficients to take into account that the independent variables, whose effects they reflect, are usually measured on different scales or metrics. Standardization allows us to make comparisons of the strength of the effects of differently measured independent variables, such as gender and risk preferences. So that although gender may be measured on a scale of zero (female) and one (male) and risk preferences on a scale from one to five (reflecting answers to attitude statements from strong agreement, through agreement, undecided, disagreement to strong disagreement), standardization establishes a level playing field of comparison. Standardization does so by simply multiplying the unstandardized regression coefficient by the standard deviation (i.e., the average deviation from the mean) of the independent variable over the standard deviation of the dependent variable. These standardized regression coefficients are also referred to as path coefficients.

A Path Analysis of the Elaborated Model

We next turn to an illustration of path analysis using an example from the power-control formulation we have introduced. Although this model specifies a sequence of indirect as well as direct effects, we will begin as if the model included only direct effects of all its independent variables on the ultimate dependent variable, police contacts (y_1). The independent variables are gender (x_1), maternal controls (x_2), risk preferences (x_3), and self-reported delinquency (x_4). The regression equation is therefore:

$$y_1 = a + b_1x_1 + b_2x_2 + b_3x_3 + b_4x_4 + u.$$

The path model that corresponds to this regression equation is presented in Figure 2.4. The lines without arrowheads on the left side of this model are unanalyzed correlations between the independent variables in the model, or in other words, the simple bivariate relationships between these variables without other variables taken into account. Like standardized regression coefficients, these correlations vary between

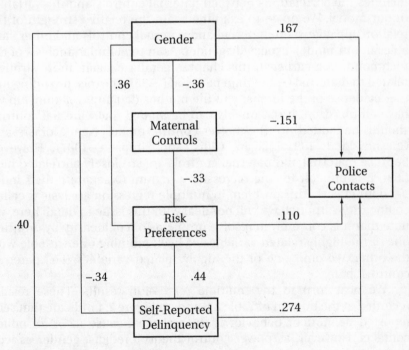

Figure 2.4   Regression Model of Police Contacts

Source: Data from John Hagan, John Simpson, and A. R. Gillis, 1979, "The Sexual Stratification of Social Control: A Gender-Based Perspective on Crime and Delinquency," *British Journal of Sociology*, vol. 30(1), pp. 25–30.

zero and one. The arrows on the right side of Figure 2.4 represent the net direct effects of independent variables on police contacts, each with the effects of the other independent variables removed.

The results of estimating this initial model with the regression equation given earlier are presented in the bottom row of Table 2.6 and on Figure 2.4. These results are based on data gathered in 1976 from 611 suburban Toronto high school students (see Hagan, Simpson, and Gillis, 1979). We can briefly describe the measurement of each variable. Gender consists of girls (coded 0) and boys (coded 1). Maternal controls are measured with answers to two summed items asking, "Does your mother know (where you are)(who you are with) when you are away from home?" Risk preferences are measured on the basis of level of agreement with the summed statements, "I like to take risks" and "the things I like to do best are dangerous." Delinquent behavior is measured with a summed six-item, self-report scale (see Hirschi, 1969) that asks about acts of theft, assault, and vandalism. Finally, police contacts are based on a self-report of the number of times the respondent has been picked up by the police.

In the far right row of Table 2.6 we have added a column that includes the correlations between paternal controls and the variables in our model. We do so to examine again the relative strength of the relationships between maternal and paternal controls and other variables in our model, especially gender. As in the tabular analysis of the Richmond data earlier in this chapter, gender is again more strongly related to maternal (−.36) than paternal (−.25) controls, providing further evidence of the intensity of the mother-daughter relationship we have emphasized. It reasonably can be argued that paternal controls should be added to the power-control model (see Morash and Chesney-Lind, 1991; Hagan, Gillis, and Simpson, 1987). However, because maternal and paternal controls are so closely correlated here (.69), it is difficult for the regression program to separate their independent effects. This problem in multiple regression analysis is called collinearity. Although we will not deal with this issue in detail here, we note that it is common to resolve problems of collinearity by omitting one of the highly related variables or by combining one variable with the other. We omit one of the highly related variables (i.e., paternal controls) here.

We next turn to the multiple regression results. These results recorded at the bottom of Table 2.6 and on Figure 2.4 indicate that self-reported delinquent behavior is the strongest cause (.274) of police contacts. However, as power-control theory predicts, gender as well has a direct causal effect on police contacts (.167). These results are helpful in evaluating a part of the power-control formulation; however, we can learn more by taking advantage of the logical sequence of

Table 2.6 Correlation and Path Coefficients*

Path Coefficient	Gender	Maternal Controls	Risk Preferences	Self-Reported Delinquency	Police Contacts	Paternal Controls
Gender	1.00	−.36	.36	.40	.35	(−.25)
Maternal Controls	−.360	1.00	−.33	−.34	−.34	(.69)
Risk Preferences	.277	−.230	1.00	.44	.34	(−.26)
Self-Reported Delinquency	.235	−.155	.304	1.00	.44	(−.31)
Police Contacts	.167	−.151	.110	.274	1.00	(−.24)

*Correlation coefficients are presented in the upper half of the table, path coefficients in the lower half; see text for a description of the variables.

Source: Data from John Hagan, John Simpson, and A. R. Gillis, 1979, "The Sexual Stratification of Social Control: A Gender-Based Perspective on Crime and Delinquency," *British Journal of Sociology,* vol. 30(1), pp. 25–38.

causal effects in the power-control model that lead from gender, through maternal control, risk preferences, and self-reported delinquency, to police contacts.

Path analysis models this sequence of effects through a series of regression equations, the last and most elaborate of which we have just estimated for police contacts. Each equation is a simplified version of the former. Therefore, the next equation we estimate takes self-reported delinquency as its dependent variable, the next takes risk preferences, and the final equation takes maternal controls as its dependent variable. We next write this full set of equations using acronyms in place of the x and y notations:

$$POLCON = a + b1GENDER + b2MATCON + b3RISK + b4SRDEL + u$$
$$SRDEL = a + b1GENDER + b2MATCON + b3RISK + u$$
$$RISK = a + b1GENDER + b2MATCON + u$$
$$MATCON = a + b1Gender + u$$

The results of estimating these equations with the Toronto data presented in Figure 2.5 indicate that there are both direct and indirect effects of gender and the other variables on self-reported delinquency and police contacts. In general, these effects are consistent with power-control theory. For example, we have already indicated that gender has a direct effect of .167 on police contacts. However, gender also has indirect effects on these contacts that operate in various ways through maternal controls, risk preferences, and self-reported delinquency.

In path analysis, the sum of a direct effect of a variable on another variable plus all indirect effects between these variables is called a "total effect." This property of path analysis and the related property that indirect effects can be calculated by multiplying intervening effects is called Wright's theorem (see Duncan, 1975; Alwin and Hauser, 1975). There are 5 indirect paths of the effect of gender on police contacts that you can follow in Figure 2.5:

$$(-.360)(-.155)(.274) = .015$$
$$(-.360)(-.151) = .054$$
$$(.235)(.274) = .064$$
$$(.277)(.110) = .031$$
$$(.277)(.304)(.274) = \underline{.023}$$
$$\text{Indirect Effects} = .187$$
$$\text{Direct Effect} = \underline{.167}$$
$$\text{Total Effect} = .354$$

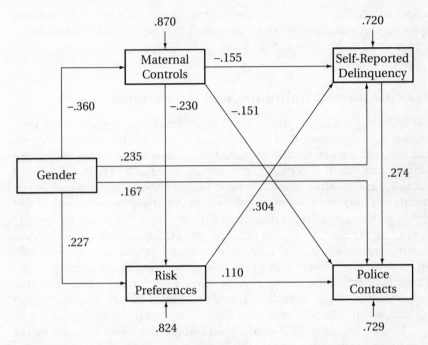

Figure 2.5 Elaborated Power-Control Model

Source: Data from John Hagan, John Simpson, and A. R. Gillis, 1979, "The Sexual Stratification of Social Control: A Gender-Based Perspective on Crime and Delinquency," *British Journal of Sociology*, vol. 30(1), pp. 25–38.

These indirect effects are all consistent with power-control theory in indicating that gender influences police contacts not only directly but also indirectly through maternal controls, risk preferences, and self-reported delinquent behavior. Said in a more general way, boys have more contact with the police not only because the police are more focused on them but also because they are less controlled by their mothers. In turn they develop higher preferences for risk, and they are therefore more involved in the delinquent behavior that generates police contacts.

You should undertake similar calculations to demonstrate to yourself that the total effect of gender on self-reported delinquency can be "decomposed" into an indirect effect of .125 and a direct effect of .235 for a total effect of .36 (this procedure is called a "decomposition of effects," and is developed further later in this chapter). These results indicate that we can account for more than half of the effect of gender on police contacts (.187/.354=.528) and more than 30 percent of the effect of gender on self-reported delinquency ($.125/.36 = .347$) with the intervening variables in the elaborated power-control model. This is progress, but still more can and should be done.

Specifications, Conditions, and Interactions

We have not yet highlighted the more controversial aspects of the theoretical ideas presented in this chapter. Some of this controversy was anticipated earlier when we noted the connection between gender-linked patterns of parental control emphasized in this theory and patriarchal family structures. Power-control theory suggests that the gender-delinquency relationship will be stronger in more patriarchal settings. Variations in patriarchy can be observed across many settings, including families, historical periods, and entire societies. When power-control theory suggests that the relationship between gender and delinquency will be stronger in more patriarchal settings, it is proposing a "specification" of the theory and the "conditions" under which it applies. Specification of the condition(s) under which a theory and its relationships apply involves "interaction effects" in regression analysis.

It is important not to confuse an interaction effect with the operation of an intervening variable. While intervening variables transmit or mediate the effects of other variables, interaction effects identify the conditions under which relationships, including links between intervening variables, operate.

Interaction effects can be extremely interesting and important but also frustrating to study. The specification of conditions under which theories apply is an important mechanism of "growth" in contemporary theory construction. However, the identification of these conditions is often frustrating because conditions change and conditions can have different meanings in different settings. This may be especially true of power relationships that specify the conditions under which power-control theory applies. Bertaux (1982:129) observed that opportunities for scientific studies exist, "when and where power relations have become stabilized, routinized, institutionalized." The problem is that as power relationships change, their effects can prove elusive, unstable, and therefore unreliable.

Interaction effects in regression analysis frequently prove unreliable as they shift in response to the variety of factors that underwrite them. A recent attempt to replicate findings from power-control theory in a suburb of Buffalo, New York (Singer and Levin, 1988), found support for the core of the power-control model introduced earlier but also found differences from the operation of this model across kinds of family power structures identified in Toronto (Hagan, Gillis, and Simpson, 1987). This can be a source of frustration (Jensen and Thompson, 1990), and Bertaux (1982:129) rightly worried that "a body of thought about social life that aims at becoming scientific is bound to move away from what has always attracted the attention of people: drama, passions, wars, the power game, uncertain struggles." However, there are also good reasons to be more optimistic about the prospects of studying such changes, particularly changes related to processes involved in power-control theory. (see Grasmick et. al., 1996)

Perhaps the most compelling reason to inquire further about such changes is that several historical studies have produced results consistent with expectations of power-control theory that links between gender and crime should vary across social settings. For example, Feeley and Little (1991) have undertaken an exhaustive analysis of criminal cases in London's Old Bailey Court from 1687 to 1912. This analysis revealed that women comprised three to four times the proportion of felony defendants during the first half of the eighteenth century (peaking at more than 40 percent of all defendants) than they have in the twentieth century (when they have accounted for less than 10 percent). The implication of such a finding is that the low contemporary involvement of women in crime may in part be a product of changes that accompanied industrialization in western societies. Although Feeley and Little's research provides the most systematic analysis to date, there are other studies which anticipate and reinforce their conclusions. Phillips (1977) in a study in Victorian England, Sharpe (1984) in an analysis of early modern England, Langbein (1983) in an examination of eighteenth century criminal trials, and Hull (1987) in a consideration of Colonial Massachusetts, all report a substantially greater involvement of women in crime prior to the twentieth century (see also Beattie, 1992). Similarly, a near century-long time series from Toronto (Boritch and Hagan, 1990) between 1859 and 1955 shows a steady and significant decline in arrests of women. It may not commonly be realized that both male and female crime rates declined in most western industrialized nations during the last century and the first part of this century (see Gillis, 1989). However, what is more impressive is that during this same period female criminal involvements declined more dramatically than male involvements, leading to a widening of the gender gap and a strengthening of the gender-criminality relationship that is observed today.

Power-control theory (see Hagan, 1989:154–158) drew on Weber (1947) to consider these changes in terms of the separation of the workplace from the home that occurred during early industrialization. A result of these changes was the separation of what Weber called the production and consumption spheres. The social reproduction of gender roles became an important part of both of these spheres with men largely assigned reproductive functions through the state (involving the police, courts and correctional agencies) in the production sphere and women largely assigned such functions through the family in the consumption sphere.

Both the state and family are involved in creating, maintaining, and reproducing gender roles, but it is particularly the patriarchal structure of the family that established a "cult of domesticity" around women during industrialization (Welter, 1966), reducing substantially female involvement in activities like crime and delinquency. Power-control theory gives particular attention to a gender division of roles that reproduces this outcome in more patriarchal families through an instrument-object relationship in which fathers and especially mothers (i.e., as instruments of social control) are expected to control their daughters more than their sons (i.e., as objects of social control). Braithwaite (1989:93) incorporated this framework into his broader theory of *Crime, Shame and Reintegration* when he wrote "we predict that females will be more often the objects and the instruments of reintegrative shaming, while males will be more often the objects and instruments of stigmatization."

Feeley and Little (1991:39) echoed this kind of explanation for the historical decline of women in crime from the eighteenth to the twentieth century. They wrote that "in the broadest terms, there was a redefinition of the female, and a shift and perhaps an intensification of private patriarchal control of women within the household." They then brought this line of argument to the following conclusion:

> By the end of the nineteenth century, there was a clear separation of home and work, a firmer sexual division of labor, the exclusion of women from the public sphere and from productive work, and the confinement of women to reproductive and domestic work in the home. Our data indicate that there was also a decline in female criminal court involvement during this period.

Feeley and Little were clear in noting that this was a period in which women lost power in the economic sphere of production and at the same time became more involved and subject to domestic social control within the family. They concluded "the trends thus point to possible explanations for our vanishing female defendant."

This study by Feeley and Little and other historical studies noted earlier encourage the expectation of power-control theory that the relationships linking crime and delinquency vary across social settings. As changes occur in gender roles in the family and in work, it is of interest to explore how these changes may alter relationships between gender and crime and delinquency. It has been argued earlier that increasing controls on women during industrialization decreased their involvement in crime. It does *not* by necessity follow that relaxation of such controls associated with changing gender roles will increase involvement in crime. This would assume a comprehensive kind of symmetrical causation (Lieberson, 1985) that power-control theory does not suggest for reasons elaborated later. However, there may be some minor and common kinds of behavior, such as smoking, that are influenced by the relaxation of controls and the movement away from patriarchal families. To examine this kind of possibility, we turn next to our use of high school survey data, this time to test a power-control theory of smoking.

Specifying a Power-Control Theory of Smoking

One of the most perplexing problems of recent decades has involved increasing rates of smoking among adolescent girls and increasing rates of lung cancer among women. Krohn et al. (1986:147) reported, "Not only does it appear that more females are smoking on a regular basis . . . but some studies have found an increase in the proportion of heavy smokers among females." Studies fluctuated in their findings and there may be signs that this pattern is levelling out; however, a concern persists about the health implications of increases in smoking among adolescent girls.

Concern is so great about the active and passive effects of smoking that strict new laws are being passed to control smoking behavior. We may even see smoking again criminalized, as it was for some age groups, times, and places in the past. In any case, it is commonly argued that smoking is analogous to forms of crime and delinquency (Hirschi, 1969; Akers, 1984; Gottfredson and Hirschi, 1990). In a social sense, it can be argued that smoking is one of the most common forms of delinquency, a kind of "common delinquency" that power-control theory was originally intended to explain (Hagan, Gillis, and Simpson, 1985).

Smoking is a form of deviant behavior where women today overall have a rough parity with men. This is reflected in a survey undertaken in 1989 of adolescents in a wealthy section of Toronto called Forest Hill (Hagan, Gillis, and Simpson, 1990). Slightly more than 20 percent of males and females in this setting smoked, as indicated in Table 2.7.

Historically, power-control theory suggests that this parity in smoking is linked to the increasing freedom and power experienced by mothers and daughters in the family, which may be most apparent in affluent communities like Forest Hill (Coser, 1985). If this is the case, it may be possible to treat differences in power relationships within the families of this community as analogues to more general changes in family power relationships over time.

A measure of marital power in Forest Hill asked who decides where to live, where to go on vacation, whether both spouses should work, and whether to move if the husband gets a job in another city. The item with

Table 2.7 Cross-tabulation of Gender and Self-Reported Smoking

Self-Reported Smoking	No	Yes	N
Female	77.5(110)	22.5(32)	142
Male	76.5(104)	23.5(32)	136

Source: Data from John Hagan, A. R. Gillis, and John Simpson, 1990, "Clarifying and Extending Power-Control Theory," *American Journal of Sociology*, vol. 95, pp. 1024–37.

greatest variance in responses in the scale indicated that while a majority (58 percent) of the wives decided alone whether to work, a large remaining proportion decided this issue with their husbands. The sample was split roughly in half on the basis of their scale scores into more- and less-patriarchal families. The sample is divided in this way in Table 2.8, and gender and smoking are again cross-classified as they were in Table 2.7.

Recall that earlier when we used this procedure to test for an intervening relationship, we observed a reduction in the percentage differences in the sub-tables. However, when we compare the percentaged results in Table 2.7 with those in Tables 2.8, we observe something different. While there is only a 1 percent difference by gender in smoking in Table 2.7, more notable percentage differences appear in Table 2.8, and the differences are in opposite directions: sons are more likely than daughters to smoke in more patriarchal families (24.6 percent versus 16.0 percent), while daughters are more likely than sons to smoke in less patriarchal families (29.9 percent versus 22.5 percent). The increase in female smoking in less patriarchal families is pronounced, nearly doubling from 16 percent to almost 30 percent.

The pattern of percentage differences is a form of interaction effect often called "suppression." It suggests that there is a relationship between gender and smoking that is suppressed in Table 2.7, which becomes apparent in Table 2.8 when differences in parental power relationships (i.e., patriarchal relationships) are taken into account.

Thus far we have used a crude measure of smoking: whether the respondents report any smoking behavior at all. You will recall that limitations of sample size and technique restrict the number of categories and variables we can use in tabular analysis. Regression analysis can take advantage of more detailed information on the number of cigarettes smoked. One way we can take advantage of the more detailed information is to construct an "interaction term" by multiplying the involved variables, gender and patriarchy. The form of the resulting regression equation is:

$$y = a + b_1x_1 + b_2x_2 + b_1x_1b_2x_2 + u,$$

Table 2.8 Cross-tabulation of Gender and Smoking by Type of Family

Type of Family	More Patriarchal			Less Patriarchal		
Self-Reported Smoking	No	Yes	N	No	Yes	N
Gender						
Female	84.0(63)	16.0(12)	75	70.1(47)	29.9(20)	67
Male	75.4(49)	24.6(16)	65	77.5(55)	22.5(16)	71

Source: Data from John Hagan, A. R. Gillis, and John Simpson, 1990, "Clarifying and Extending Power-Control Theory," *American Journal of Sociology,* vol. 95, pp. 1024–37.

where y is the number of cigarettes smoked, x_1 is gender, x_2 is patriarchy, and x_1x_2 is the interaction of these variables.

In estimating this regression equation, daughters and less patriarchal families are coded 1, so that the product interaction term assumes a value of 1 for those subjects who are female and from less patriarchal families. The results of estimating this regression can be presented as follows with the unstandardized coefficients assuming their positions in the equation:

$$y = 1.891 + (-1.064)x_1 + (-.648)x_2 + (2.0)x_1x_2 + u.$$

The coefficient for the product interaction term (2.0) has a t-value of 2.577, which would occur by chance fluctuation in sampling less than 1 out of 100 times. By letting smoking in a regression equation assume the continuous value of the number of cigarettes smoked a day, we are able to more convincingly demonstrate that an interaction effect is operating.

However, not only the relationship between gender and smoking may be affected by the conditioning influence of family structure but also the intervening variables in the power-control model may be affected. To explore this possibility we employ an elaboration of regression techniques called LISREL, or the Linear Structural Relationships Model (Joreskog and Sorbom, 1984). It is not necessary or appropriate to discuss this statistical modeling program in detail here. We can simply note that it allows researchers to use multiple measures or indicators of concepts that are treated as unobserved. That is, this statistical modeling program allows us to test and improve the measurement of our concepts with multiple measures (beyond simply adding the measures), while also acknowledging that there is always a gap between theoretical concepts and actual measurements of them. As we will see next, the paths in a structural LISREL model can be interpreted in the same fashion as the path model previously noted.

The results of this more elaborate path model are presented in Figure 2.6. With the exception of gender, which is indicated only by reported sex, the other concepts in this model are measured with 2 indicators each. Instead of these indicators being summed, as they sometimes were earlier, LISREL treats each indicator as a distinct entity. In addition, a concept is added to this model, maternal relational control, which is measured by student's reports that they talk with their mothers about their thoughts and feelings and that they want to be the kind of person their mother is. These relationships are assumed to be formed early in life and to therefore precede maternal instrumental controls, which are now measured with reports of not only whether mothers are perceived to know where their children are but also whether they know who their children are with. Finally, smoking behavior is measured in

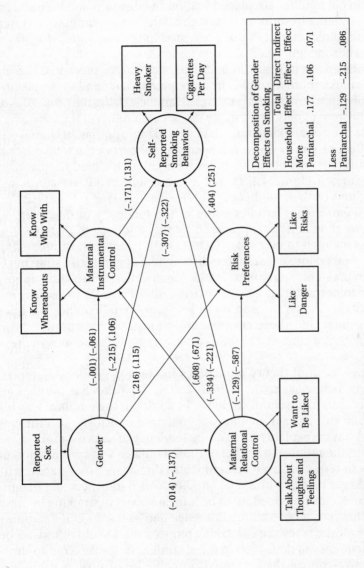

Figure 2.6 A Power-Control Model of Teenage Smoking

Source: John Hagan

terms of whether the students report heavy smoking (seven or more cigarettes a day) and in the terms of the actual number of cigarettes
smoked on average per day.

As earlier, the sample is divided into two groups of students from
more and less patriarchal families. Path coefficients for students from
less patriarchal families are placed first on the diagram and followed by
those for students from more patriarchal families. A summary of total,
direct and indirect effects is also presented in the accompanying lower
right hand box in Figure 2.6.

The total effects indicate (as in the tabular analysis presented earlier)
that boys smoke more than girls in more patriarchal families, while girls
smoke more than boys in less patriarchal families. Using the properties of
Wright's theorem of path analysis we can see that much of the total effect
that results in boys smoking more than girls in more patriarchal families is
a direct effect of gender. However, a substantial part of the total effect is
also a result of sons in these families being more inclined to take risks
than daughters $[(.115)(.251)]$, as well as these sons being less controlled
than daughters by their mothers $[(-.137)(-.587)(.251)+(-.137)((-.221)]$.

In less patriarchal families some of the tendency of daughters to
smoke more than sons is suppressed by the tendency of daughters to
still be less inclined to take risks $[(.216)(.404)]$. When this counteracting
tendency is taken into account, the direct effect of gender on smoking is
larger than previously apparent: $-.215$. Meanwhile, there is little opportunity for maternal relational or instrumental controls to reduce the
smoking of daughters, since in these less-patriarchal families the links
between gender and these controls are minuscule, indicating that in
terms of maternal control daughters are treated much like sons in these
families.

So power-control theory anticipates interesting gender differences
in smoking behavior in the more- and less-patriarchal families of
wealthy Toronto high school students. In addition, the emphasis of this
theory on links between gender and maternal controls and attitudes
toward risk-taking explains some of the tendency of sons to smoke more
than girls in the more-patriarchal of these families. The specification of
the theory in terms of family structure also directs us to a different pattern of linkages in less-patriarchal families, which indicates that daughters, like sons, can gain freedom to become involved in smoking in these
families. However, a continuing difference between sons and daughters
in terms of attitudes toward risk taking reduces what might otherwise be
a greater tendency of daughters in these families to smoke. This application of power-control theory would probably be of further value if it
included measures of perceptions of the risks of smoking per se. It
would also be relevant to have measures of perceived "benefits" of
smoking, such as weight loss and weight control. Pressures involved in

dieting may be of special importance to adolescent girls. Unfortunately, these measures are not available in the data set and must await further research.

Liberation, Patriarchy, and Delinquency

We turn finally to an issue that has caused confusion in interpretations of power-control theory. At least one critic (Naffine, 1987) interpreted this theory as suggesting that the *ideas* of the women's liberation movement will lead to increased criminality among women. This is not the point of this theory, but consideration of this interpretation does suggest another interesting possibility. This is, that *un*liberated, patriarchal attitudes may play a role in explaining some *male* delinquency.

While it is unlikely that identification with egalitarian sex role attitudes (e.g., the sharing of power in the family and in occupational roles) causes delinquent behavior, it may be that more-patriarchal attitudes do directly and indirectly cause some delinquency (e.g., violence) and help further to explain the tendency for males to exceed females in delinquency. We pursue this last possibility to illustrate a procedure often used in regression analysis called "the decomposition of effects." This procedure was partially introduced earlier in this chapter and now can be demonstrated more fully.

This demonstration again uses data drawn from a 1988 survey of Toronto high school students, in this case students from the more general population. These students were asked about their agreement/disagreement with the following sex role attitude statements:

■ A man can make long-range plans for his life, but a woman has to take things as they come.

■ Men should share the work around the house with women such as doing dishes, cleaning, and so forth.

■ A woman should have exactly the same job opportunities as a man.

Student agreement/disagreement with these statements was ordered so that when summed student scores ranged from less- to more-patriarchal in orientation. These scores were then included with measures like those introduced above in a regression analysis of self-reported assaultive behavior. This behavior was indicated by answers to an item that asked how often the students had "beaten up someone on purpose?"

The resulting regression decomposes the effects of gender, patriarchal attitudes, and other power-control variables on self-reported assaultive behavior by estimating five equations. Each equation adds another variable in sequence from gender, through maternal relational control, maternal instrumental control, patriarchal attitudes, to risk preferences. The results are presented in Table 2.9.

As each equation adds a variable that intervenes between gender and assaultive behavior, the effect of gender declines by the amount (of the gender effect) that the intervening variable transmits. Note that patriarchal attitudes (.5 − .365=.135) transmit the largest intervening effect but that maternal instrumental control (.625 − .5=.125) and risk preferences (.365 − .291=.074) also play notable mediating roles. Overall, these three variables account for more than half of the tendency for boys to exceed girls in their involvement in assaultive behavior (.334/.632=.528). Patriarchal attitudes do not have a strong impact on assaultive behavior in this model: the standardized effect is .131 before the introduction of risk preferences, and .102 after. Nonetheless, these attitudes play a notable intervening role, and a net direct effect remains even when all other variables are included in the model. There is therefore further evidence that can be incorporated within a power-control model, which assumes that patriarchy plays a causally significant role in the causation of male delinquency.

Conclusions

This chapter is an introduction to issues of causality that form a central part of a social science of crime. In the chapters that follow, principles and techniques introduced in this chapter are developed further in relation to several controversies that focus on criminological research. Each of these chapters is concerned with issues of causation, and the logic and methods introduced form a basis for most causal arguments you will encounter not only in these chapters, but as well in the larger criminological literature that this book makes accessible to you.

One way to place in perspective much of what we have considered to this point is to compare our presentation with past introductions to the methods of our field. These introductions also have been concerned with issues of causation. They characteristically suggest that to demonstrate causation it is necessary to establish that the variables considered are associated (i.e., that they are related or covary), that there is an identifiable sequence to the association (i.e., that the cause precedes the effect), and that the association is nonspurious. The last criterion is the familiar reminder that correlation does not mean causation and typically involves a demonstration that an alleged causal relationship between variables does not disappear when added relevant variables that precede the correlated variables are taken into account.

Table 2.9 Decomposition of the Effects of Power-Control Variables and Patriarchal Attitudes on Self-Reported Assaultive Behavior

Variable		Eq.1	Eq.2	Eq.3	Eq.4	Eq.5
Gender	b(se)	.632(.112)	.625(.109)	.500(.112)	.365(.119)	.291(.116)
	B	.232	.230	.183	.134	.107
Maternal Instrumental	b(se)		-.167(.734)	-.120(.036)	-.108(.036)	-.099(.035)
Control	B		-.200	-.136	-.126	-.116
Patriarchal Attitudes	b(se)				.071(.023)	.055(.023)
	B				.131	.102
Risk Preferences	b(se)					.177(.030)
	B					.245
Intercept		.403	1.250	1.951	1.549	
R^2		.054	.092	.120	.134	.184

A classic spurious correlation involves the relationship between storks and human fertility in northern Europe. Fertility is apparently higher in some regions of northern Europe where storks are more common. The explanation of this correlation is that fertility is higher in rural areas of these nations where storks also happen to flourish. So the "real" causal association is between rural location and fertility.

Although we have emphasized the importance of association and sequence in this chapter, we have not focused on spuriousness. Rather, we have emphasized the role of intervening variables in mediating/transmitting/interpreting and therefore in accounting for causal effects. We have done so because we believe these intervening processes are more common and more important than issues of spuriousness in criminological analysis. Most correlates of crime have real causal effects, but the mechanisms by which these effects operate often are unclear. This is often the case in the social sciences. For example, few people would believe that storks cause fertility, while the interesting causal issues have to do with intervening variables that mediate the causal influence of rural residence on fertility (i.e., do farmers have more time for sex? Do they need children to help farm?).

We also have given considerable attention to interaction effects that specify conditions under which relationships hold and/or are modified. We have noted that these effects can be unstable, often varying across time and place. This instability makes interaction effects interesting, but often frustrating to study. A controversial interaction we have observed in this chapter involves variation in the relationship between gender, smoking, and perhaps other forms of common delinquency among adolescents in more- and less-patriarchal families. We are less concerned here with the reliability of these findings than with the exposition of the methods involved in their investigation. The interactions explored derive from a power-control theory that these methods help to make explicit and to test. This brings us to our final point: perhaps the most important attraction of the application of scientific methods in the study of crime is that these methods encourage us to articulate our ideas in clear and testable ways.

Urbanization, Sociohistorical Context, and Crime

A. R. Gillis

It is my belief, Watson, founded upon my experience, that the lowest and vilest alleys of London do not present a more dreadful record of sin than does the smiling and beautiful countryside.

Sir Arthur Conan Doyle (1856–1930), in *Copper Beeches*

The Chicago School of sociology emerged on the 1920s and 1930s in the works of Burgess, McKenzie, Park, Wirth, and Shaw and McKay, among others, and provided an explanation of the relationship between urban disorganization and crime for several generations of American sociologists. However, one of the knocks against the Chicago School is that the research that they did in that city in the 1920s and 1930s was in fact bound by time and space but represented as universal nevertheless (see, for example, Sjoberg, 1970). Apart from underestimating the contribution of context to cause, overgeneralization adds undeserved credibility to arguments and imparts an aura of inevitability to situations that can in fact be changed. Since most social scientific research is done on America by Americans, overgeneralization amounts to applying theories of the present-day American situation to other places and periods. This can annoy historians, social scientists, and the people who live in these places, and this can confuse U.S. tourists who expect Paris, London, or even Toronto to be the same as metropolitan areas in the U.S. Such social scientific ethnocentrism can also blind U.S. researchers and policy makers to realistic alternatives to American patterns.

Part of the problem originates with the need of sociologists to generalize. Social scientists are supposed to generalize. It's our job. Moving beyond particular concrete cases to more abstract and universal levels enables us to build a broad body of knowledge (see, for example, Berelson and Steiner, 1964). This distinguishes us from historians and other disciplines in the Arts, where an emphasis on unique events and detailed description of populations and periods inhibits the development of more abstract theory and its application elsewhere (see Kiser and Hechter, 1991).

In one respect social scientists are very careful about generalizing. We typically exercise a great deal of scientific rigor in drawing samples and generalizing back to the populations from which they are drawn.

Unless social scientists are confident that relationships shown in samples are unlikely to occur by chance, we refuse to believe that these patterns actually exist in the population. (Tradition in sociology holds that reasonable doubt disappears when the probability of chance is at or below 1 in 20: i.e. $p \leq .05$.)

In spite of this rigor in generalizing back to our populations, we are often rather casual when we infer from them to the universe beyond. Experiments on undergraduates in university courses, surveys within particular cities, and analyses of national census data produce findings that may or may not hold for other people, other cities, other nations, or other historical periods. Obviously evidence from one population bound in time and space is far better than no information at all for making general statements. However, human conditions can differ markedly across populations as well as over time to produce dramatically different results. Since it is impossible to conduct research on a sample representing all populations in all historical periods, social scientists rely on replications of studies on *different* populations to establish the reliability of results over time and space. Successful replication increases confidence in original findings, sometimes to a point where propositions are viewed as laws, or "invariant." (See, for example, Hirschi and Gottfredson, 1983, on age and crime; c.f. Greenberg, 1985.)

On the other side, failure to replicate original results casts doubt on them and typically produces an argument about whose measures are more reliable, whose analysis is more sophisticated, or whose implications are more moral. Although this can be entertaining, unless one of the studies is seriously flawed, the situation usually does more to produce two antagonistic camps instead of contributing to a general body of knowledge. This is unfortunate, since the failure to replicate research findings does not necessarily mean that the findings of one of the studies is wrong. Instead, the second investigation may simply indicate that the results of the original analysis are not universally applicable. The circumstances under which the original proposition is supported (or the conditions in the second population that negate it) should be investigated and specified. In fact, discovering the *circumstances* under which propositions hold is as theoretically and practically important as the propositions themselves (see Walker and Cohen, 1985 on scope statements).

One of the most vivid examples of the importance of context as a causal factor can be seen in two of Shakespeare's tragedies. Although *Hamlet* and *Othello* were named after the heroes, the tragedies resulted as much from the circumstances in which the two found themselves as the "tragic flaws" in their personalities. Hamlet, an intellectual, was more a man of words than deeds. His delay in taking action (which is entirely understandable to any empiricist, when you consider a ghost was prompting him to murder his uncle) allowed the villain to take countermeasures and almost everybody (including Hamlet) winds up seriously dead. On the other extreme, Othello was a military man and far more given to action than to deep thought and free-floating anxiety. His circumstances involved a suspicion that his wife, Desdemona, was unfaithful. ("Evidence" was supplied by a false friend, Iago.) Othello killed Desdemona. Once he realized his mistake, he conceded that he "loved not wisely but too well," and then took his own life.

The interaction of personality and context is demonstrated by the idea that in Hamlet's position, Othello would have quickly dispatched his evil uncle, become king, and lived happily ever after (at least until he got married): no tragedy. On the other side, if Hamlet suspected his wife of infidelity, his character could not take such rash action on such weak evidence: no tragedy. Thus, the tragedies of both Hamlet and Othello were brought about by the interaction of specific personalities in particular contexts. Neither, by themselves, caused tragic outcomes, but when you combine the two together in the right way it's a different story.

In social science, similar interactions can occur between independent variables in quantitative analyses. For example, research in Germany found that multiple-unit housing contained a disproportionate number of residents who experienced stress. Further, the higher their dwelling-units were located in buildings, the greater the levels of stress reported by respondents. Since they had been unable to choose the location of their dwelling units, the probability of selection was low, leading the researcher to conclude that high living is stressful (Fanning, 1967). Subsequent research in Hong Kong failed to support this finding (Mitchell, 1971). It is possible that one or both of the studies has produced inaccurate results. It is also possible that differences in the populations under analysis caused the anomaly—an obvious possibility here being culture. Since the German research included only women, while the Hong Kong study included both sexes, another possibility was gender. A third study, in Canada, supported this reasoning, showing that while high living may be stressful for women, it may be beneficial for men (Gillis, 1977). Combining both sexes in an analysis would fail to show this, because the positive relationship for the females would be cancelled out by the negative relationship for the males.

The discovery of the conditions or limitations under which propositions hold, then, is an integral part of building social scientific knowledge, while taking into account contextual differences emphasized by cross-cultural researchers and historians.

Urbanization

The substantive focus of this chapter is the relationship between urbanization and crime, and the arguments developed by students of cities to explain the relationship. Most of the explanations were developed by twentieth-century sociologists to account for the patterns they observed around them in Chicago and other U.S. cities (for a discussion see Archer and Gartner, 1984). In view of the national and temporal constraints of this research, this chapter examines generally the urbanization of Europe and its relationship with the emergence of civilization. The chapter also presents a time-series analysis of urbanization and rates of crime in nineteenth-century France and concludes that, at least with respect to serious offenses, urban life is not by itself criminogenic. Synthesizing these findings with those produced by contemporary research suggests that social and demographic changes in Western nations in the last half of the twentieth century may have provided an essential context for the emergence of a direct relationship between urbanization and rates of serious crime.

Explanations of Contemporary Urban Crime

The relationship between urbanization and crime is probably close to invariant, at least in the minds of most students of crime (see, for example, Berelson and Steiner, 1964: 628). Cities are viewed as dangerous, and the bigger they are, the greater the threat. However, scholars have traditionally disliked cities (White and White, 1962), and sociologists and criminologists are no exception (Mills, 1942). Whether this antipathy promotes or follows from their analyses of urban/rural differences is uncertain, but the volume of critical prose is large. The following explanations focus on crime and delinquency and represent only a fraction of the literature that reflects this aversion of intellectuals to cities. Most of the explanations are locational versions of arguments that account for the social distribution of crime and delinquency.

Selection and Migration

Urbanization refers to the proportion of a region's population that resides in areas designated as urban. So an increase in urbanization could result from either an increase in the urban population or a decrease in the rural population. In fact both typically occur, through rural to urban migration. Because of their relatively low rates of fertility, cities depend on migration from rural areas for their survival and growth. It is unlikely that migrants are randomly selected to move to urban areas—some types of people are more likely to migrate to cities than are others. So it is possible that people who leave rural areas for the bright lights of the city are also more inclined to become involved in criminal behavior than are those who stay behind. The effect of this selection would be to lower crime rates in rural areas while simultaneously increasing them in urban areas, producing a positive correlation between urbanization and rates of crime.

Selection could occur for any number of reasons, including demographic, economic, and social and social psychological factors, such as the strength of ties to family, friends, and the local community. Individuals who migrate may have weaker ties to other people, be relatively immune to social control, more likely to take risks, and have a greater tendency to engage in deviant behaviors, including crime (see Gillis, 1994a). Similarly, cities may attract excitement seekers or criminals who originate in rural areas but go to cities to engage in their misdeeds (see, for example, Gibbs and Erickson, 1976).

Deviant Subcultures

Small, dispersed populations, such as those in rural areas, villages, and towns and villages restrict support for highly specialized goods and services. This includes unusual or deviant interests. For example, if only 1 out of every 100 people has an interest in regularly using illicit substances and 50 clients are required to make drug-pushing an economically viable career, it follows that all things being equal, towns with populations of less than 5,000 will not support a full-time professional drug-pusher. On the other hand, a large metropolitan area offers viable careers for hundreds or even thousands of drug dealers, as well as organization with specialized roles. Further, once drug networks are established, a subculture can emerge that can recruit members and increase demand. In this way, then, cities can harbor a wide range of unusual, deviant, and criminal interests, with larger cities offering and encouraging support for even more infrequently occurring urges and impulses, including illegal activities (see, for example, Fischer, 1984).

Informal networks of urbanites may also develop to offer social support and protection in the face of an unpredictable and unfriendly social environment (see, for example, Suttles, 1968, 1972). However, by engaging in conflict, even for protection, these networks may produce strong distinctions between insiders and outsiders, and link network loyalty to both indifference and hostility toward strangers (see Gillis and Hagan, 1990).

Urban Environments and Social Disorganization

The relationship between city life and the human condition attracted the attention of social scientists from the very beginning. Tönnies, Simmel, and other nineteenth-century scholars described the urban condition in terms of loss of community. This lead continued in twentieth-century America and was amplified in the works of Wirth (1938) and Milgram (1970).

As noted earlier, the specific relationship between crime and urban life was probably most widely disseminated by the Chicago School. These urban ecologists, including Wirth, Burgess, Shaw and McKay, and

Thrasher viewed the size, density, heterogeneity, and mobility of urban populations as infertile ground for social organization and the development and maintenance of self-control. The cultural heterogeneity of the urban scene eroded traditional norms, and the freedom and anonymity of crowded and constantly changing neighborhoods promoted bystander apathy. This could not only allow people to get away with their criminal behavior but may have even inspired individuals to engage in non-conforming behavior in an effort to assert their individualism in an aloof and uncaring social environment (see, for example, Rainwater, 1966).

Some students of cities oppose this view of urban community as too dismal (see, for example, Jacobs, 1961) and assign too much importance to the physical environment while ignoring social networks and "community without propinquity" (see Wellman, 1979). However, recent research indicates that urbanites are in fact more tolerant of differences and nonconformity, draw a sharper distinction between friends and strangers, and treat the latter with greater indifference than do their rural counterparts (see Stephan and McMullin, 1982, Wilson, 1985; Tuch, 1987). Further, the social disorganization contention has been reformulated in terms of network analysis and supported empirically with data from Great Britain (see Sampson and Groves, 1989; Bursik, 1988; Sampson, 1988).

Thrasher (1927) argued that deviance can be exciting and even a form of entertainment (see, more recently, Katz, 1988) and when combined with social disorganization and reduced control, produced crime, delinquency, and a breakdown of social order. In 1972 Oscar Newman published an architectural variant of this argument. He suggested that specific aspects of urban design create unsupervised locations by inhibiting or preventing surveillance and control in neighborhoods and even within apartment buildings. High walls around buildings, underground parking areas, long corridors, and secluded spaces such as stairwells provide opportunity for deviant or criminal activity. This is because these locations are concealed from formal policing on streets, while at the same time, residents do not feel obliged to maintain surveillance on these areas either because they lie outside their own dwelling units. As with the perspective developed by the Chicago school, Newman's argument accounts for the location of criminal activity and suggests that structural barriers (in this case physical) block the local social ties that represent community and prevent crime and delinquency.

Urban lifestyles may also exacerbate criminal activity by depressing social control. In rural areas, traditional occupations for husbands and wives revolved around the home, where passersby would have been noticed and surveillance maintained. In contrast, occupations and cosmopolitan activities in modern urban areas frequently draw adults away from home, leaving an unattended store of valuable goods (see Cohen and Felson, 1979).

Social Reaction

Social reaction arguments alert us to the possibility that variation in rates of crime may reflect different patterns of enforcement and recording of offenses rather than variation in actual criminal behavior. In the case of urban crime, the likelihood of detection, apprehension, and recording of offenses may be higher in urban than in rural areas. Rather than seeing cities as places to commit crime with impunity, then, the reaction perspective suggests that because of their high density and more extensive surveillance, urban areas are more dangerous for criminals than for more conforming citizens. Like William Whyte (1943) before her, Jane Jacobs (1961) argues that although lots of urban neighborhoods look disorganized, the communities they contain are alive and well, with strong informal controls. In addition, police are more likely to patrol high-density areas and detect any offenses that occur in them (see generally Stinchcombe, 1963, and more specifically Hagan, Gillis, and Chan, 1978; Gillis and Hagan, 1982). Further, the bureaucratized urban police seem more likely to process and record the offenses they detect than are their more informal rural counterparts (see, for example, Wilson, 1968). So between the informal control of residents and the formal control of urban policing, higher rates of crime in urban areas may be the result of an excess of social control rather than an excess of criminal activity.

Urbanization and the Civilization of Western Europe

Although social scientists often disagree about the causes, then, they generally concur that crime is coincident with modern urban life (see Berelson and Steiner, 1964). This is not surprising since the arguments were developed in twentieth-century North America to explain findings produced by cross-sectional analyses of rural/urban differences in crime in the United States (Archer and Gartner, 1984). However, except for the last few decades, serious crime has been in decline in the West since the waning of the Middle Ages (Chesnais, 1981; Gurr, 1979, 1981, 1989; Gurr, Grabosky, and Hula, 1977; Stone, 1983. See also Lane, 1974, 1979, 1989, on more recent periods). Since it was during this epoch that Europe urbanized, the growth of cities is more likely to have been a cure than a cause of serious crime.

The Temper of Medieval Times

The merits of the Middle Ages have been extolled by twentieth-century scholars as well as nostalgic romantics. Europe was largely rural during the period, having gradually de-urbanized with the fall of the Roman

Empire. The scale of community life was small, political power was relatively diffuse (Mumford, 1970), and kinship ties and interpersonal relationships were more concrete, encompassing, and enduring (M. Becker, 1988; Mumford, 1961). People were more religious (Huizinga, 1924), honor and loyalty were highly regarded (M. Becker, 1988), and suicide was exceedingly rare in this heroic epoch (Masaryk, [1881] 1970: 126–7). However, as gratifying as all this may have been, Eco's (1983) *The Name of the Rose* probably gives a more balanced portrayal of medieval life. Although he focused on the clergy, Eco's description of superstition, intemperance, passions, and violence evidently applied to the wider social sphere as well.

The expansion of Christianity throughout medieval Europe was ineffective in deterring crime. In fact, with its focus on mutilation, mortification of the flesh, and repression of natural urges, medieval Christianity may have contributed to feelings of fatalism, personal instability, and unpredictable outbursts of violence. (See also, Davis, 1975, on ritual violence associated with rites of passage.) Life was hard and death was ubiquitous during the Middle Ages. Famines, epidemics, plagues, and the wild animals of fairy tales were realities that maintained high rates of premature mortality (McEvedey, 1988; McNeill, 1976; Zinsser, 1963). This, and the personal insecurity it engendered, may have also helped to desensitize medieval people to physical cruelty, for they frequently injured or killed one another with unpredictable outbursts of extreme violence (Gurr, 1979; Stone, 1983), particularly in rural areas (Given, 1977).

> Medieval men had little control over their immediate impulses; they were emotionally insensitive to the spectacle of pain, and they had small regard for human life, which they saw only as a transitory state before Eternity; moreover, they were very prone to make it a point of honour to display their physical strength in an almost animal way (Bloch, 1964: 411).

Cities as Concentrations of Capital and Organized Centers of Civility

The burgeoning cities that heralded the end of the Middle Ages were more than simply large concentrations of people. They contained populations in specialized occupations or trades that were controlled by guilds, as well as a court of law (see M. Weber [1921] 1958; Chirot, 1985). Consequently, cities were able to be much more than the sum total of the production of their individual residents. In this respect, urban areas were not only accumulations of human and economic capital, they were concentrations of social and cultural capital as well (see G. Becker, 1964, on human capital;

Coleman, 1987, 1988a, 1990, on social capital, and Bourdieu, 1977, 1980, 1984; DiMaggio and Mohr, 1985, on cultural capital).

From the standpoint of the individual, access to urban markets demanded the possession of physical, human, and/or cultural capital for which there was demand and the willingness to observe habitually the laws, norms, and obligations of the city (see Hirschman, 1977, on the surrender and sublimation of passions to interests). However, on a macro level, whether civility preceded or followed urbanization is unclear. On the one hand, a minimal level of order and social stability would have been required to enforce the obligations, agreements, contractual arrangements, and civil behavior that were cities. In view of the relationship between the expansion of state power and urban wealth discussed earlier, the coercive power of the State may have provided the basis for the social order of the city. Further, towns and cities often maintained their own sergeant of arms or constabulary, whose task was the maintenance of order. On the other hand, the explicit use of force and policing is not always effective for some types of behavior, including violence (see, for example, Gillis, 1989), to the point where such efforts may even elicit the very reaction they are intended to deter (Henry and Short, 1954). Perhaps as a consequence, patterns of control evolved from direct coercion to more indirect, integrative control through the use of the economy and information systems. Granovetter (1985) suggests that normative order may be "embedded" in social organization, and Coleman (1987) notes that norms can be seen as social capital, so civility may have been inherent in the emerging organizations that were cities. It is noteworthy that civility and civic derive from the same Latin word, *civis*. (See Berman, 1983, and more generally, Braithwaite, 1989, on the constraints of interdependence, and the emergence of shame as a mechanism of maintaining conformity and consistency. See also Bayley, 1986; Etzioni, 1975; Foucault, 1975; Gibbs, 1989; Giddens, 1981a; 1985; Skocpol and Finegold, 1982.) So urbanization may have been both cause and consequence of the development of a specialized economy, the formation of an organized system of social control and an increasing degree of public safety, especially for those willing and able to abide within the walls and the rules of the city (see Gillis, 1994b).

By the eleventh century European re-urbanization was well under way and continued (with some short-run setbacks due to epidemics of bubonic plague, smallpox, and cholera) well into the twentieth century (see Hohenberg and Lees, 1985; Tilly, 1990). During this period, urbanization may have further eroded violence as a strategy for settling disputes. From nineteenth-century Strasburg, Simmel (1970) observed that the relatively personal and spontaneous style of living in sparsely populated rural environments was not as apparent in cities. He suggested that city life required adaptation to an environment that included large numbers of personal contacts and a greater demand for predictability and punctuality associated with a more complex division of labor (see also Durkheim, [1893] 1964). In response to this, urbanites learned to avoid overload by developing a blasé attitude and ignoring irrelevant stimuli. Feeling was divested from the majority of social relationships, which became more task-specific, superficial, and emotionally inconsequential.

> (T)he sophisticated character of metropolitan psychic life becomes understandable—as over against small town life which rests more upon deeply felt and emotional relationships. These latter are rooted in the more unconscious layers of the psyche . . . The intellect, however, has its locus in the transparent, conscious, higher layers of the psyche; it is the most adaptable of our inner forces . . . Thus the metropolitan type of man . . . reacts with his head instead of his heart . . . They (metropolitan people) share a matter-of-fact attitude in dealing with men and with things (Simmel, 1970: 778).

According to Simmel, then, the metropolitan mind was governed more by thought than by feelings. This urbane self-control became part of the cultural capital of the city, increasing the "trustworthiness of the social environment," which is social capital (see Coleman, 1988a: S103. See also MacAulay, 1963, on the necessity of trust for the viability of contract).

To summarize, during the Middle Ages, Western Europe was rural and experienced high rates of serious crime. However, the Renaissance coincided with reurbanization, the emergence and growth of states, and the civilization of the population. This seems to have continued through to the eighteenth and nineteenth centuries, but the causal sequence is uncertain. The pacification of Western Europe may have occurred as a result of the monopolization of violence by states, with urban areas simply an unimportant correlate of the whole process. Similarly, cultural changes initiated by the Renaissance may have pacified Western Europe with urbanization occurring as a consequence rather than a cause of increasing gentility. On the other hand, urbanization may have generated civility either independent of or in conjunction with other factors, including the growth of states. In any case, there is little empirical support for the idea of cities as a cause of serious crime, at least until the eighteenth and nineteenth centuries, when industrialization was in full flight, and conditions of the urban working poor were critical.

Nineteenth-Century France

To examine more closely the relationship between urbanization and crime, we turn to a distinct historical context: France during the second half of the nineteenth and first part of the twentieth centuries. In view of the topic of the research, France during this era is a particularly appropriate case to analyze. Urbanization continued throughout the period, yet crime rates were a source of considerable public concern. An obsession with decadence and crime "endured at all levels of French society throughout the nineteenth century " (Beirne, 1987: 1145). It was during this period that Durkheim provoked considerable controversy by declaring at least some social pathology inevitable and locating its origins in society and its moral boundaries (see Wright, 1983). At the time, the prevailing belief focused on the emergence and growth of "dangerous classes" as the cause of both criminal and political upheaval (Tombs, 1980). All of this suggests that in nineteenth-century France urbanization was a positive rather than a negative correlate of the *public perception* of crime. Whether this perception is a reflection of the actual rate of crime is unclear. In any case, the fact that the population for analysis seems not to be in accord with our expectations makes it more rather than less appropriate to study.

The specific focus of this research is urbanization and its impact on rates of major and minor crimes in France between 1852 and 1914. This period is marked on one end by the rebellion of 1848 and Louis Napoleon's *coup d'état* of 1852, and on the other end by the massive disruption of World War I.

Although criminal statistics must be approached with care even when they are recently compiled, "Frenchmen in the nineteenth century did possess one of the world's best statistical records of that era for making educated guesses about trends in crime" (Wright, 1983: 96–97). Criminal statistics were published annually from 1826 in the *Compte générale de l'administration de la justice criminelle.* The Penal Code was revised in 1863 for the last time in the nineteenth century, reducing some serious crimes to misdemeanors, and further restricting the discretionary power of judges (Wright, 1983).

French population statistics for the nineteenth century are also relatively high in quality. Because France led the decline in European fertility, French population statistics receive a great deal of attention from historical demographers, so limitations are known and correction factors have been developed. (For the most part, French census enumerations, first published in 1851, converge convincingly with other estimates of population characteristics, especially since 1856. See, for example, Van de Walle, 1974.)

The last half of the nineteenth and early twentieth centuries was an era of widespread technical, economic, and demographic change in France. Although there was only one major war (the Franco-Prussian War, 1870–1871), the age can hardly be described as peaceful. It was a period of intense and extensive social challenge and conflict, which occurred for the most part within the country, pitting an emerging proletariat against their employers and, increasingly, the state.

Throughout the nineteenth century, and particularly during the latter half (the *fin de siècle*), elites perceived that the nation was in decay and that their class position was weakening (see Weber, 1986). Perhaps more in response to this, then, and in the interest of maintaining order and the *status quo*, the nature and extent of state control also changed, with the advent of national policing. (See, especially, Lyman, 1964; Lane, 1967; Silver, 1967; Monkkenon, 1975; and more generally, Black, 1976; Cobban, 1961, 1965; Magraw, 1983; Tilly, 1986; Weber, 1976, 1986; and Wright, 1981 for more general treatments of this period of French history.)

Courts and Crime Rates

There were three court systems in France during the nineteenth century. The *cours d'assises* dealt with *crimes* (serious offenses such as index crimes or felonies in the United States). The *tribunaux correctionnels*, adjudicated *délits* (more minor offenses, corresponding to misdemeanors); the *justice de paix* was concerned with *contraventions*. These were petty violations such as traffic, hunting, and customs offenses. *Contraventions* were heard by justices of the peace, who could impose fines or prison sentences up to two years. (See also Cohen and Johnson, 1982; Tilly, Levett, Lodhi, and Menger, 1975; and Wright, 1983.)

Research on patterns of crime during the nineteenth century converges in some respects and diverges in others. Some studies suggest that rates of serious personal violence were higher in rural than in urban areas and declined during the last half of the nineteenth-century, while property crime was more of an urban offence and increased over the same period (see Cohen and Johnson, 1982; Lodhi and Tilly, 1973; Shelley, 1981; Weber, 1976; Zehr, 1975; and more generally, Fischer, 1976, 1984). However, these studies were for the most part cross-sectional analyses and/or relatively confined in the periods on which they focused. Longitudinal research shows that rates of serious crime declined while rates of minor offenses increased over the last half of the nineteenth and first half of the twentieth centuries (Davidovitch, 1961; Chesnais, 1975, 1981). So researchers agree that rates of serious violence declined and that rates of minor property crime increased but disagree on whether rates of serious property crimes and minor acts of violence increased or decreased during the nineteenth century. In view of this, it is empirically as well as theoretically important to distinguish major from minor crimes of violence (e.g., homicide, rape vs. assault), as well as major from minor property crimes (e.g., robbery vs. theft).

This research examines the relationship between urbanization and the changes in crime in France during the 61-year period between 1852 and 1913. The analysis focuses on charges for *crimes* and *délits* which resulted in appearances before the *cours d'assises* and the *tribunaux correctionels*, respectively. So the study concentrates on charges for both serious and minor offenses, and excludes petty violations. (Data are transcribed from the *Compte Général de l'Administration de la Justice Criminelle en France* in the *Ministère de la Justice,* and the *Annuaire Statistique,* in the *Bibliothèque Nationale,* both in Paris.)

In order to control for the effects of changes in population, units for the analysis are expressed as rates. The dependent variables are rates of major and minor crimes per unit population, and the independent variable is the proportion of the total population living in areas designated as urban. The control variable is industrialization, indicated by the national consumption of fossil fuels (coal and petroleum products). This variable will also be expressed as a ratio variable, with total population as the denominator. This avoids possible problems arising from analyzing the relationship between variables expressed as rates and others that are not (see Firebaugh and Gibbs, 1985, 1987; Bradshaw and Radbill, 1987; and Kraft, 1987 for an extensive discussion of this issue.)

Scatterplots

Scatterplots show the data points representing the different values taken on by two variables and can often provide a visual representation of the relationship between them. When one of the variables is time, indicated in our study by year, the plot shows the change over time of the other variable, in this case urbanization.

The French population gradually escaped what Marx called "the idiocy of rural life" by abandoning or being forced off the land and agricultural occupations and joining the industrial proletariat in urban areas (see McQuillan, 1984). During the nineteenth century the number of people living in urban areas in France almost tripled. In 1821 urban France contained just over 6 million, which represented about 20 percent of the total population. By the end of the century almost 16 million (15,957,000 in 1901) lived in urban areas, representing 41.0 percent of the population, and by the beginning of the war this was about 45 percent. The urbanization of France proceeded in a generally linear fashion over the nineteenth and early twentieth centuries, except for a slight depression during the war in 1870. (The old definition of urban, a settlement of at least 2,000 people, is used across all years here.) (See also, Braudel, 1988; Tilly, 1986. See Figure 3.1.)

Between 1852 and 1914, rates of serious crime showed an overall decline in France. The rate of crime against persons fell gradually between 1852 and 1869 and dropped precipitously in 1870 thanks to the Franco-Prussian War. Following the war, the crime rate increased for several years before resuming the same general decline displayed in the years preceding 1870 (Figure 3.2).

Rates of major property offenses also declined between 1852 and 1914, falling steeply up until 1870. They rose sharply during the post-war

Urbanization

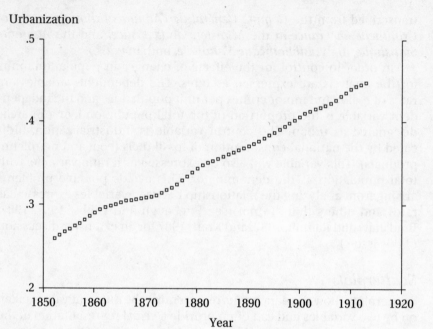

Figure 3.1 Urbanization in France, 1952–1914

Source: Data from the *Complete Généneral de l'Administration de la Justice Criminelle en France* in the *Ministère de la Justice,* and the *Annuaire Statistique,* in the *Bibliothequè Nationale,* both in Paris.

France, 1852-1914

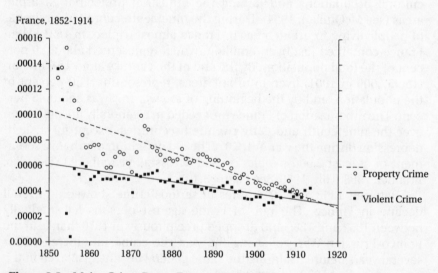

Figure 3.2 Major Crime Rates: France, 1852–1914

Source: Data from *Complete Général de l'Administration de la Justice Criminelle en France,* p. 76, in the *Ministère de la Justice* in Paris.

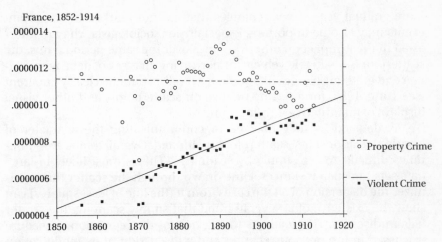

Figure 3.3 Minor Crime Rates: France, 1852–1914

Source: Data from *Complete Général de l'Administration de la Justice Criminelle en France*, p. 76, in the *Ministère de la Justice* in Paris.

period and then declined just as abruptly before levelling off in a gradual decline by 1880 (Figure 3.2).

In contrast to rates of major crime, minor offense rates increased between 1852 and 1914. Except for a drop during the Franco-Prussian War, the rate of common assault increased dramatically throughout the period (Figure 3.3).

Rates of minor property offenses (theft) followed a more varied pattern than did the minor assault rate. Except for the drop during the war in 1870, theft rates increased up until the end of the century and then declined until just before World War I (Figure 3.3).

The scatterplots suggest that urbanization, which steadily increased in France between 1852 and 1914, is inversely related to rates of major crime, which gradually decreased over the same period. On the other side, minor offense rates generally increased between 1852 and 1914, suggesting a direct association with urbanization.

Scatterplots illustrate the association of two variables. In our analyses, one of these variables is year, so the relationship between year and the other variables can be interpreted as the direction and rate of change in these variables over time. Scatterplots show both temporary and permanent changes in direction, as well as the presence of outliers—data falling outside an established pattern. (Outliers in the present analyses reflect specific years in which unusual, but time-specific events occurred, such as the Franco-Prussian War in 1870.) When changes are dramatic and long-standing (not short-run blips), they may mark the end of one political, social, or historical period and the beginning of another, and are therefore especially noteworthy for historians.

More gradual year-to-year changes that are not marked by important events may also be important, especially for sociologists who are interested in their impact on other variables over the same period. Thus, the scatterplot is a valuable vehicle for portraying an array of data, with sudden and gradual changes in direction as well as outliers clearly apparent (see Tufte, 1983, for a terrific treatise on scatterpolots and other visual displays of quantitative information).

As detailed as they may be in communicating the character of bivariate relationships, scatterplots are limited. Overall trends are sometimes difficult to see simply by scanning. (This is most likely in large data sets.) In such instances a line drawn through the scatter that minimizes the dispersion of all the cases from it (the line of least squares) can show the existence of an overall trend that simply scanning the scatter fails to discover. This leads us to a review of the regression procedure discussed in the previous chapter and a discussion of its modification for the analysis of time series.

The line of least squares is a line drawn through an array of data in a scatterplot that minimizes the sum of the squared deviations of each dat point from the line. Like a mean or standard deviation, dat point is a statistical model or construct that in this case represents the relationship between two variables and is drawn through a scatterplot to illustrate a general trend. The *intercept* (α in a regression equation) indicates the starting point, located on the y (vertical) axis, and the *slope* (b in a regression equation) shows the angle of incline. This shows on average how many units of change in one variable are produced by a unit of change in the other. In the case of urbanization and year, for example, this amounts to indicating how much France urbanized per year between 1852 and 1914 (about .3%, or b=.00306). In the case of crime and urbanization, it involves showing on the average how much the crime rate changes per unit change in urbanization (major property offenses, b=−.00045; serious crimes of violence, b=−.00011).

As with the arithmetic mean (average), which functions as a portrait of the character of an array of numbers, the slope presents a *general* visual image (the line of least squares) or a numeric representation (the intercept and the ratio of change in one variable to change in the other, i.e. angle of the line). Compared to the scatterplot, then, the slope sacrifices detail to characterize general relationships.

Apart from showing trends that may be obscured by wide scatters, numeric representations of the line of least squares also allow mathematical logic to be used to force even more knowledge from the available facts. (In extreme form this is known as "torturing the data until it confesses.") For example, numeric generalizations about the nature of associations between variables are also helpful in determining how likely an observed relationship is to have been produced by chance (i.e., whether it is *statistically significant*). The stronger the association between the variables, the less likely it has been produced by random error (including flukes in sampling and random errors in measurement). The other factor that affects the significance of associations is the spread of the scattered data around the line of least squares. The *standard error* is the numeric indicator of this spread or the "goodness of fit" of the line of least squares. (If the slope is more than twice the magnitude of the standard error, the likelihood that the slope is a distortion of reality is $p \leq .05$.)

In relationships between two variables (bivariate relationships) the correlation coefficient is the slope presented in standardized form. (The slope is standardized by multiplying it by the ratio of the standard deviations of the independent and dependent variables. This may be done when the units of change in variables have no meaningful interpretation, or when analysts want to compare the slopes of different variables within a population, or in the case of multivariate analyses, within a single equation.) A correlation coefficient normally ranges between 1.00 and -1.00, and can be given a proportional reduction in error (PRE) interpretation by squaring it to get r^2, which is the "proportion of variance 'explained'" (i.e., the PRE). Bivariate correlation coefficients are sometimes called zero-order correlation coefficients because they do not involve *controlling* for the effects of other variables.

Being able to control for the influence of other independent variables represents another important advantage that the numerical expression of a line of least squares has over its visual presentation. With the mathematical illustration, it is possible to estimate the angle or strength of the association between one independent or predictor variable and the dependent variable, hold it constant, and then calculate the correlation or slope for the dependent variable on another independent variable. This approach produces *partial correlations* or *partial slopes* for each independent variable and provides an assessment of their relative strength as predictors of the dependent variable.

Partial slopes and correlations are useful for evaluating arguments. For example, if both urbanization and industrialization are associated with a changing rate of crime, it is possible with *multiple correlation/regression* to estimate both their combined and individual strength as predictors of change in the rate of crime. So if one argues that any impact that urbanization has on crime is due only to the dependency of both of these variables on the growth of industrial capitalism, any association between urbanization and crime should be attenuated if not eliminated by controlling for industrialization. If, on the other hand, it is not industrialization but urbanization that affects crime, holding industrialization constant should not affect the slope for crime rates on urbanization.

Multicollinearity, Autocorrelation, and Autoregression

Apart from issues of measurement and difficulties in locating data, there are two problems that often plague analyses of macro-level historical data. These are *multicollinearity* and *autocorrelation/regression*.

Sometimes independent variables are not so independent. If they are strongly correlated, the situation is called collinearity (two variables), multicollinearity (more than two independent variables), and estimates of their independent associations with the dependent variable become unstable (almost as if the sample size became much smaller). In such cases, tests of significance may be more important than partial correlations or slopes as indicators of relative predictive power. So if our measures of urbanization and industrialization are strongly correlated, it may be imprudent to place much confidence in our estimates of their independent associations with rates of crime.

When standard (*ordinary least squares* or OLS) regression or correlational analyses are used to analyze temporally ordered data, the possibility of distortion from autocorrelation increases. Trouble occurs when a variable's error term and one or more of its own lags are correlated, either positively or negatively. (Autoregression, the correlation of a variable with itself over time, is similar, though conceptually distinct.) If autocorrelation or autoregression occurs to the extent that the adjacent case is a better predictor of a randomly selected case than is the mean, then an important assumption of OLS regression is violated, and standard estimates of stability cannot be trusted. (It is noteworthy that autocorrelation/regression is also possible, though less common, in cross-sectional analyses. This occurs when adjacent cases, such as census tracts, are better predictors of a randomly selected case than is the mean.)

For example, inertia could affect urbanization, making the best predictor in a specific year the level of urbanization in the preceding year. Also, contagion and inertia could make the crime rate in a specific year the best predictor of the crime rate in the following year. In a sense, these situations would mean that each variable affects itself over time, and this should not be attributed to another source (i.e., the independent variable). This could happen with OLS regression estimates of slopes for rates of crime on urbanization, because OLS regression does not assume that the best predictor of a randomly selected case is the mean rather than the adjacent case.

The Durbin-Watson d statistic was developed to show whether positive or negative autocorrelation and autoregression is present. This statistic has a range between 0 and 4. Values around 2.0 indicate no autoregressive distortion. When values stray too far from 2, autocorrelation/regression is present, and a way of estimating the impact and significance of slopes that will not be mislead by this situation must be used instead of standard OLS procedures. One such technique is a *gen-*

eralized least squares (GLS) regression procedure to estimate slopes and partial slopes. GLS strategies essentially produce an estimate of autocorrelation/regression, remove it from the investigation, and analyze the covariation that remains. Accordingly, the following analysis is based on two versions of GLS regression. One type, the Prais-Winsten time-series analysis is used to estimate standardized slopes and Durbin-Watson scores, and the other type, a maximum-likelihood technique gives estimates of autoregressive processes, standard errors, and partial slopes. If auto-regressive processes occur at all, most involve a one-year lag. Our focus will be confined to searching for such first-order autoregressive processes. (See Johnston, 1984; Kmenta, 1971; and especially Ostrom, 1990 for more detailed discussions of time-series analysis.)

Results

As the scatterplots indicate, urbanization is negatively related to both rates of serious crimes of violence and major property offenses. The OLS zero-order correlation coefficient for violent crime and urbanization is $r = -.47$ and is statistically significant. (The likelihood that such a coefficient could be produced by chance is less than 1 in 1000, or $p \le .001$.) The Durbin-Watson d statistic for this equation is 1.56, indicating that autoregressive processes are present, but not severe. This is reflected by the similarity of the findings from the Prais-Winsten GLS regression analysis (β). The unstandardized slope is $b = -.00011$, with a standard error of s.e. $= .00003$. Since the slope is negative, we can conclude that urbanization is a negative predictor of rates of serious crimes of violence in France between 1852 and 1914, and because the slope is more than twice the value of the standard error, the relationship is statistically significant (Table 3.1).

Table 3.1 OLS Correlation Coefficients (r), GLS Standardized Slopes (*B*), and Partial Slopes (b) for Annual Rates of Major Crimes of Violence and Property Crimes on Urbanization, France, 1852–1914

	Rates of Serious Crimes of Violence				Rate of Major Property Crimes			
	r	*B*	*b*	*s.e.*	*r*	*B*	*b*	*s.e.*
Urbanization	−.47[a]	−.47[a]	−.00011	.00003	−.81[a]	−.56[a]	−.0004	.0001
r² (adjusted)	.21	.19			.64	.29		
Durbin-Watson "d"	1.56	1.57			.35	1.53		

[a] $p \le .001$

Source: Data from the *Complete Général de l'Administration de la Justice Criminelle en France*, in the *Ministère de la Justice* in Paris.

Urbanization is also a negative predictor of the rate of major property offenses. The OLS zero-order correlation is very high, with $r = -.81$, and $p \leq .001$, indicating a close correspondence between urbanization and decline in rates of this type of crime. However, in spite of this, and a corresponding "explained variance" of $r^2 = .64$, the Durbin-Watson statistic of $d = .35$ warns of the presence of strong autocorrelation/regression. Consequently, we use a time-series procedure to take into account the possibility of this type of distortion. However, although the standardized slope produced by this time-series analysis with the autocorrelation/regression removed is considerably smaller than the estimate produced by the OLS procedure, the slope is still moderately strong with $\beta = -.56$ and significant, with $p \leq .001$. In the end, then, urbanization is also a reasonably strong negative predictor of major property offenses.

At this point we know that the relationships between urbanization and rates of major violent and property crimes are negative and not based on autoregressive processes. However, before we can feel confident that the relationship between urbanization and these variables is indeed negative, we should examine the potential contribution of several other factors.

The Franco-Prussian War

The Franco-Prussian War, and its aftermath, the destruction of the Paris Commune in 1870–1871, were turbulent events in French history. In fact, both urbanization and crime rates fluctuated during these years, and swings in crime were dramatic. Since, like averages, slopes are sensitive to extreme values (outliers), it is possible that even though the events of 1870–1871 only represent two data points, because they are so extravagant that they have an extraordinary influence on the slopes of the lines of least squares. To examine this possibility, we create a "pulse variable" or *dummy variable* for the Franco-Prussian War. This variable is simply year, reclassified as two categories: one for 1870–1871 and the other containing all other years. By including this variable in an equation with urbanization as predictors of crime rates, we can see whether urbanization continues to be a significant predictor of crime rates after the contribution of 1870–1871 has been removed (Table 3.2).

However, controlling for the Franco-Prussian War increases rather than decreases confidence in the reality of the relationship between urbanization and rates of serious crime. In the case of serious crimes of violence, the slope with urbanization is unchanged at $b_1 = -.00011$, with s.e. $= .00003$. In the case of major property offenses, the removal of the disruption of the war actually intensifies rater than attenuates its association with urbanization ($b_1 = -.0005$) and lowers the standard deviation

Table 3.2 Maximum Likelihood of GLS Regression for Annual Rates of Major Crimes of Violence and Property Offenses on Urbanization, Controlling for War, Industrialization, and Rates of Minor Crimes, France, 1852–1914

	Serious Crimes of Violence						Major Property Offenses					
	b_1	s.e.	b_2	s.e.	b_3	s.e.	b_1	s.e.	b_2	s.e.	b_3	s.e.
AR(1)	.01	.13	.01	.13	.67	.11	−.88	.05	−.83	.07	.67	.11
Urbanization	−.00011	.00003	−.00011	.00006	−.0002	.00004	−.0005	.0001	−.0003	.0001	−.003	.00001
War (1870–1871)	−.000004	.000009					−.00002	.00005				
Industrialization			−2.89	518.7					−1322.2	1366.5		
Minor Offenses:												
Violence					23.47	9.48						
Property											40.21	8.3

Source: Data are from the *Complete Général de l'Administration de la Justice Criminelle en France*, in the *Ministère de la Justice*, and the *Annuaire Statistique*, in the *Bibliothèque Nationale*, both in Paris.

to s.e.=.0001. Thus, the association between urbanization and these rates of crime cannot be said to be an artifact of the events of 1870–1871.

Industrialization

Industrialization began in rural areas, then moved to the cities, and eventually became associated with urbanization. Because of this, factors associated with industrialization may account for the relationship between urbanization and crime. To test for this possibility, we examined national consumption of fossil fuels as an indicator of industrialization. Unfortunately, the correlation of this variable with urbanization is so strong (r=.96, p≤.001) that they are virtually identical empirically. Consequently, the results of any effort to estimate their independent association with any dependent variable would not be reliable. In view of this collinearity between energy consumption and urbanization, we used another measure of industrialization that could be distinguished empirically from urbanization to examine their independent associations crime rates—the number of steam engines. This measure of industrialization has face validity, inasmuch as it began with the invention and proliferation of the steam engine.

The proliferation of steam power has been used in other studies as a measure of industrialization (see, for example, Lodhi and Tilly, 1973). In fact, steam engines may be an even better measure of industrialization than the consumption of fossil fuels, since the latter encompasses both private and industrial consumption, whereas few steam engines were in non-industrial use. (By the end of World War I, however, the ascendency of the internal combustion engine would eventually displace steam power. Consumption of fossil fuel would probably be a better measure of industrialization for this period.)

The number of steam engines is also useful for present purposes because it is a correlate of fuel consumption (r=.54, p≤.001), supporting its use as an alternate indicator of industrialization. Of equal importance, number of steam engines is associated with urbanization (r=.57, p≤.001), but not to a degree that completely defies disentanglement.

Industrialization has no significant impact on rates of serious crimes of violence ($b_2=-.2.89$, s.e.=518.7), and controlling for it has no effect on the power of urbanization to predict violent crime (still at $b_2=-.00011$). However, the addition of industrialization into the equation increases the standard error to s.e.=.00006. In light of the failure of our measure of industrialization to act as a significant predictor of the dependent variable and the fact that the slope for violent crime on urbanization is unchanged with industrialization in the equation, it seems unlikely that industrialization is the reason for the association between urbanization and crime. Industrialization is also a weak predictor of property crime and has no impact on its relationship with urbanization. (It is noteworthy that autocorrelation/regression continues to be a strong and significant factor in the case of major rates of property offenses $(AR(1) = -.83, p \leq .001)$.)

It is tempting to conclude that urbanization is clearly more important than industrialization as a predictor of rates of major crime. The analysis suggests that this is indeed the case for France between 1852 and 1914. However, it is important to remember that the collinearity between urbanization and the use of fossil fuel indicates that energy consumption was an essential element of urbanization during this period, and that although separating their effects may be mathematically possible, the results may be neither reliable nor theoretically astute. Although industrialization began in rural areas, urbanization and industry became strongly correlated and may not only have affected each other, but joined in their effect on crime as well.

Minor Offenses

The impact of urbanization on the declining rate of serious crime may be more apparent than real. As rates of serious crime declined, rates of minor offenses seem to have increased (Figure 3.3). It is possible that urbanization or forces associated with it, such as liberalism, increased a tendency for offenders to be charged with minor offenses for committing acts which in previous years would have elicited more serious charges. If this happened, rates of serious crime would have declined as rates of minor offenses simultaneously increased, and the decline in serious crime associated with urbanization would be less a matter of increasing civility than a matter of changing classification.

To test for this possibility, the rate of minor crimes is included in equations. If the reclassification hypothesis is accurate, the addition of this variable ought to attenuate or eliminate the original associations between urbanization and major crime rates. But this does not happen. Rates of minor offenses are *directly* rather than inversely related to rates of serious crime. In the case of violent offenses, the partial slope is $b_3 = 23.47$, s.e.$= 9.48$, and controlling for minor crimes of violence actually *increases* the association between urbanization and serious crimes of violence ($b_3 = -.0002$, s.e.$= .00004$). For property crimes, the slope for major offenses on minor offenses is $b_3 = 40.21$, s.e.$= 8.30$, and urbanization persists as a significant predictor of the rate of major property crimes, $b_3 = -.0003$, s.e.$= .00004$.

In view of the positive relationship between major and minor rates of crime, it is noteworthy that although urbanization is a negative predictor of major crimes, it has no association with rates of minor property offenses and is in fact a strong *positive* predictor of rates of minor crimes of violence ($b = .00000277$, s.e. $.00000035$), as discussed below.

Recursive Regression Analysis

Time-series analysis takes into account the possibility of auto-regressive processes within a specific interval. However, historical contingencies causing sudden or gradual shifts in context can alter the nature of relationships at any point during the period of the analysis. Because of this, the statistical properties of a series may not be constant (stationary) and may change dramatically over time (see Priestly, 1988; Isaac and Griffin, 1989). Thus, the means and variances of individual variables may fluctuate, and associations between variables may become stronger or weaker over time. One way of checking on this uses a moving time series analysis or "recursive regression analysis" that examines the temporal stability of the relationship between rates of major crimes against persons and property and urbanization (see Brown, Durbin, and Evans, 1975; Griffin and Isaac, 1992).

The analysis begins with the equations for the whole period and continues by dropping the first year of the series and re-estimating the equations. The procedure then continues sequentially. In the present study, the initial equations were estimated for the time series 1853–1913, inclusive. The second equation is based on the 1854–1913 series, then, the third for 1855–1913, and so on. This backward procedure uses 1913 as the anchor and continues until the period for analysis is 1884–1913, and the n has been reduced to 30 (Table 3.3).

Urbanization is a strong, negative predictor of property crime throughout the period. The ratio of the standard error to the slope improves in the later part of the period, suggesting that the relationship between urbanization and rates of major property crime was somewhat stronger during that period of time.

The opposite situation emerges in the case of violent crime. With the exception of the series including 1854, which seems to be a bit of an outlier for both types of crime, the relationship between urbanization and property offenses weakens toward the later part of the period. Slopes decline and standard errors rise, until the last five years the ratio deteriorates to non-significance, with $p \leq .05$ (of course the smaller size of the sample contributes to this). Whether urbanization eventually became a non-predictor or even a positive predictor of violent crime can only be determined by analyzing data since 1913. As it stands, the recursive regression analysis suggests a higher level of stationarity with the relationship between urbanization and property crime than crimes of violence. However, urbanization is a negative correlate of both types of serious crime for the entire period.

Discussion and Conclusions

This analysis of France, 1853–1913, indicates that urbanization and rates of major crimes are *negative* rather than *positive* correlates, and that this association is not the result of specific historical events, such as the

Table 3.3 Moving Time Series Analysis, Rates of Property Crime and Violent Crime on Urbanization: 1853–1884 to 1913

YEAR	Property Crime b	Property Crime s.e.	Violent Crime b	Violent Crime s.e.	n
1853	−.45	.10	−.11	.03	61
1854	−.51	.12	−.06	.04	60
1855	−.37	.07	−.09	.03	59
1856	−.31	.06	−.12	.02	58
1857	−.29	.05	−.12	.02	57
1858	−.25	.04	−.12	.02	56
1859	−.24	.04	−.12	.02	55
1860	−.25	.05	−.11	.02	54
1861	−.25	.05	−.11	.02	53
1862	−.25	.05	−.12	.02	52
1863	−.25	.05	−.11	.02	51
1864	−.24	.05	−.11	.02	50
1865	−.25	.05	−.11	.02	49
1866	−.27	.05	−.11	.03	48
1867	−.28	.04	−.11	.03	47
1868	−.29	.05	−.11	.03	46
1869	−.29	.05	−.11	.03	45
1870	−.29	.04	−.09	.04	44
1871	−.33	.03	−.12	.03	43
1872	−.38	.05	−.12	.03	42
1973	−.35	.03	−.12	.04	41
1874	−.33	.03	−.12	.04	40
1875	−.30	.03	−.12	.04	39
1876	−.30	.03	−.12	.04	38
1877	−.30	.03	−.09	.04	37
1878	−.31	.03	−.09	.04	36
1879	−.32	.03	−.10	.05	35
1880	−.33	.04	−.07	.05	34
1881	−.34	.03	−.09	.05	33
1882	−.36	.03	−.09	.06	32
1883	−.34	.04	−.08	.05	31
1884	−.35	.03	−.08	.06	30

Source: Data are transcribed from the *Complete Général de l'Administration de la Justice Criminelle en France* in the *Ministre de la Justice*, and the *Annuaire Statistique*, in the *Bibliothèque Nationale*, both in Paris.

Franco-Prussian War. Further, the data suggest that this relationship between urbanization and crime is neither the result of reclassification of offenses, nor an association between urbanization and industrialization.

Because this analysis focused on France as the unit of analysis, it is not certain that these declines actually occurred in urban areas even, though urbanization is related to a reduction in rates of major crime. It is possible that urbanization of France somehow generated a decrease in rural crime rates, and that this was responsible for the drop in crime rates for the country as a whole. If this were indeed the case, concluding that urban areas had lower crime rates than rural areas would be an example of an *ecological fallacy* (see Chapter 1, and Robinson, 1950). This is always a possibility when arguments developed at one level of analysis (e.g., the community) are tested with data drawn from another level of analysis (e.g., the nation). This involves *aggregation-disaggregation* problems (see Hannan, 1971). However, in the present case the probability that our thesis is fallacious seems low, since there is no logical explanation for why urbanization would have generated declining crime in rural areas (except by attracting criminals to cities). Moreover, cross-sectional analyses of urbanization and violence in nineteenth-century France contradict the idea that urbanization supressed crime more in rural than urban areas (Lodhi and Tilly, 1973). (However, major property crimes may have been more prevalent in urbanized areas. Therefore the possibility of an aggregation-disaggregation problem cannot be totally disregarded, especially in the case of property crime.)

The relationship between urbanization and serious crime may be causal, as the civilization argument suggests. On the other hand, the relationship may also hold because of a mutual dependence on a third factor which is not yet apparent. Whether such a variable (or variables) will ever be discovered is unknown. We were unable to find such a variable. So for the present, we are left with tentative findings for a specific time and place. Similarly, the discovery of a negative association between urbanization and rates of major crime is consistent with the civilization argument and therefore supports it. The relationship is also consistent with other structural explanations (see, for example, Gillis, 1989). Thus, although the analysis of these data strongly suggest the existence and direction of the relationship between urbanization and major crime rates, the reasons for the relationship (i.e., the *intervening* variables) are unknown, and await discovery by subsequent research.

In one respect, our findings support current assumptions and findings concerning the relationship between urbanization and crime in present-day America. Minor offenses became more numerous than major crimes in nineteenth-century France, so urbanization may actually have contributed to an overall increase in the amount of crime by inflating minor crimes of violence. In this respect, then, the French data are in accord with modern arguments and evidence. However, the patterns shown by the facts concerning rates of serious offenses diverge sharply from the findings produced by cross-sectional analyses of North American studies. Since our conclusions are in general accord with those produced by other studies on nineteenth-century populations (see, for example, Lodhi and Tilly, 1973), it seems unlikely that the results of our research are invalid. On the other side, research in the twentieth century includes a plethora of highly competent cross-sectional analyses, all of which cannot be unreliable. In view of this, it is probably more reasonable to conclude that socio-historical context is an important variable affecting the relationship between urbanization and rates of serious crime. The drift from stationarity in the relationship between urbanization and serious crimes of violence gives a measure of support for this notion within our data set.

The idea that the relationship between urbanization and crime is historically contingent may bring little consolation to residents of modern America, who are distressed about rising rates of crime in *their* cities. Similarly, social scientists who are working to develop explanations for this contemporary pattern may question the utility of attending to information and arguments from other continents and other centuries. The answer to both of these concerns has to do with generalization and theory. The French data demonstrate that urbanization *per se* need not necessarily increase rates of major crime. In fact, these data show that urbanization can even be associated with a decrease in rates of serious crime. This should give a measure of hope for the occupants of beleaguered cities and affect the way in which social scientists try to explain present relationships between urbanization and crime.

One possibility for the contemporary relationship between urbanization and rates of major crime is that cities themselves changed, particularly those that had been concentrations of industrial, human, and social capital. One of the most dramatic demographic phenomena of the last half of the twentieth century in North America has been the continuing suburbanization of urban populations. Suburbanization took off with the end of World War II and may have had a devastating impact on the nature of life in the cities that were most affected. Unlike Canadian and other patterns of suburbanization, in the United States suburbanization often resulted in the abandonment of inner city areas by industries and by people with jobs. This left behind an unemployed urban underclass who were in great need of public assistance and protection. But the erosion of capital that accompanied the exodus of industry and taxpayers removed the financial basis for meeting these needs. This combination of social disorganization and economic hardship, absence of opportunity and assistance, and too few exits may have turned modern American cities into repositories of crime instead of the fortresses against it, which they had been in earlier times (see Wilson, 1987). If this is indeed what happened, urbanization and city life may be taking the blame for a major demographic change with severe economic and organizational consequences. Urbanization *per se* may be innocent, or if it is guilty, not acting alone. (Recall how strongly industrialization and urbanization were associated in nineteenth-century France.)

The arguments that have developed in twentieth-century North America linking crime with urbanization are not necessarily wrong, so much as they are bound by time and space. They are also incomplete as explanations. By ignoring the fact that urbanization has not increased rates of serious crime in other places or even in other times, the arguments also ignore the importance of socio-historical context and other variables that produce the relationship between urbanization and crime. Just as with Shakespeare's two tragedies, contextual factors are more than simply scope limitations. They are as much a part of the causal process as is urbanization in decreasing or increasing crime, and should be specified and included in any explanation of the relationship. After all, this is how social scientific knowledge is accumulated.

4 Initial and Subsequent Effects of Policing on Crime

A. R. Gillis

Sequence and time are the structure around which historians build explanation, but these factors are largely ignored by social scientists, including criminologists (Garofalo, 1977). This chapter shows how including time can sharpen images of changing patterns of crime and illuminate the contributions of competing theories developed to explain them.

When sociologists and criminologists predict, they draw on past research and logic to propose that a change in one variable produces a change in another. If they test such a proposition as a hypothesis, social scientists typically use a cross-sectional research design to find out whether units of analysis scoring high on one of the variables in their hypothesis also tend to score high (or low, in a negative relationship) on the other. If there is an association and it is unlikely to be the result of chance (i.e., $p \leq .05$), the hypothesis and the argument from which it was derived have received empirical support. On the other side, if the prediction is false, the proposition and the more general thesis that generated it are viewed as disconfirmed.

Inability to find factual support for an argument may indicate that it is indeed unsupported by the data from a particular sample. At the very least this would clearly disprove the idea that the proposition will hold for *all* populations. It may even mean that the hypothesis will not hold in *any* population. However, failure to find supporting evidence can also occur when arguments are actually valid. For example, there may indeed be a relationship between the *concepts* in a proposition, but if there is weak correspondence between indicators and the concepts they are supposed to measure, there may be no observable association between the *variables* in the hypothesis. Thus, invalid measurement can nullify accurate propositions.

Good Theory and Bad Timing

Invalid measurement is not the only enemy of valid arguments. Testable theories in sociology typically involve the specification of a variable that is supposed to intervene between an independent and dependent variable. (The intervening variable "explains" why they were related in the first place.) These statements either implicitly or explicitly invoke the notion of cause. Causality does not occur instantly, in fact by definition, changes in

75

a causal agent must temporally precede its effect (see Nettler, 1970). Although sequence is sometimes clear, timing is not. Depending on the processes involved, the interval of time between cause and effect could range between nanoseconds and generations. The implicit question within every causal argument then, is how long must we wait before a cause produces an effect? The answer is not only an important aspect of explanation, it may also determine whether an argument receives empirical support. If a proposition is tested before a cause has had a chance to generate its results, the hypothesis is unlikely to be supported by the data.

Unfortunately, social scientists typically display no interest in time or even the sequence of the empirical events with which they test their arguments (Garofalo, 1977). There are probably several reasons for this. For one thing, much of the sociological tradition is ahistorical and following these thoughtways may lead students of social processes away from concerns about time and sequence. When and in what order events occurred is an obsession of historians. This is the essence of historical explanation, and precision on these questions as well as measurement is the basis of historical accuracy. (In fact, Stewart MacAulay once suggested that if they think of it at all, most social scientists view history as "just one damn thing after another.") Even sociologists who are inclined to favor historical explanations and view the present as the product of the past, forget to tell us how long it will all take to happen. For example, Marx neglected to tell us how long it would take for the state to wither, signaling the transition between the socialist and communist stages of social evolution. This temporal uncertainty gave skeptics the opportunity to jump the gun in declaring the dictatorship of the proletariat permanent and the story that it would eventually wither a big lie. On the other side, the uncertainty about how long everything was going to take allowed the faithful to hang on for generations.

We should be sympathetic to the problems faced by social scientists in specifying the timing of causal processes. For historians, who look backward, this is a difficult, but empirically possible piece of detective work. On the other side, temporal specification for social theorists may be more difficult and depend on logic more than on clues from prior research. Nevertheless, any thought at all about the duration of causal processes would represent a distinct improvement over the current situation and reduce the likelihood of rejecting of hypotheses that would be accurate if the time for completion of causal processes were taken into account.

Methods and Time

In some respects, sociological disregard of time and sequence may arise less from the theories social scientists prefer than from the methodologies they employ. Although their arguments typically involve causality or at least the idea that change in one variable precedes change in another, propositions are rarely tested in this form. Instead, as noted earlier, sociologists tend to test arguments with cross-sectional research designs, where sequence is implied by argument, but the order of variables is temporally identical (see Lieberson, 1985). This may not make much difference in some research. For example, it is obvious in a study of the relationship between social integration and suicide among individuals, that as a final act, suicide cannot precede a change in social integration. However, when the unit of analysis is a collectivity, such as a census tract, province, or state, sequence can become more difficult to determine. Durkheim's analysis in *Suicide* was of aggregates, not individuals. Because of this, suicide does not have to be causally prior, because increasing rates of suicide may affect the level of social integration in the areas that were the units of analysis.

In view of the causal and temporal nature of the arguments they make, and since logic as a determination of sequence can get so complex, social scientists would be well-advised to use longitudinal designs focusing on change over time, instead of relying on cross-sectional research designs comparing the values of variables across units within one time period. Longitudinal analyses not only permit the possibility of determining sequence but enable students of social processes to examine how long a cause may take to produce an effect. These questions are important, since propositions and the theories from which they are deduced may live or die with their answers (see generally, Lieberson, 1985). (See Abbott, 1983; Aminzade, 1992; Bryant, 1994; Griffin, 1992, for more general discussions of sequence and time.)

The present chapter illustrates this point by examining the competing claims of deterrence theory and reaction arguments concerning crime and punishment. Specifically, we investigate whether the presence of police represses crime, as deterrence theory would maintain, or whether policing is more likely to inflate offence rates, as reaction arguments suggest. Once again, the analysis focuses on the emergence of civilization of Europe in general, and on France between 1852–1914 in particular. In fact this chapter follows from the earlier analysis showing the relationship between urbanization and crime and can be viewed as an examination of the growth of policing as the reason for this association.

This chapter focuses on the relationship between policing and crime, an issue that is of considerable importance in contemporary America. However, as with the preceding chapter, our analysis focuses on data from a different place and period. As we noted earlier, this type of examination is useful because the propositions derived from theory are typically seen to apply across time as well as across space, and continually testing hypotheses with data from the same place and period can give a false sense of credibility to these generalizations. Many empirical generalizations in zoology such as the whiteness of swans and the incapacity of mammals to lay eggs had to be modified with the discovery of Australia by Europeans. This had little bearing on day-to-day life in Europe, where there were no black swans or duck-billed platypusses embarrassing scientists with their egg laying. However, knowledge of the existence of these animals forced Western zoologists to expand their thinking on these matters. This expansion can be important in determining how to conceptualize problems. For example, the results of the analysis in the previous chapter tell us that urbanization need not necessarily be associated with serious rates of crime. This expands conceptual horizons for contemporary students of crime in urban America.

Cultures of Violence

The long decline in rates of serious crime described in the chapter on urbanization was a transformation that began with the European Renaissance. As noted in that chapter, the end of the middle ages coincided with an increasing accumulation of capital in cities. The Renaissance was also associated with an increase in the concentration of coercive force in states (Tilly, 1990). According to Elias ([1939] 1978), nobles who typically maintained standing armies moved from isolated castles, rural estates, and martial arts to life at court, where disputes were settled with intellectual rather than physical contests.

As monarchs monopolized coercive power within their domains, they not only limited the capacity of the nobility to execute political rebellion but reduced their inclination to engage in criminal activity as well. This was doubly important because during the medieval period, the nobility were not only the most dangerous class, but because of their social prominence, they also served as bad examples for the lower strata.

> A spiral of aristocratic violence, of vendettas, rebellions and counter-rebellions obviously laid the way open to a serious degree of destabilization in society. Under the shadow of the quarrels of the great, lesser men could too easily follow their example and pursue their own quarrels by violent means . . . (Keen, 1990: 195).

With their loss of military power, the nobility found that avenues of influence had moved from violent confrontation on the battlefield to the monarch's court, located near (if not in) the royal residence (Elias [1939] 1978). Contests at court were more indirect and symbolic, with power allocated on the basis of emotional control, social grace, and diplomatic intrigue rather than the martial arts. So as the necessity of civility became apparent, non-violent skills became more highly valued. This culture of the court (courtesy) gradually diffused downward through the bourgeoisie and beyond, sensitizing the population to displays of passion and violence, and creating gentle men and women (see Elias, [1939] 1978, [1939] 1982, [1969] 1983; Gurr, 1979).

The Growth of States and the Centralization of Coercive Power

The civilization of Europe seems certainly to have involved changes in patterns of public preference. But whether these changes caused or merely accompanied the pacification of European populations is unclear. It is noteworthy that Elias ([1939] 1978, [1939] 1982) frames his analysis of the emergence of civilization in structural change, beginning with the repression of the nobility by monarchs. The centralization of authority and the increasing coercive power of states, particularly within their own borders, may have produced changes in social values and norms and had an impact on rates of crime as well. In England, for example, King Henry VII started the largely successful Tudor campaign to disarm the nobility and suppress private violence (see Stone, 1967), and by 1850 previously accepted forms of violent settlement of disputes, such as the duel, had also died out.

With the decline of feudal estates and local autonomy, the size of political units increased, as did the power of rulers to resist external challenges (see Tilly, 1987). The invention and use of artillery, and the development of roads on which to transport the cannons of the state probably facilitated this, while at the same time demolishing the utility of most stone castles as strongholds against the new military might of the state (see Tilly, 1985). This could have been why diplomacy at court replaced confrontations in the field as a more effective avenue to power, prestige, and property for the nobility. As states grew in size and strength, power also became more centralized, through the encapsulation of local authority structures by "more encompassing auspices," and "the total amount of sanctioning to which individuals are subject grows as more encapsulating levels of authority undertake sanctioning" (Bayley, 1985: 41; Black, 1976). The growth of states may not have replaced local organization and control, then, so much as it expanded and intensified the integration and regulation of individuals by broader collectivities. (An increase in the national tax rate, for example, rarely brings reductions in provincial or municipal rates. See also Foucault, 1975.) So as nation-states emerged, they consolidated their power and extended their capacity to sanction while at the same time reducing the capacity of opposition to resist. This, is "the very essence of government," and its "defining activity" is "the maintenance of order" (Bayley, 1985: 45).

Giddens (1985) concurred. Generally following Max Weber, he viewed the nation-state as a "power container," defining it as "a set of institutional forms of governance maintaining an administrative monopoly over a territory with demarcated boundaries (borders), its rule being sanctioned by law and direct control of the means of internal and external violence" (Giddens, 1985:120). He added that "in nation-states surveillance reaches an intensity quite unmatched in previous types of societal order, made possible through the generation and control of information, and developments in communication and transportation, plus forms of supervisory control of 'deviance'" (Giddens, 1985:312). Giddens recognized the importance of the state in the civilization of Europe when he stated that "the development of the absolutist state was undoubtedly associated with major advances in internal pacification" (Giddens, 1985: 189; see also Bayley, 1975; Gillis, 1987; Tilly, 1987).

The expansion of state surveillance was also tied to urbanization. According to Giddens (1985: 190), "Modern policing with its characteristic mixture of informational and supervisory aspects of surveillance was both made possible and seen to be necessary by the wholesale transferral of populations from rural to urban environments." (He sees "heightened surveillance" as one of four "institutional clusterings associated with modernity"—the others are centralized control, industrialization, and capitalistic enterprise.) In fact Giddens (1985:15) goes so far as to argue that "only in cities could regular surveillance be maintained by the central agencies of the state" (see also Stinchcombe, 1963; Foucault, 1975). On the other side, Hay (1975) argued that until the eighteenth century, surveillance in England was embedded in the social relations between the landed gentry and the peasantry. So the growth of formal policing in the nineteenth century may represent less of a change in the amount than in the form of state surveillance, going from a local, more encompassing mode to a more formal and specific institutional form. If this is the case, policing could represent a change in form of surveillance by emerging states either in response to the decline of a rural, agrarian social order, and/or by the emergence of the urban industrial conditions that succeeded it.

Public Order, Punishment, and Policing

During the Middle Ages punishments were severe by today's standards. However, authority was haphazardly organized, arbitrarily administered, and thinly distributed within and between the many localities that now constitute modern Europe. Sanctions were severe, even for minor offenses, and included displays of dramatic cruelty, public spectacles such as the pillory and stocks, and permanent stigmatization, including branding and amputation. These harsh sanctions may have represented an attempt to offset weak links of communication and irregular enforcement of laws with exemplary punishment. However, stern retribution may have been deemed appropriate by medieval people for whom violence was a common occurrence (see Given, 1977; Foucault, 1973; Stone, 1977). In any case, probably because of an increasing aversion to brutality associated with increasing civility, official approval of severe punishment faded. In fact, this occurred to such an extent that juries began to refuse to convict offenders when punishment for a crime was seen as too extreme. As this sentiment was more frequently expressed through jury trials (the outcome of which could not be appealed by the prosecution), the state had to begin easing sanctions in order to get convictions (see Beattie, 1986, and Garland, 1990, on the evolution of punishment).

This imposition of law, order, and political control is consistent with deterrence theory and the use of punishment as repression. In fact, the emergence and growth of state police coincided with this change from a model emphasizing the severity of punishment to one that featured its certainty, and from the standpoint of the evidence on deterrence, this made sense.

Punishment, Compliance, and Defiance

When Moses told his followers that retaliation for personal injury was appropriate, he added the caveat that the severity of a penalty should fit the offense that precipitates it. The guideline provided by the prophet was "an eye for an eye, a tooth for a tooth." Later, Christians interpreted Mosaic law liberally, emphasizing compassion and tolerance rather than punishment, even to the extent of "turning the other cheek." Although most Western populations eventually embraced some version of Judeo-Christian values, medieval Europe displayed little of the restraint prescribed by this religious tradition. On the contrary, the level of violence among medieval populations was only exceeded by the force applied by emerging states in attempting to maintain control and suppress it. Guilt or lack of it was far more important than was the nature of an offense in determining punishment. In fact, beyond exile and execution, there were not many punishments available for serious crimes. Once guilt was pronounced, the question was not so much *whether* an execution should take place, but how dramatic it should be. (Rulers did not pick up nicknames such as "the Terrible" or "the Impaler" through an aversion to stern measures.)

During the eighteenth century Cesare Beccaria (1738–1794), Jeremy Bentham (1748–1832), and other utilitarian philosophers formulated deterrence theory as both an explanation of crime and a method for reducing it. As an ethical system, deterrence theory is more Mosaic than Christian, authorizing punishment, but limiting its severity. Moses would have approved. But unlike Moses, the utilitarians did not base their idea of reasonable retribution on a simple exchange between individuals. Beccaria argued that crime was not only an attack on an individual but on society as well. This extended the issue of punishment beyond retribution and restitution to aggrieved individuals. Society was cast as victim, not merely bystander, and what had been seen as an issue of tort, or dispute between individuals, expanded to an issue of criminal law. Further, since the utilitarians believed in "the greatest happiness for the greatest number," the interests of society preempted those of individuals. For the utilitarians, then, the purpose of punishment became the protection of society through the prevention of crime.

As an explanation of crime, deterrence theory uses a rational economic model of behavior. Action persists if it is rewarding to the actor. Thus, people engage in criminal behavior when its benefits are greater than the costs of discovery and punishment. Like other activity, illegality is seen as motivated by the pursuit of pleasure, even if it was intangible, such as the release of passion or anger (see Katz, 1988, for a contemporary description of the delights of delinquency). The point of punishment for deterrence theory is less retribution than utility: the neutralization of the rewards of crime. A "just" measure of pain offsets any pleasure associated with a particular offense, without going overboard. Excessive punishment will deter crime, but is offensive to humanists as a "waste" of suffering.

Deterring crime has two dimensions. One is specific and focuses on the reduction of repeat offenses (recidivism) in individual offenders through the administration of appropriate punishment. The other is general and focuses on preventing similar offenses in the general population by demonstrating through the punishment of individual offenders that crime does not pay. The two dimensions are related, but they may also vary independently. For example, although it may be viewed as inhumane, execution is obviously effective as a specific deterrent. In any case, perhaps because of their focus on the collective good, the utilitarians were more interested in deterring crime in the general population than preventing recidivism in individual offenders (see, generally, Hagan, 1985). Whether punishment is indeed effective as a general deterrent is uncertain. Even punishment that acts as a specific deterrent in one population, may not inhibit other offenders from recidivating. Whether punishment acts as a specific deterrent seems to depend, among other things, on age and personality type of the offender, as well as on the nature of the offense. In fact, punishment may even act as a reinforcer instead of an inhibitor and increase the likelihood that offenders will recidivate. For example, Keane, Gillis, and Hagan, (1989) found that contact with the police reduced recidivism among juvenile females, but increased it among juvenile males, and that the intervening variable was "taste for risk." In summarizing the research on the deterrent effect of punishment, Sherman (1993) notes that when it is per-ceived as unjust, punishment can elict defiance rather than compliance. Thus, if excessive severity is perceived as inappropriate or cruel, individ-ual recidivism may be increased, rather than decreased.

Punishment varies in its severity, certainty, and celerity (swiftness). Because of this, it also varies in its capacity to act as a general deterrent. According to deterrence theory, punishment that is too mild, uncertain, or slow in application will by definition fail to deter. In fact, although the issue of capital punishment has attracted more attention to the question of severity, its sustained deterrent value is uncertain (Tittle, 1980; Hagan, 1985; Sherman, 1993). The situation with non-capital sanctions is also equivocal. For example, Ross (1986) notes that when penalties for drunken driving are made more severe there is an immediate deterrent effect, but that this typically levels off and disappears within a few months. The impact of celerity is also questionable, not so much because of discrepant or conditional research results, but due to an absence of research altogether (Hagan, 1985). This leaves us with the certainty of punishment, and it is here we find the greatest degree of empirical support for deterrence theory. It is the likelihood of apprehen-sion and punishment more than its severity that is the most salient fac-tor in deterring criminal behavior. Certainty, or more precisely the perception of it, has not only been shown to be a negative correlate of crime in *post factum* analyses, but with experimental designs as well. This suggests that its impact is indeed causal (Hagan, 1985).

In spite of this empirical support for deterrence theory, it is notewor-thy that many social scientists are ambivalent about the idea. This seems particularly the case with Marxists. Jack Gibbs (1978) observes that although Marxist theory assumes coercion and repression by the state to be effective, there is a disinclination among Marxists to even use the term "deterrence," let alone acknowledge its efficacy. He calls this "the secret scandal" of Marxist theories of criminal law (see Gibbs, 1978:106–107).

The reason for this ambivalence is probably a well-founded suspi-cion that political and economic repression is justified with concepts such as "dangerous classes" and the need for law, order, and deter-rence. Turk (1982) notes that vague laws and blurred distinctions facil-itate the prosecution of political crimes and further entrench the power of the state. However, it may have been the political repression involved in the growth of European states that also deterred crime.

Definitions of Crime and Patterns of Enforcement

Whether viewed as serving the whole or a few, deterrence theory pre-dicts that given a minimal combination of severity and certainty, pun-ishment is both a specific and general deterrent. However, both the argument and the data used to support it have been challenged by sociologists who focus on official reactions to crime as more inflationary than deflationary, particularly with respect to the issue of certainty.

Historical analyses are typically confined to official records or published accounts of incidents, arrests, charges, and the like. Although these accounts may give a generally accurate portrayal of visible crime, their validity as a measure of hidden crime and actual levels of criminality is uncertain. The five-century decline in rates of serious crime, then, is "real" only inasmuch as recorded sources of information reflect it, and a variety of factors besides an actual decline in serious criminal behavior could have deflated the official rates of major crimes. The emergence of bureaucratic urban states and modern legal systems resulted in much more than intensified law enforcement. As the legal apparatus became more complex, patterns of enforcement, punishment, as well as the law itself changed. These alterations resulted from wider cultural, social, and economic changes (see, for example, Chambliss, 1964), but also had an impact on both the nature and volume of criminal statistics, independent of actual criminal activity. As European states expanded over the last five centuries, and people became more civil, both the penalties for infractions and the definition of illegality became more specific. If punishment is used as the basis for classifying crime as serious, the frequency of serious crime may have declined more because of reclassification than pacification (although this seems unlikely in view of post-Enlightenment transformations in penal strategies). Data on convictions or charges, then, may reflect not only a decline in rates of serious criminal behavior, but a growing inclination to redefine specific criminal behaviors as less serious. Changes in legal classification can be found in official records, but an increasing inclination to charge, convict, and punish offenders for less serious crimes may not be easy to identify, appearing only as a decline in the rate of major crimes and a corresponding increase in the rate of minor offenses. (Juries may also be more inclined to convict offenders for minor than major offenses. See, for example, Beattie, 1986; Wright, 1983:96. See also Foucault, 1975; Ignatieff, 1978; and O'Brien, 1982, on changing patterns of punishment.)

Changes in judicial procedure and patterns of police discretion may also have had an independent effect on the nature and volume of official crime statistics. In the case of minor offenses, the growing concentration of people in cities may have combined with escalating surveillance to increase rates of arrests and charges, independent of any change in rates of behavior that would be adjudicated criminal if detected and processed (see Cicourel, 1968; Foucault, 1975; Perrot, 1975; Stinchcombe, 1963; and Monkkonen, 1975, 1981). Also, as population grew, especially in urban areas, the increasing number of offenders may have resulted in a growing tendency to reduce charges in an effort to clear overburdened courts, particularly those hearing serious offenses, which consumed more time (see Alschuler, 1979; Ferdinand, 1967; Friedman, 1979; Haller, 1970; Heumann, 1975). If this occurred, declines in official rates of serious crimes would have been purchased with increases in official rates of minor offenses.

In summary, the five-century decline in serious crime may have resulted from several factors. Broad cultural change associated with the pacification of the nobility and the concentration of population in cities may have increased general civility and a public preference for non-violent settlement of disputes. Alternatively, the emergence and growth of states and their monopolization of coercive power may have led to the imposition of law and order on European populations. On the other hand, increased policing may have inflated the volume of offenders, overburdening courts and increasing pressure on officials to reduce charges to speed up processing. Any or all of these explanations could actually account for the decline in rates of serious crime in Europe over the centuries.

These three perspectives imply different consequences for crime rates from the expansion of policing. If policing is irrelevant, and increasing civility is the principal cause of the decline, there should be little or no correlation between policing and crime rates, unless the growth of policing is also a consequence of increasing civility. But if policing deters crime, the correlation should be negative. However, if reaction arguments hold, the most immediate effect of increased policing should be increased arrests, charges, convictions, and official rates of crime because of a greater capacity to detect crime. If this is the case, the correlation between policing and crime rates will be positive. These three alternatives seem on the surface to be mutually exclusive: correlations are either positive, negative, or nonexistent. All three outcomes could coexist, however, at different points in time.

Contemporaneous and Long-term Effects and Types of Crime

As we noted earlier, historians are well aware of the importance of time, and construct their explanations around sequences of events that are lead up to a particular event (see Griffin, 1993, on historical narratives). However, most social researchers give little attention to time, if indeed they consider it at all (see Abbot, 1983; Garofalo, 1981; and Lieberson, 1985). Yet, the causes and effects described by their theories do not by definition occur simultaneously (Nettler, 1970). Instead, a change in an independent variable (cause) is followed some time later by a change in the dependent variable (effect), and the length of time involved may be an essential factor in shaping the outcome. For example, the temperature of the shower you take before entering a swimming pool can affect how warm or how cold the water in the pool will feel. A hot shower makes the pool seem cold, while a cold shower has the opposite effect. But this is only the case if you go immediately from the shower to the pool. If unfinished pool cleaning or locked doors extend the time between shower and swim, the impact of shower temperature diminishes, and may decline and even reverse. Standing around after a hot shower will eventually cause you to feel cold, so by the time you jump into the pool its water will feel warm, and hanging around after a cold shower will have the opposite effect.

The influence of policing on crime may also depend on the length of time between cause and effect. The immediate impact of an expansion of policing is most likely to be an increase, not a decrease in arrests (see, for example, Gatrell, 1980). If increased policing produces more arrests and yet also deters crime, these countervailing forces may confound correlations within the same time period. However, it is reasonable to expect any deterrent impact to follow both the immediate appearance of the police and their initial inflationary effect on arrests. So the initial impact of policing on crime may be positive, and subsequent effects negative. If these eventual deterrent effects outweigh the initial inflationary impact, crime rates will decline with increased policing.

Policing may also have different effects on different types of crime. Violence is typically more spontaneous and passionate than is property crime, which makes property crime a better candidate for deterrence. Further, since major crimes typically leave less room for discretion (Nettler, 1984) and are by definition more severely sanctioned than minor offenses, violence may be less susceptible to initial inflationary effects and more susceptible to eventual deterrence from increased policing.

In view of this, the following analysis examines the relationship between policing and crime within the same period of time, where an inflationary impact is most likely to prevail (supporting reaction arguments), as well as over an extended period of time, where deflationary effects are more likely to be exhibited (supporting deterrence theory). Since major property offenses are the most susceptible to deterrence, and minor offenses, particularly those involving violence, are the most likely to be inflated by changes in policing, the analysis also distinguishes crimes of violence and property offenses, in both their major and minor forms.

Nineteenth-Century France

As noted in the chapter on urbanization and crime, French population statistics for the nineteenth century are relatively high in quality. Because France led the decline in European fertility, French population statistics receive a great deal of attention from historical demographers, so limitations are known and correction factors have been developed. (For the most part, French census enumerations, first published in 1851, converge convincingly with other estimates of population characteristics, especially since 1856. See, for example, Van de Walle, 1974.)

The last half of the nineteenth and early twentieth centuries was an era of widespread technical, economic, and demographic change in France. Although there was only one major war (the Franco-Prussian War, 1870–1871), as noted earlier, the age can hardly be described as peaceful. It was a period of intense and extensive social challenge and conflict, which occurred for the most part within the country, pitting an emerging proletariat against their employers and, increasingly, the state.

> Sometime in the nineteenth century the people of France shed the collective-action repertoire they had been using for about two centuries and adopted the repertoire they still use today. A definitive shift to the new repertoire did not become complete until the 1850s (Tilly, 1986:391).

The new repertoire supplanted traditional and parochial forms of collective protest, such as seizures of food ("food riots"), serenades, and *charivaris* (noisy demonstations), which were usually directed against local patrons. Strikes, mass meetings, petitions, demonstrations, and social movements became the new ways of protesting, and these typically challenged wider authority rather than local patrons (Tilly, 1986). Further, urban industrial societies were more sensitive to these new forms of protest (Polanyi, 1944), so they were often effective. Throughout the nineteenth century, and particularly during the *fin de siècle*, elites perceived that the nation was in decay and that their class position was weakening (see Weber, 1986). Perhaps more in response to this, then, and in the interest of maintaining order and the *status quo*, the nature and extent of state control also changed with the advent of national policing.

The Expansion of State Surveillance

Policing had existed on a small scale for centuries in European communities, but state policing began in France, early in the nineteenth century. From well before the Revolution, an elite regiment of the army, the *Maréchaussée*, (from which "marshall" is derived) had served as the military police in rural areas, and later as Napoleon's bodyguard as well. During the nineteenth century, the military duties of this regiment were greatly eroded as policing became more and more its *raison d'être*. These *gens d'armes* (men at arms) became the *Gendarmerie Nationale*, the national police force of France. They still patrol the countryside, highways, and towns of less than 10,000 in population, act as the bodyguard of the president, and continue to be administered as a regiment of the French army by the Ministry of Defense in Paris.

The task of policing the larger towns and cities of France fell to the *Sûreté*, a national civilian police force administered by the Ministry of the Interior in Paris. In 1829, several months before Bobbies began patrolling the streets of London, one hundred uniformed officers appeared on the streets of Paris. Giddens (1985: 230) notes that uniforms indicate to civilians that the wearer is a "specialist purveyor of the means of violence." According to Stead (1983) the uniform would also "keep in the public's mind the presence of policemen" and encourage the public to assist the police when they were in need of it. The Prefect of Police, Debelleyme, also hoped uniforms would discourage officers from frequenting taverns and openly engaging in "bad habits" such as intemperance and gambling, and reduce the frequency of policemen vanishing into the crowd when trouble started (Stead, 1983: 54–55).

Both national police forces grew throughout the nineteenth century, with the *Sûreté* (now the *Police Nationale*) consistently increasing with urbanization. The size of the *Police Nationale* eventually exceeded that of the *Gendarmerie*, the growth rate of which had levelled off by 1880 (see Figure 4.1). The *Gendarmerie Nationale* now numbers over 80,000, with the *Police Nationale* at 108,000. In view of the size of the French population (about 52 million) the ratio of police to public is relatively high in comparison to other Western countries, such as Britain or the United States.

The growth of state policing in France involved far more than a specific focus on crime control. Tilly (1986) notes that the growth of national policing brought three important changes:

> First, the surveillance, control, and repression of popular collective action became the business of the national government's specialized local representatives: police, prosecutors, spies, and others. Second, the procedures of surveillance, control, and repression, bureaucratized and routinized, became objects of regular reporting and inspection. Third, anticipatory surveillance increased greatly: authorities watched groups carefully to see what collective action they might take in the future, and be ready for it (Tilly, 1986:36).

Courts and Crime Rates

This following analysis examines the relationship between the expansion of state control, as reflected by the changes in formal policing, and the changes in crime in France during the 61-year period between 1852 and 1914. To control for the effects of changes in population, the units for the analysis are expressed as rates. The dependent variables are rates

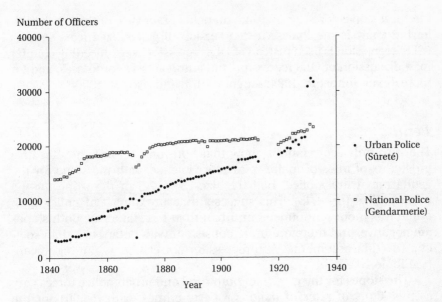

Figure 4.1 Growth of Policing: France, 1845–1935

Source: Data are transcribed from the *Compte Général de l'Administration de la Justice Criminelle en France in the Ministère de la Justice in Paris.*

of major and minor crimes per unit population, and the independent variables are number of gendarmes and number of police (*Sûreté*) per unit population. This makes sense theoretically, and avoids possible problems arising from analyzing the relationship between variables expressed as rates and others that are not (see Firebaugh and Gibbs, 1985, 1987; Bradshaw and Radbill, 1987; and Kraft, 1987, for an extensive discussion of this issue.)

Contemporaneous Effects

As noted in the chapter on urbanization, analyses of temporally ordered data are more likely than others to be distorted by autocorrelation, which violates an assumption of ordinary least squares (OLS) regression, making slopes difficult to interpret. In the following analysis, for example, bureaucratic inertia could have an impact on the size of police forces, so the best predictor of the number of police officers in a specific year is the number in the preceding year. Also, contagion and inertia could make the crime rate in a specific year the best predictor of the crime rate in the following year. This situation would confound attempts with OLS to interpret slopes for rates of crime on policing. In view of this, in the following analysis the Prais-Winsten version of generalized least squares (GLS) regression is used instead of OLS regression (see preceding chapter for a discussion of OLS regression and autoregressive processes, and for more details Johnston, 1984; Kmenta, 1971; and Ostrom, 1990).

Results

The zero-order correlations show that both police forces are negative predictors of rates of major crimes of violence, with the slope for the gendarmes (rural police) half the size ($\beta=-.22$) of the slope for the urban police ($\beta=-.45$). This suggests that any impact of policing on crime was more pronounced in urban than in rural areas. Both slopes are negative, and therefore more consistent with deterrence than societal reaction arguments. Autoregression/correlation is not significant (see Table 4.1).

The slopes for the growth of both rural and urban police forces vary as predictors of rates of major property crimes, with $\beta=.001$ for the urban police and $\beta=.23$ for the gendarmes. Neither is statistically significant with $p\leq.05$. Autoregressive processes are present in both equations (see Table 4.1).

The negative relationship between the growth of policing, especially in urban areas, and major crimes of violence is consistent with a deter-

Table 4.1 Time Series Analysis of Rates of Serious Crimes of Violence and Major Property Crime on the Ratio of Police and Gendarmes per 100,000 in France, 1852–1914

	Rates of Serious Crimes of Violence			Rate of Major Property Crimes		
	B	b	s.e.	B	b	s.e.
AR(1)		.071	.129		.978	.018
Police (urban)	−.45[a]	−.067	.018	.001	.059	.029
r^2	.20			.000		
Durbin-Watson	1.62			1.20		
Ar(1)		.182	.128		.983	.091
Gendarmes (rural)	−.22	−.132	.086	.23	.257	.091
r^2	.048			.055		
Durbin-Watson	1.51			1.55		

[a]$p\leq.001$

Source: Data are transcribed from the *Compte Général de l'Administration de la Justice criminelle en France* in the *Ministère de la Justice* in Paris.

rence argument. However, the direction and significance of slopes suggest that the growth of the state may have inflated rather than deflated rates of major property crime. This can be explained in two ways. The increasing crime rate may have resulted in the growth of policing, or as noted earlier, the growth in policing may have resulted in a more charges being laid. The latter seems more likely because the response of the state to an increasing crime rate is unlikely to have been so sudden.

Distributed Lags and Long-Term Effects

It is possible that the impact on rates of major crime of the growth of policing may have not have been immediate and may have been distributed over a longer period of time than one year. If this is the case, the effects could show up in an equation with distributed lags. Here the dependent variable is regressed on observations of the independent variables taken at an earlier point in time (see Dhrymes, 1971; Stewart, 1984). These different observations begin with the present and extend back four years. That is, the current size of the police force as well as its size in each of the preceding four years can be estimated as predictors of crime. So any contemporaneous effects (the relationship between the size of the police force and the crime rate within the same year) will show up with no time lag (t). On the other side, more long term effects will become apparent when the observations of an independent variable. In this case, the size of the police force for an earlier period (t − n) is introduced in its lagged form as another predictor. (The other way of looking at this is that we are examining the impact of present policing on crime rates in subsequent years.)

The intercorrelations between the different observations of the independent variable do not produce any problems of multicollinearity. The largest single correlation coefficient is r=.34 for the police, lagged 0 and 1 years as predictors of rates of major offenses. (These correlation coefficients are listed in single columns headed by a 0. It is unnecessary to show all possible intercorrelations, since the correlation between lags 0 and 1, for example, will be the same for lags 1 and 2, lags 2 and 3, and so on. See Table 4.2.)

The distributed lags provide no additional support for the argument that the growth of policing repressed serious crimes of violence. Most of the slopes are in the expected direction (negative), but none are significant, and little is added to the predictive power of the equation as indicated by r^2. The contemporaneous effect of the urban police is the only significant slope, suggesting that if policing had an impact on rates of major crimes of violence, it was repressive, but immediate and temporally confined.

The case of property crime is more complex. The growth of the urban police force appears to have been unrelated to rates of major

Table 4.2 Time Series Analysis with Distributed Lags of Rates of Serious Crimes of Violence and Major Property Crime on the Ratio of Police and Gendarmes per 100,000 Population

	Serious Crimes of Violence			Major Property Crimes		
	B	b	s.e.	B	b	s.e.
Surete (urban)						
AR(1)		.066	.14		.898	.06
Lag in years:						
0	−.31	−.044	.06	.27	.064	.03
1	.01	.000	.06	.01	.002	.03
2	.01	.002	.06	−.26	−.064	.03
3	−.02	.003	.06	−.41	−.102	.03
4	−.01	.001	.06	−.44	−.107	.03
5	−.13	−.021	.06	−.20	−.049	.03
r^2 (adjusted)	.071			.216		
Durbin-Watson	1.61			1.55		
Gendarmes (rural)						
AR(1)		.188	.14		.981	.02
Lag in years:						
0	−.10	−.046	.16	.23	.262	.10
1	.02	−.001	.20	.12	.166	.10
2	−.21	−.132	.20	−.07	.030	.10
3	.13	.008	.20	−.04	.045	.10
4	−.07	−.044	.20	−.14	−.041	.10
5	−.04	−.022	.17	.00	.070	.10
r^2 (adjusted)	.06			.04		
Durbin-Watson	1.52			1.19		

Source: Data are transcribed from the *compte Général de l'Administration de la Juscice Criminelle en France* in the *Ministère de la Justice* and the *Annmaire Statistique* in the *Bibliothèque Nationale,* both in Paris.

property crime, at least as indicated by its contemporaneous (non)effect of $\beta=.001$ (this, of course, is not statistically significant). However, the distributed lag model reveals that the impact of the urban police force is initially positive with no lag ($\beta=.27$), but switches to negative over time, with $\beta=-.26$ for a 2-year lag, $\beta=-.41$ for a 3-year lag, and $\beta=-.44$ and $\beta=-.20$ for 4 and 5-year lags, respectively. Thus, the initial inflationary impact of urban policing on crime within the same year is more than offset by deflationary effects in subsequent years. This suggests that the impact of urban policing on rates of major property crime fits at one point in time with societal reaction arguments, and at other points in time with deterrence theory. Further, the overall impact of urban policing on this type of offense is deflationary. Neither this nor the initial inflationary effect would have been revealed without an analysis of distributed lags, because the contemporaneous effect of $\beta=.001$ gives no indication of any impact at all.

Overall, the findings are consistent with deterrence arguments, and suggest that growth of the urban police force may have been a substantial contributor to the decline in rates of major property crime in nineteenth-century France.

As noted earlier, there were no important changes in the law itself during the period under analysis. However, a gradual move toward leniency may have produced a shift in patterns of charges, where offenders were more likely to be charged for more minor offenses before the *tribuneaux correctionals* than more serious crimes before the *cours d'assises*. However, as the rates of minor property offenses and crimes of violence are positive rather than negative correlates of their more serious counterparts, the facts are not consistent with this argument. The relationship between rates of major and minor offenses is statistically significant (zero-order correlations in the neighborhood of r=.40) but positive, rather than negative. These data do not suggest that there was an increasing tendency to charge major offenders with minor crimes. In any given year, then, an increase in charges for major property crimes was directly, rather than inversely related to an increase in charges for minor offenses. This suggests that either major and minor criminal activities tend to increase or decrease simultaneously, or that changes in the police behavior initially affects charges for both major and minor crimes in the same way. However, since rates for minor and major crimes of violence were rising and falling, respectively, the latter seems more likely than the former. So the zero-order relationship between rates of major and minor offenses seems most likely to be based on a mutual dependence on policing.

It is with rates of minor offenses that we find greatest support for reaction arguments. Increases in the number of both urban police and the gendarmes are strong and significant predictors of rates of minor crime. These are contemporaneous, and the effect holds, even in distributed lag models, which display no subsequent offsetting deterrence effect. Thus, policing may have inflated rates of minor offenses either by increasingly discovering minor crimes, or by actually manufacturing arrests, as more critical reaction theorists suggest.

These data are consistent with deterrence theory for some crimes under specific temporal circumstances (e.g., a 3- and 4-year lag for urban police on rates of major property crime). But reaction arguments also receive support from contemporaneous analyses of the impact of both urban and rural policing on rates of both minor property offenses and minor crimes of violence.

Discussion

The growth of state policing in France between 1852 and 1914 may have had an important impact on changes in rates of crime. The immediate effect seems likely to have been an increase in the number and rate of arrests and charges, particularly for minor offenses, but also for major property crime. However, in the case of major crimes of violence, a negative contemporaneous relationship suggests that policing may have also instantly had an effect as an deterrent. It is possible that by charging more people with minor assault, police surveillance increased the rate of charges for minor crimes of violence, but that this prevented these minor offenses from becoming more serious. Thus, policing may have been directly responsible for some of the increase in minor crime rates, and at the same time, produced decreases in rates of major crime. However, since rates of major and minor crimes of violence are positive correlates, the best one can conclude is that if this happened, this effect was a small one, and was more than offset by other factors that inflated minor assaults and repressed major crimes of violence. (The effect of policing is not statistically significant when its distributed impact is examined over a period of 5 years, and is too weak to account for much of the decline in major crimes of violence over the nineteenth century.)

Although policing is a negative predictor of major crimes of violence, its impact is relatively limited in strength and duration. The importance of policing as a predictor of major crimes of violence could result from several factors. As noted earlier, increases in population density associated with urbanization may have amplified informal public surveillance, and this surveillance, rather than formal policing deterred serious violence and/or prevented minor incidents from becoming more serious (see Jacobs, 1961; Stinchcombe, 1963; Hagan, Simpson, and Gillis, 1979; Gillis and Hagan, 1982). However, what seems most likely is that the irrationality of most expressions of serious violence make major crimes of violence relatively impervious to deterrence, which depends on a minimal level of reasonable thought. In view of this, the civilizing changes in cultural patterns described earlier were more likely to have been the major factor in reducing serious crimes of violence in nineteenth-century France (see Gillis, 1994b).

From the standpoint of theory, the most interesting case is the effect of urban policing on rate of major property crime. An equation with lagged variables showed that there is an immediate positive relationship within the same year, consistent with the idea that increased policing inflates official rates of crime. However, lagging suggests that this may have been followed 3 and 4 years later by substantial negative effects for policing on crime, and this is consistent with a deterrence argument. Thus, one equation containing lagged values of one variable is consistent with two opposing theories.

The fact that property crime seems to have been more sensitive to policing than violent crime, which is often more expressive than goal-oriented, is consistent with deterrence/repression theory. The essence of deterrence theory is punishment. When it is sufficiently severe, certain, and swift, punishment is supposed to counter the rewards of crime and, at least in rational people, repress criminal behavior. Certainty has more general deterrence value than has severity (see Tittle, 1969; Chiricos and Waldo, 1970; Bailey, Martin, and Gray, 1972; and for a recent summary, Ross, 1986), but these elements of deterrence theory are essentially non-additive. Logically, neither certainty without sanctions nor sanctions without certainty deters, so a measure of both is necessary.

In earlier periods, when nation-states were weak and poorly organized, the certainty of punishment was probably low. By present standards, exemplary punishment was typically severe, but current research suggests that the general deterrence value would also have been low. However, with the expansion of state policing, the certainty of punishment probably increased, giving it a greater capacity to deter, especially for crimes that continued to carry severe punishment. Although the severity of punishment was in general decline over the nineteenth century (O'Brien, 1982; Wright, 1983), juries in France continued to give relatively severe sentences to property criminals (Donovan, 1981). In view of the relatively severe sentences given to property criminals, the fact that policing had its greatest impact on rates of major property crimes is consistent with deterrence theory.

As noted in the chapter on urbanization and crime, rates of minor crime increased in France over the period of analysis. Several factors may have contributed to this. Industrialization produced more items to steal, and urbanization may have produced more opportunities to steal them (see Cohen and Felson, 1979; and, recently, Messner and Blau, 1987). Declining employment may have combined with this to tip the balance still further in favor of larceny. Increasing size, density, and social heterogeneity of populations may not only have provided greater opportunity for people to become involved in minor altercations, but also the aggravation to do so (see Milgram, 1970; Simmel, 1970; Wirth, 1938). An increase in the use of alcohol and morphine following the Franco-Prussian War (Weber, 1986) may have made the situation worse. Finally, following Sherman's (1993) view, people may have had difficulty accepting police presence and surveillance as just and reacted with more defiance than compliance.

Although these factors may have produced a greater number of minor offenses, increases in arrests and charges may also have occurred independently of any actual increases in rates of minor criminal behavior. As noted earlier, the growing concentration of the population in cities combined with the proliferation of public space to reduce privacy, and most behaviors, legal and illegal, may have become more visible. These conditions could result in an escalating rate of arrests and charges without any real increase in frequency of infractions. Research in other places and periods suggests that rates of minor offenses are highly susceptible to changes in police organization, procedures, and discretion (see, for example, Boritch and Hagan, 1987; McCleary, Nienstedt, and Erven, 1982; Monkkonen, 1981; Slovak, 1986), and France during the nineteenth century seems to have been no exception. Adolphe Quetelet ([1842] 1969) observed that it is likely that in the case of major crimes, official data are more reliable measures of actual criminal activity than are official data for minor offenses, which to a much greater extent reflect other variables in the judicial process, including the activities of the police (see Beirne, 1987, on Quetelet). The fact that β with 0 lag is much greater for policing as a predictor of minor than major offenses supports this.

Whether the patterns shown by this analysis hold for other states in the nineteenth century, or for France during earlier or later periods is uncertain. In some ways France was unique. For example, the orientation to surveillance by the French police was more explicit than in the police forces of other countries (Emsley, 1983). Also, it is obvious that the expansion of state policing in France could not be responsible for declines in crime during earlier periods, since state policing did not exist. However, like patterns of protest, surveillance and repression take various forms, evolving together over time, and involving both cultural and structural changes. So different structures will be salient in different periods, as well as in different nations (see Bayley, 1985). Giddens (1981b, 1985) for example, notes that patterns of control in western countries seem to have evolved from direct repression/deterrence to a more indirect, integrative control through the use of information systems and the industrial economy (see Foucault, 1975, and Skocpol and Finegold, 1982). In view of this, the impact of policing in France may have lost much of its punch even by the end of World War I. Ross (1986), notes that the deterrent effect of certainty often decays over time, and Loftin and McDowall (1982) found no relationship between policing and crime in twentieth-century Detroit. This shows that the relationship between policing and crime in nineteenth-century France is not universal. Thus, subsequent declines in crime, even in France, may have resulted from the emergence and growth of different forms of repression and control.

Conclusions

In general, deterrence theory does not get much empirical support from research. This may be due to the fact that it is an argument constructed around the interaction of several variables, including how soon the punishment is administered. In modern democratic states, if serious punishment comes at all, it is typically long after the associated offense has occurred. This is because democracies like the U.S. enable the accused to engage in a lengthy series of appeals to try and safeguard against punishing an innocent person. Similarly, people in modern industrial national states in the West are more repelled by violent punishment than were their ancestors in the distant past. Even in the seventeenth century, English juries refused to convict offenders when punishments were seen by the public as excessive (Beattie, 1986). Thus, when severity was too high, certainty declined.

On the other hand, when punishment is swift, severe, and certain, it may indeed act as a general deterrent. Wallachia (now part of Romania) was ruled in the fifteenth century by a despotic prince named Vlad (1431–1476), son of Vlad Dracul. During a 14-year reign, Prince Vlad may have executed as many as 20 percent of his population, using methods that were highly likely (if not certain), swift (no lengthy trials there), and severe (by today's standards, cruel and unusual). His frequent use of one macabre style of execution earned him the nickname "Vlad the Impaler" as well as a malevolent reputation. (This infamy has survived over the centuries thanks in part to Bram Stoker, who wrote *Dracula* based on Vlad and his bloodthirsty disposition. See McNally and Florescu, 1972.)

Evidently Wallachians' fear of Vlad the Impaler was so intense that he was able to provide solid gold drinking-cups at public fountains, and no one would steal them, even though they were not chained down. This suggests that when punishment is severe, certain, and swift, deterrence works. However, in fifteenth-century Wallachia, people may have had more to fear from the authorities than the criminals. It is possible that deterrence theory *can* work only under totalitarian conditions, and whether law-abiding citizens are safer or feel more secure in these circumstances is questionable.

When the dust finally settles, the question of whether policing, or any other dimension of punishment, prevents or promotes criminal behavior will probably have as much to do with contextual factors, including the nature of the offense, as with the severity, certainty, and swiftness of punishment. Further longitudinal studies should also be advised by the fact that any impact of independent variables need not be immediate. The deflationary effects of policing on property crime would not have shown up in this study without lagging variables. In fact, without *lagging variables,* the conclusions of this analysis would have been that there was no impact of policing on serious property crime. It is only when we take into account the passage of time, that some secrets of social life are revealed.

In the final analysis, time is a methodological issue: the questions social scientists typically ask are often incongruent with their orientation to data. As noted earlier, part of the problem lies with social thinkers who neglect to specify the duration of their causal processes and fail to alert researchers to the importance of time. Yet whether explicit or implicit, statements of causality at least designate sequence. However, in spite of this, and the general superiority of longitudinal analyses, most social scientific research is still cross-sectional (Lieberson, 1985). Even in much longitudinal research, cross-sectional reasoning continues to prevail, and students of social processes ignore how long they take to occur, thereby missing the opportunity to examine sequence. Any thought at all would reveal the inadequacy of these approaches for addressing research questions, especially when they are formulated on the macro level, where processes may take longer to produce measurable results. If their goal is empirically-supported theory and a body of knowledge, then social scientists would be well advised to assume some of the historian's obsession with sequence and with time.

Subcultural Theories of Crime and Delinquency

David Brownfield

Subcultural theories were once among the predominant sociological explanations of crime and delinquency. Most versions of the theory state that crime and delinquency are caused by adherence to a set of values shared by the group that reinforce deviant behavior. For example, Walter Miller (1958) argued that the focal concerns or central values of the lower class culture encourage gang delinquency.

Culture is a set of values, ideas, and actions learned by individuals from the people who matter to them. Thus, culture is shared and transmitted from one person to another, and from one generation to another. This is how culture endures longer than the lifespan of the population who lives it. To the extent that it defines identity, helps people to cope with impinging reality, and extends the viability of a population, culture can be viewed as a type of capital (see Bourdieu, 1986). In addition, adhering to the rules of one culture can violate the norms of another. For example, Thorsten Sellin (1938) argued that many fundamental "conduct norms" are universal or apply to all people, but that other norms or rules may vary across cultural groups. When people from these different populations come into contact, through immigration for example, the immigrants would be seen as deviant from the perspective of those in the host population, and *vice versa*.

In some cases, this may result in assimilation and the obliteration of differences. However, a pluralist accommodation of different behaviors is also possible, where deviant or even illegal patterns continue indefinitely, passed from those "in the know" to novices, and from old to young as subculture. In fact, according to Sykes and Matza (1961), some of the values and norms of the dominant cultural group may even generate "subterranean values" in reaction to the straight world, which are adopted by both rebels with and without causes. For example, the Hell's Angels disdain for bourgeois life more than matches the rejection of society by academic rebels and has attracted both media coverage and new members for decades (see Thompson, 1967).

Although the Angels now have a business orientation as well, the origin of the motorcycle culture is rooted more in romantic anarchy and a rejection of post-war suburbanism than in material acquisitiveness.

However, there may also be a criminal subculture that offers material gain as well as an escape from conventional bondage to those who risk it. According to Sutherland (1937), one can move into a life of professional crime through "differential association" with those who supply the motivation as well as the human and social capital needed for success in the field.

The human, cultural, and social capital that entice and enable people to engage in deviant or criminal activities may exist as an explicit rejection of dominant mores, folkways, and laws. Subcultures can also be generated by independent, long-standing differences by social class, age, gender, and even geographic region.

Combining Structure and Culture

Subcultural theories have had an impact on structural theories in criminology that focus mainly on economic conditions as the cause of crime. Albert Cohen's (1955) version of strain theory, for example, is a mixed model incorporating elements of both cultural deviance theory and anomie theory. Recently, however, subcultural theories have become much less popular and influential in criminology than processual and individual level explanations such as social learning theory. Processual and individual level theories tend to focus on correlates of crime such as reinforcement and imitation of deviance; such theories tend to ignore structural factors that may affect crime such as social class, gender, and age.

One of the fundamental problems with subcultural theories may have been their failure to incorporate effectively structural factors into an explanation of crime and delinquency. The notion of combining structure and culture in a single explanatory framework is not new. Toby (1950) argued that ethnic values and economic opportunity structures may both be causes of crime. This combined perspective dates back at least to Weber, who argued that the intersection of culture (the Protestant ethic) and structure (urbanism, the accumulation of wealth, banking innovations, and so on) influenced the rise of capitalism in western Europe.

In a recent essay, Wilson (1991) has advocated an integrated structural and cultural theoretical approach to the study of social dislocations among the ghetto underclass. He asserts that analyses framed in terms of a forced and simplistic choice between cultural and structural factors have not increased our understanding of social problems among the urban poor. Wilson distinguishes between the unemployed living in blue collar or working class neighborhoods and the unemployed who live in ghetto neighborhoods with high rates of poverty. While structural factors may restrict opportunities for the former, the unemployed in the slums are also affected by cultural factors of learning and community influence. In particular, Wilson argues that frustration created by the inability to control one's life chances will, in turn, create a sense of futility and lack of self-confidence. Thus, self-efficacy is reduced by what Wilson terms "weak labor-force attachment," which is influenced by the attitudes and beliefs of others in the ghetto.

The transmission of these attitudes and beliefs among peers and neighbors is part of a cultural process which, according to Wilson, merits further study. In *The Truly Disadvantaged* (1987), he describes "concentration effects" of the cultural impact of living in ghetto communities, where the role models and reference groups may develop a sense of fatalism. The absence of conventional role models is produced and compounded in its effects not only by the lack of stable jobs, but also by poor schools and the absence of desirable partners for marriage (Wilson, 1991: 11). Hagan (1993) summarizes several recent ethnographic studies that depict increasingly limited structural or economic opportunities for urban youth, who seem to be turning to a deeper subcultural commitment to gangs.

When structure and culture have been combined in criminological theories, there may have been an overemphasis on the structural factor of social class in subcultural explanations. Rather than an almost exclusive concern with class, it might be more productive to examine additional structural factors—particularly age and gender—as these are interrelated with cultural causes of crime.

In this chapter, we will summarize several subcultural theories of crime and delinquency, and we will examine the potential and the weaknesses of these theories. We will discuss subcultures in terms of possible differences by social class, geographic region, age, and gender. The elements of a subcultural explanation will be explicitly considered, with the purpose of attempting to revive interest in and research about subcultures in criminology.

Subcultures and Social Class

Albert Cohen (1955) states that a delinquent subculture is part of the crime problem among the working class. His description of the subculture is perhaps the best example of what Yinger (1960) defined more precisely as a "contraculture," with norms and values in opposition to the conventions of society. The delinquent contraculture according to Cohen is "nonutilitarian, malicious, and negativistic." Violence and vandalism are typical offenses committed by subculture members, who seek to repudiate the middle class values and institutions, such as the school, that have rejected them and defined them as failures.

The values that are instilled in lower class children by their parents are described by Cohen as the initial cause of failure in middle class institutions such as the school. Working class children are not taught to be self-disciplined; their parents are more permissive than are middle class parents. Working class parents are less likely than middle class parents to stress the use of reason in settling disputes, and they are also less likely to emphasize to their children the importance of cognitive skills. Love and affection are given unconditionally in the working class, while middle class parents give love and affection conditional upon achievement in school. These differing types of socialization generate differing levels of success in school, which are in turn correlated with crime and delinquency.

Walter Miller (1958) has been more clearly identified as a subcultural theorist than has Cohen. Miller depicts the lower class culture as a more independent entity or phenomenon than does Cohen, who describes the delinquent subculture as forming in reaction to middle class values. The lower class culture in Miller's theory has a long history of well-established traditions defined by the focal concerns of trouble, toughness, smartness, fate, autonomy, and excitement.

At the other end of the class distribution, many of those who have studied white collar crime (dating back to Sutherland) have emphasized the causal role played by values stressed within corporate and business culture. Coleman (1989: 205) discusses a culture of competition, in which wealth and success (achieved by whatever means necessary) are the primary goals. Makkai and Braithwaite (1991) report a modest level of support for a subcultural explanation of violation of regulating norms in the nursing home industry.

Research on the Lower Class Subculture

Most empirical research has focused on the issue of a distinctive lower class subculture. For example, Short and Strodtbeck (1965) measured the values of middle- and lower-class black and white males in gang and non-gang contexts. They selected values (or "semantic-differential" images) intended to test subcultural theories of Cloward and Ohlin (1960). Contrary to all of these subcultural theories, Short and Strodtbeck found that regardless of social class and gang membership, all of the groups studied evaluated middle class lifestyle values equally highly. For example, regardless of social class and gang membership, respondents tended to evaluate highly those who work for good grades in school and those who save money.

Nevertheless, Short and Strodtbeck did find significant differences by class and gang membership that were consistent with subcultural theories. Lower class and gang boys were more likely than middle class, non-gang boys to endorse loitering or hanging out on street corners. Black gang boys were particularly likely to endorse a sexually active lifestyle. Gang boys, black and white, were more likely to positively evaluate someone who is a good fighter with a tough reputation (consistent with Miller's focal concern of toughness). In contrast, nearly all respondents expressed little tolerance for those who use drugs to get high. Cloward and Ohlin's concept of a retreatist subculture received almost no support in the Short and Strodtbeck study; Short and Strodtbeck observed that it was difficult to locate gangs whose activities centered around drug use.

Gang boys were found to positively evaluate criminal images to a greater extent than non-gang boys. An ethical orientation endorsing those who have connections to avoid trouble with the law was found to be most common among gang boys and the lower class respondents. Short and Strodtbeck reported a somewhat greater tendency for gang members versus non-gang members to be utilitarian and materialistic in their attitudes. Overall, they find that acceptance of deviant behavior is inversely correlated with social status. Thus, Short and Strodtbeck conclude that there is widespread acceptance of middle class prescriptive norms, but middle class proscriptive norms are not so universally held; in particular, lower status respondents express greater tolerance for deviant behavior.

Short and Strodtbeck argued that their findings support the notion that legitimate and illegitimate behaviors need not be perceived as mutually exclusive by gang boys. Gang boys are ambivalent in their values, expressing support for both middle class ideals and deviant values. Miller's argument that these findings merely reflect adherence to "official" ideals is rejected by Short and Strodtbeck. They point out that gang boys also expressed approval of deviant images or values (and that gang boys were more likely to express such approval than non-gang boys). Further, Short and Strodtbeck state that Miller's reliance on actual behavior to measure values may preclude recognition of the possibility that values and behavior may be discrepant.

While Hirschi (1969) also draws similar conclusions to those of Short and Strodtbeck, in some respects Hirschi's empirical analysis is supportive of cultural deviance theory. For example, Hirschi finds that delinquents are less likely than nondelinquents to express support for legal or conventional moral norms. Delinquents are less likely to endorse conventional achievements than are nondelinquents. Hirschi also reports that delinquents are more likely than nondelinquents to be fatalistic and to desire the autonomy of premature adult status, including activities such as drinking and driving a car (though not necessarily at the same time).

On the other hand, Hirschi reports substantial evidence inconsistent with Miller's theory. For example, Hirschi finds little support for the

idea that the female headed household is a significant factor in producing subcultural values and delinquency. Further, Hirschi argues that
members of the lower class do not strongly adhere to the tenets of the
subculture delineated by Miller, and that personal characteristics such
as academic ability have a stronger impact on delinquency than cultural
factors or variables. We elaborate these arguments further by discussing
Hirschi's (1969: 212–223) evidence and arguments in greater detail.

Hirschi begins by pointing out that parental occupational status is
not related to delinquency (neither in the Richmond Youth Study nor in
other self-report studies). This finding undermines Miller's entire argument. However, Hirschi goes on to examine possible linkages between
family status and the focal concerns described by Miller.

The focal concern of trouble implies an instrumental attitude
toward the law. An instrumental attitude toward the law may be characterized by the person who only weighs the rewards of crime versus the
risks of punishment (rather than whether a particular action is right or
just). Miller argues that lower class culture members are less likely to
obey the law due to moral compunction than simply due to the desire to
avoid the complications and hassle of being arrested. Hirschi finds that
family status is unrelated to the probability of agreeing with the statement "it is all right to get around the law if you can get away with it."
Contrary to Miller's discussion, this measure of instrumental attitudes
toward the law is not significantly related to status.

A value placed on "smartness" implies a positive evaluation of the
ability to manipulate others and to obtain as much as possible with the
least possible effort. Again, Hirschi finds little support for Miller's theory.
Family status was not related to the pattern of responses to the following
item: "Suckers deserve to be taken advantage of."

Hirschi did not have direct measures of the focal concerns of toughness and excitement in his study. Consistent with the pattern of findings
in Hirschi's study, Ball-Rokeach (1973) reports that socioeconomic status (measured by income and education) is weakly correlated with
approval of violence. While lower-status respondents were less likely to
attach significance to a sense of accomplishment, being independent or
self-controlled than higher status respondents, none of these values was
significantly associated with approval of violence or with participation
in interpersonal violence.

The observed indicators of subcultural values used by Ball-Rokeach
have been criticized by Curtis (1975: 112–113) for a number of reasons.
For example, the slogans and phrases used by Ball-Rokeach are characterized as being relatively abstract rather than concrete depictions of
realistic situations. Curtis argues that such abstractions may be appropriate measures for highly educated respondents, but not for typical
subculture members. The statements selected by Ball-Rokeach include

some conventional, dominant culture values (such as emphasizing free-dom or independence, social recognition, and being courageous), which are hardly limited to a criminal subculture.

Miller argues that lower class subculture members emphasize inde-pendence from authority, the freedom to do as one pleases. This focal concern of autonomy was measured in a number of ways by Hirschi, including measures of drinking, dislike of criticism by adults, and the significance of a car. Neither drinking nor degree of dislike of criticism by adults (measured by the item "I don't like being criticized by adults") were significantly associated with family status. Youths from lower sta-tus families were more likely than youths from higher status families to consider a car important. (Hirschi argues that middle class children are just as interested in cars as lower class children, but that middle class adolescents are more likely to take the availability of cars for granted. Further, Hirschi finds that controlling for measures of academic ability eliminates the relationship between family status and perceived signifi-cance of cars.)

Lower class people have been found to be more fatalistic and present-oriented than middle class people (cf. Banfield, 1968). Planning for the future is perceived by lower class people to be relatively worth-less since such plans rarely materialize. Hirschi does find that lower sta-tus respondents were somewhat more likely than higher status subjects to agree with statements such as "a person should live for today and let tomorrow take care of itself" and "there is no sense looking ahead since no one knows what the future will be like." Hirschi argues that such atti-tudes may be generated more by personal circumstances and prospects than by cultural transmission of values. To test this argument, he again controls for measures of academic ability to see if the original relation-ship between status and fatalism persists. While such controls reduce the magnitude of the original relationship to some extent, status contin-ues to influence fatalistic attitudes in the direction predicted by Miller. Academic ability does enhance the lower status child's feelings of self-determination, but there remains a significant effect of status (and pos-sibly subcultural influence).

An Experimental Proposal

It is possible that additional research on fatalism and social class may point to structural rather than cultural causes. Consider the following proposed series of experiments (see Henslin and Reynolds, 1979, for a discussion of fatalism). In the first experiment, lower class and middle class children are presented with a choice of being given one candy bar immediately without condition or two candy bars following the perfor-mance of a simple task, such as adding a column of numbers. If theorists such as Miller and Banfield are correct, we might expect lower class children in the first experiment to be somewhat less likely than the middle class children to defer gratification (and therefore be more likely to choose to receive one candy bar immediately).

In the second experiment, both lower and middle class children are told that these same terms or conditions will apply in receiving either one or two candy bars; but for those children who choose to perform the simple task, the promise of receiving the two candy bars is broken by the unscrupulous experimenter and the children are not given any candy. In a third experiment (with the same initial conditions as the first experiment) among the children who were promised candy but not given any, would we continue to observe substantial social class differences in the percentages of children choosing to defer gratification? It is unlikely that there would be. Further, we would expect that relatively few of the children would continue to defer gratification after experiencing the broken promise.

Lower class children may be more fatalistic and less inclined to defer gratification than middle class children because lower class children have experienced more broken promises, not because they devalue the conventional Protestant ethic. Lower class children are probably well aware that the promise of the American dream of success for those who work hard seems too distant and is often unkept. Structural rather than cultural factors may account for the fatalism and lack of deferred gratification among the lower class.

Kornhauser (1978) also criticizes the notion that apathy or fatalism is a shared value of the lower class. Rather than representing some valued motivational disposition, fatalism and apathy represent the absence of motivation which is determined largely by structural rather than by cultural factors. Kornhauser also questions the lack of distinctive values in the lower class culture other than those specifically concerned with crime and delinquency. The absence of distinctive values with respect to class solidarity and social welfare undermines the argument for the existence of a class based subculture. Kornhauser asks (1978: 212), are the members of the lower class subculture the most pro-union and the most concerned with social welfare, or are they the most indifferent to the needs of their social class?

Reviving Class-Based Subcultures

The analysis and arguments of Short and Strodtbeck, Hirschi, and Kornhauser persuaded many criminologists that the effects of a delinquent subculture are weak or nonexistent. However, Messner (1983) reports findings that may lead us to believe that rumors of the death of subcultural theory were premature. Messner found persistent effects of region on homicide rates controlling for structural variables such as socioeconomic indices. This finding suggests the possibility of a regional subculture of violence, a topic we will consider later.

Further, nearly all of the research on subcultures in criminology has defined class in terms of income, education, or parental occupation. Brownfield (1987) advocated the use of underclass measures, such as unemployment and welfare status, to reassess cultural deviance theory. Hirschi had found that both of these underclass measures are significantly associated with delinquency in the Richmond Youth Study. Brownfield also found that indicators of subcultural focal concerns in the Richmond study were correlated with these underclass measures. For example, children in the underclass were more likely to agree with the statement "it is all right to get around the law if you can get away with it" than children of higher status families.

Behavioral measures of autonomy, including smoking, drinking, and dating, were also significantly associated with underclass measures. These behavioral measures are flawed as indicators of values since it is possible to feel remorse for one's actions (for lying, cheating, and gluttony). Remorse or guilt felt over one's actions does not constitute positive evaluation of the behavior. Attitudinal measures of autonomy (assessing the importance of cars and dislike of criticism by adults) were significantly related to unemployment, but not to welfare status. Brownfield also found that measures of fatalism and smartness were correlated with underclass measures. In multivariate analyses, the underclass measures tended to have significant effects on both focal concerns and delinquency in a manner consistent with predictions derived from cultural deviance theory.

However, not all of the evidence in Brownfield's study was found to be supportive of subcultural theory. Jensen and Rojek (1980) argued that cultural deviance theory portrays delinquency as a consequence of successful socialization into a subculture. Delinquency is actually a manifestation of conformity to the norms and values of the subculture. Social control theory portrays delinquency as a consequence of the failure of conventional institutions to socialize children. Brownfield constructed a test of these competing depictions of delinquency by observing the effects of attachment to a member of the subculture. If the portrayal of cultural deviance theory is correct, attachment to or identification with an unemployed father should enhance the process of socialization into the norms and values of the subculture. If the control theorist's depiction is correct, attachment to the father (regardless of employment status) should reduce acceptance of deviant values.

Brownfield found the evidence is far more consistent with the socialization propositions derived from social control theory than with predictions based on cultural deviance theory. Regardless of employment status, attachment to the father tends to reduce acceptance of deviant or subcultural values.

However, there are at least two limitations of this test of cultural deviance theory. First, the father is not the central role model or agent of socialization in Miller's version of cultural deviance theory; the focus is more on peer influence than on parental socialization patterns. Also, the assumption that unemployed fathers adhere to subcultural focal concerns themselves may be incorrect. Unemployed fathers very likely convey similar conventional messages to their sons as fully-employed fathers convey.

Subcultural Theory and the Origins of Law

Empirical research has focused on other important issues regarding class based subcultures. Kornhauser (1978) discussed the cultural deviance theory interpretation of the origins of criminal law in relation to social class. Sellin (1938), one of the first cultural deviance theorists, asserted that laws are completely variable historically and across cultures. Similar to Marxist theory, Sellin argued that laws represent the interests of powerful segments and these laws are imposed on people within society with little or no power. The laws supposedly do not reflect common interests of all people in society.

The evidence on the evaluation of common law crimes across a variety of groups and cross-culturally suggests an overwhelming consensus in proscribing theft and violence (see Rossi et al., 1974; Hagan, Silva, and Simpson, 1977; and, ironically, Sellin and Wolfgang, 1969, who seem to ignore the implications of their own findings for subcultural theory).

Kornhauser points out that no culture or subculture can promote values which might threaten its own existence. Values which condemn force and fraud are nearly universal because the continued existence of society requires such values. Hence, Kornhauser concludes that subcultures of crime and delinquency are nonexistent. Her argument does not ignore the considerable evidence on greater toleration of deviant behavior among some segments (e.g., Short and Strodtbeck, 1965). Kornhauser argues that mere toleration of deviance is not what subcultural theorists such as Miller described. Instead, Miller and others emphasize preferred and positively endorsed values requiring criminal behavior. Kornhauser sees the absence of commitment to conventional values as indicative of anomie and amorality rather than a subcultural system of values. Offenders are portrayed as indifferent to morality and merely instrumental rather than adhering to subcultural values.

Concluding Remarks on Class-Based Subcultures

Since culture is a group property, in order for subcultures to exist they must be linked to an identifiable group (Kornhauser, 1978: 210). To establish the existence of a group rather than a mere aggregate, it must be shown that individuals are capable of concerting their actions. People must be able to interact with each other directly or indirectly to be able to form an identifiable group and a subculture. Felson et al. (1994) hypothesize that violent subcultures are more likely to develop in small groups with extensive interpersonal interaction, such as in schools and neighborhoods rather than in large aggregates such as social classes, ethnic groups, or geographic regions. They find that high schools seem to provide a meaningful subcultural context that significantly affects delinquent behavior. Felson et al. measure subcultural values that focus on approval of aggression in response to some form of provocation. They report that the prevalence of these subcultural values within a school affects delinquent behavior independent of the individual's own personal values. Kornhauser asserts that the lower class is better conceived as a collectivity or loose aggregate rather than as a group; hence, she concludes that it is unlikely that the lower class has a subculture.

Despite Kornhauser's trenchant criticism of class based subcultures, we have seen some evidence in partial support of a lower class subculture explanation. Further, subcultures may be linked to age, gender, and region.

A Regional Subculture of Violence

Sociologists have attempted to apply a subculture of violence thesis specifically to the American South. (Fischer [1975] also discusses deviant subcultures based on place of residence or urbanism.) Homicide rates in the South have been observed to be substantially higher than in other regions of the United States (Huff-Corzine, Corzine, and Moore, 1991). Some theorists (Hackney, 1969; Gastil, 1971) argue that there is a regional culture of violence in the South which endorses a vigorous defense of one's honor, glorifies military skills, and reflects the historical need for coercion in the antebellum, slave economy.

Reed (1972: 10) argues that the South retains a distinct identity as an "ethnic subsociety." The Southern ethnic subsociety functions much like other ethnic groups according to Reed. The ethnic subsociety (a) serves as a source of group identification for individuals, (b) provides a network of groups and institutions which allow individuals to limit their significant group interactions to their own ethnic subsociety, and (c) filters the national cultural behaviors and values through its own cultural heritage.

Reed presents evidence from opinion polls administered from the 1930s to the 1960s that supports his contention of a persistent Southern subculture. For example, the South retains its distinctive religious heritage; Reed (1972: 57–81) found that Southerners are still more likely to be Baptists, more frequently attend church, and are more likely to abstain from alcohol than non-Southerners. Reed also finds a higher probability of gun ownership and a higher probability of the use and approval of corporal punishment of children among Southern versus non-Southern respondents (1972: 45–55).

Hackney (1969) finds that there is a significant effect of region on 1940 homicide rates, holding constant factors such as urbanization, education, income, unemployment, and age. He argues that Southerners are more likely to have a passive attitude toward their environment, which in turn is related to feeling less self-responsibility and "a greater use of projection in ego defense" (1969: 923). Historical experiences of guilt and defeat have likely contributed to the development of a "siege mentality." Hackney theorizes that high Southern homicide rates may reflect the aggression and frustration of a defeated colony. He states (1969: 924–925) that Southerners are most conscious of their identity as Southerners "when they are defending their region against attack from outside forces: abolitionists, the Union Army, carpetbaggers, Wall Street and Pittsburgh, civil rights agitators, the federal government, feminism, socialism, trade-unionism, Darwinism, Communism, atheism, daylight-saving time, and other by-products of modernity."

In a recent study of the Southern subculture of violence, Ellison (1991) concludes that prior research (e.g., Dixon and Lizotte, 1987; Reed, 1972) has yielded contradictory findings because diverse measures of approval of violence have been used. Ellison argues that Southerners are more likely than non-Southerners to approve of violence only in specific situations related to defensiveness and responses to affronts to honor (cf. Reed, 1982). Southerners do not approve of violence carte blanche or for all situations to a greater extent than non-Southerners.

Ellison argues that a "public" religious culture in the South that emphasizes a vengeful deity may condone violence if committed in retribution for certain affronts to honor. ("Public" religious culture is emphasized because religious attendance was found [(Ellison, 1991:1236–1237)] to have a greater effect on attitudes toward defensive violence than measures of personal devotion such as individual prayer.) Fundamentalist religion condones retributive justice or "an eye for an eye" retaliation. However, Ellison (1991:1230) finds that regional differences in support of defensive violence may be declining over time, given lower levels of support for such behavior in more recent (or younger) Southern cohorts.

Like Hackney, Gastil (1971) traces high Southern homicide rates to cultural traditions developed in the antebellum period. The prolonged existence of a frontier society (supposedly indicative of a lack of civilizing influences), a tradition of dueling and an exaggerated sense of honor, extreme social class differences (between black and white and between aristocracy and poor tenant farmers), and a tendency to carry weapons are all cited as components of a regional culture of violence. In contrast to Hackney, who defined the South as the former Confederate states, Gastil constructed an Index of Southernness to take into account the diffusion of Southern culture to border and western states. Gastil's regression analysis yields a significant correlation between the Index of Southernness and homicide rates in 1960, holding constant factors such as racial and age composition, median income, health facilities (hospital beds and physicians per 1,000 persons), urbanization, and median education levels.

Other researchers find that either the apparent regional variations in homicide rates can be explained by the high incidence of structural poverty in the South (Loftin and Hill, 1974), or that personal crime rates in the South are converging with personal crime rates in the non-South (Smith and Parker, 1980). Loftin and Hill argue that both Gastil and Hackney failed to accurately assess the effect of structural variables (such as poverty, education, and age distribution), thus biasing the results of their statistical analyses in favor of finding regional or cultural effects.

Messner (1983) also uses the structural poverty index, but he finds that region (using the Index of Southernness and the Confederacy measure) continues to have a significant effect on homicide rates (averaged for the period 1969–1971) for a sample of 204 Standard Metropolitan Statistical Areas (SMSAs). Messner argues that states (used in previous analyses) are arbitrary statistical aggregations, whereas SMSAs represent more meaningful social communities.

Huff-Corzine, Corzine, and Moore, (1991) conclude that the South is more completely defined by remarkably high homicide and low suicide rates. This conclusion, suggested by Hackney and by Henry and Short (1954), draws attention to an attribution hypothesis, wherein homicide is acceptable if personal frustrations may be blamed on external forces and suicide is acceptable among those with an internal locus of control. Both blacks and Southerners are likely to have an external locus of control and are more likely than whites and non-Southerners to harm others in response to frustration.

We turn next to a consideration of subcultures based on age and gender. While there is considerable consensus that age and gender are consistently correlated with criminal behavior (Nettler, 1984), subcultural theorists (with a few notable exceptions) have failed to focus on age and gender subcultures.

Adolescent Subcultures

England (1960) suggests that an adolescent culture emerged from the withdrawal of young people from productive economic roles, due to compulsory education, child labor laws, and a shift away from agricultural production. Withdrawal from the economy produced an ambiguous status for teenagers, separating them from adults but not conferring a clear childhood status. Adolescents face contradictory expectations. England states that the teenager "is not expected to engage in productive labor, but neither is he encouraged to loaf; he is discouraged from early marriage, but is allowed to engage in proto-courtship; he cannot vote, hold public office, or serve on a jury, but is expected to be civic minded" (England, 1960:536).

England writes that post-World War II changes have speeded creation of a youth culture, especially the development of a large market for goods and services directed at teenagers (including music-related products, cosmetics, and car-related products) and mass communication directed at teens (including radio, television, and magazines). Minority group psychology has developed among teenagers with separate leadership figures (often entertainers), feelings of antagonism and alienation among those identified by a conspicuous trait (age), and feelings of exclusiveness toward the dominant group (adults).

Attitudes and values may develop in the adolescent subculture that focus on a leisure class lifestyle and hedonism. To a certain extent, status among adolescents becomes defined in terms of the ability to participate in hedonistic activities. Hebdige (1976) describes part of the British youth culture in terms of dress, consumerism or a materialistic ethic, and by distinctive language or vocabulary. In the early 1970s, Hebdige observes that youth culture in Britain adopted a vocabulary labeled "Wolverine," based on the writings of novelist Tom Wolfe. This distinctive vocabulary was primarily sarcastic and irreverent in tone.

Many observers of youth culture, including England, also stress that there are strong connections between adolescent and adult cultures, though distortions and caricatures of adult values occur. Vaz (1965) describes a subculture among middle-class boys as peer oriented, anti-intellectual, and focused on status and pursuit of thrills and leisure. Rather than depicting these values as a contraculture, Vaz writes that these values reflect adult values and institutions, and that indeed adults encourage their development. Socialization and popularity are encouraged by parents and by teachers. Participation in athletics, dating, parties, and driving are encouraged, while being overly studious is discouraged. Much of adolescent male behavior derives from attention-seeking competitions, according to Vaz, while excessive conformity to peer expectations also generates some delinquent behavior. Delinquency evolves out of some acceptable middle-class activities; middle-class adolescents may rarely define themselves as delinquent. Corsaro and Rizzo (1990) also emphasize continuity in socialization of children in adult and peer settings. Yet extreme forms of misbehavior are attributed to personality problems, according to Vaz, rather than as a natural outgrowth of middle class culture.

Westley and Elkin (1957) suggest that adolescence is not a period of storm and stress, nor are adolescents completely segregated from adult values and adult control. Instead, these researchers find (in a study of an upper middle class suburb of Montreal) considerable similarity in values and continuity between adult and adolescent social worlds. Adolescents experience a relatively protective, supervised lifestyle, including limited unstructured time and participation in supervised athletics. The Protestant ethic of hard work, thrift, and savings is emphasized among adolescents; conventional adult values are mirrored among adolescents in terms of assessments of ideal marriage partners (with occupation and social status as important criteria). Westley and Elkin conclude that conventional peer groups do have different tastes than adults in dress, music, and so on, but there is no significant rejection of adult values regarding achievement and career goals.

Coleman's (1961) study, *The Adolescent Society*, reflected the public perception of a distinctive youth culture. Coleman depicted the adolescent society as separate from and in opposition to the adult society; the values and norms of adolescents were supposedly very different from those of adults. For example, Coleman found that high school boys wanted to be remembered most for being a star athlete, while high school girls wanted to be remembered as being popular. The leading crowds in high schools were also perceived to be composed of athletic boys and popular girls. Social activities rather than academic achievement were valued among adolescents.

Berger (1963) criticized Coleman's conclusions regarding a completely distinct and separate adolescent culture. Berger argued that middle-class adults share most of the same values as adolescents. The admiration of athletics and the desire to engage in social activities are widespread among adults. Sporting events, cars, sex, and drinking are all part of the middle-class adult world. Tanner (1988) suggests that although peers influence tastes in fashion and music, parents have a greater influence on important issues such as career and marital decisions. Perhaps, as Short and Strodtbeck (1965) have argued with respect to class differences in values, there may be little variation by age in terms of prescriptive norms but considerable variation by age in terms of proscriptive norms. Hence, young people may be more tolerant than adults of engaging in deviant or criminal activity, but adolescents may also value educational and occupational goals as highly as adults do.

Abuses of the automobile by adolescents, including a variety of traffic offenses and joyriding, reflect the adult obsession with cars in terms of speed and power status symbols rather than as mere transportation (England, 1960). The competitive spirit of the adult world may degenerate into violence and destruction among teenagers, often in conjunction with athletic contests. The adult obsession with sex is reflected in sexual relations among teenagers; restraint and self-control among adults are not popular themes in the media. Adult norms of alcohol consumption regarding moderate use and appropriate occasions are not easily observed by adolescents, who by necessity usually consume alcohol secretly (which may lead to abusive patterns outside the supervision of adults).

Maddox and McCall (1964) conclude that there is no widely shared youth culture that supports drinking. Instead, they found considerable disapproval of alcohol use among adolescents (as well as among adults) regarding drinking by teenagers. Maddox and McCall argue that adolescents seeking adult status were likely to drink. For example, adolescents who sought autonomy from adult control and those who had spending money and jobs, which confer such independence, were likely to drink frequently. Likewise, those adolescents who planned to assume adult role responsibilities immediately following high school were more likely to drink than those planning to go to college. These findings are consistent with social control theory.

Tanner (1988) observes the emphasis on age stratification in modern society, with groups divided into periods of infancy, childhood, adolescence, middle age, and the elderly. The concept of "youth culture" emerged as there came to be more emphasis placed on the problematic aspects of adolescence. Deviant youth traditions of delinquency, bohemianism, and radicalism have been identified. Tanner suggests that this preoccupation with deviant youth cultures ignores the fact that the majority of adolescents refrain from serious acts of deviance or extensive involvement in deviant subcultures.

As England suggested, young people since the late nineteenth century have been made more marginal to economic production and their status has become more ambiguous over time. Young people are required to spend more time training to work in advanced industrial societies, and their segregation in schools helps to foster what Empey (1982) terms a middle class youth subculture. Tanner argues that the post–World War II baby boom has encouraged the development of a youth subculture, wherein there is a higher ratio of children to be socialized relative to adults needed to socialize children. Divisiveness along age lines, symbolized by the phrase "generation gap," displaced older conflicts based on class and ethnicity to a large extent (Tanner, 1988: 330).

Tanner suggests that streaming or school tracking has a particularly strong and negative influence on students in non-university bound programs. As students in the lower streams perceive their lack of future life chances, they are more likely to become involved in deviant youth cultures. However, Wiatrowski et al. (1982) find that streaming or tracking in itself has little impact on students after controlling for antecedent measures of academic ability (i.e., controls for test scores recorded before high school tracking even begins eliminates the effects of tracking on adolescent delinquency).

Tanner (1988: 355) rejects "quick fix" strategies to deal with the problems of youth culture. In particular, the banning of song lyrics in rock music is very unlikely to affect adolescent behavior or prospects. Prinsky and Rosenbaum (1987) find that most teenagers do not even understand the lyrics of most rock songs; it seems unlikely that their behavior would be greatly influenced by such incomprehensible material.

Tanner questions the utility of subcultural explanations of deviance given the transient level of commitment to the youth culture. Adolescent deviance, is characterized by its lack of sophistication, its situational and episodic nature, and by a lack of group cohesion (see Gottfredson and Hirschi (1990), for a similar view). The subcultural explanation therefore does not seem to be consistent with these characteristics of adolescent deviance.

Research on Adolescent Subcultures

According to the Schwendingers (1985), automobiles are a central part of adolescent subcultures, symbolizing independence, status, and power. Cars also provide opportunity for trouble, including drunken driving, sexual encounters, and a variety of traffic offenses (cf. Chambliss, 1973). Yet Higgins and Albrecht (1981) point out there are very few sociological studies of cars and adolescents.

Recent research has focused on the diverse nature of adolescent subcultures. For example, Hagan (1991b) identifies two distinct adolescent subcultures. First, a delinquency subculture is defined by attitudes toward activities such as stealing, vandalism, and fighting (measured by respondents ranking "how much fun" these activities are). Second, a party subculture is defined by attitudes toward parties, drinking, dating, and driving around in a car. The party subculture embodies subterranean values that emphasize risk taking in terms of activities that mirror adult society's obsession with cars, sex, and alcohol.

Hagan reports that identification with a party subculture actually enhances attainment of occupational status among the sons of non-working class fathers. Participation in a party subculture may help to develop networks or social contacts for non-working class males. (College fraternities recruit members with such promises.) In contrast, identification with the subculture of delinquency only has significant negative consequences for the status attainment of sons of working-class fathers. These findings are also consistent with Chambliss's (1973) ethnographic study of the differential long-term consequences of delinquent involvement for middle-class and lower-class boys, with middle-class boys being largely unaffected while lower-class boys were, in some instances, very adversely affected.

Kennedy and Baron (1995), in a field study of a youth punk rocker group, conclude that subcultural theory provides a good explanation of street violence (combined with rational choice and routine activities perspectives). Other youth groups such as skinheads and skaters also seem to follow patterns similar to those of punk rockers. Subcultural norms among such youth groups seem to encourage violence by placing a premium on a tough reputation and, more specifically, by endorsing the acquisition of desired material goods by force or threat of force.

Kennedy and Baron (1995:217) quote one punker's approach: "I wanted his shirt, so we were following behind. Then he got on his skate (skateboard) so we ran him down. I said, 'Hey, I really like your shirt; I'll trade you my ring.' He said no, so I said, 'I'll trade you my Jesus Christ Superstar shirt.' He said no. So I said, 'Which do you value more, your shirt or your life?'"

Weak or compliant victims defined as "geeks" are deemed to be appropriate victims within the punk rocker subculture—and they are viewed as easy targets who are unlikely to call the police (Kennedy and Baron, 1995). The presence of third parties in potentially violent confrontations provides for subcultural norms that endorse aggression and may confer the sheer physical strength needed to be successful in carrying out such attacks.

As suggested earlier, along with age, gender has been one of the most consistent correlates of crime. We turn next to a consideration of a subcultural explanation of gender and criminal behavior.

Gender and Subcultural Theory

Nancy Chodorow (1974) dismisses biological factors as the primary influence on sex roles and instead attributes most gender differences to the fact that women, nearly everywhere and throughout history, are held responsible for early child care. The feminine personality largely develops in relationships with other people far more than the masculine personality, which develops in greater isolation from others.

Gender differences derived from the maternal relationship are extended by peer groups in childhood. Lever (1976) found that the games children play reflect and reinforce gender differences in personality. While boys tend to play competitive, zero-sum games that often involve quarreling and disputes, girls tend to play non-competitive, turn-taking games (jump rope and hopscotch) that tend to have few clear winners and losers and that involve fewer disputes. Lever reports that when disputes occur during girls' games, the game is usually ended. In contrast, boys seemed to revel in the legalistic arguments incident to games almost as much as in the game itself.

Sutherland and Cressey (1978: 131–135) conclude that biological predisposition is insufficient in explaining gender variations in crime rates. The gender ratio in crime varies by a number of non-biological factors, including cross-culturally, over time, and by place of residence. However, Sutherland and Cressey (1978: 135) argue that perhaps "the most important difference is that the girls are supervised more carefully and behave in accordance with anticriminal behavior patterns taught to them with greater care and consistency than do boys." Turk (1969) also attributes the low rate of female crime to a higher level of agreement with legal norms among females compared with males, and to the tendency for female activities to be more restricted than the activities of males. Turk suggests that relative power has a negligible effect on male versus female rates of crime.

Jensen and Eve (1976) find that controls for measures of attachment to the law and parental supervision do not entirely account for the effect of gender on delinquency. However, they report that controls for these and other variables did reduce the effect of gender on delinquency considerably.

Hagan, Gillis, and Simpson (1985, 1987) also emphasize parental supervision as a key intervening variable helping to account for gender differences in delinquency. In addition, power-control theory suggests that taste for risk and perceived risk are significant factors in helping to account for variation in rates of delinquency by gender. The specification of several intervening variables will likely be necessary for a full explanation of gender differences in crime and delinquency. Both structural and cultural factors may need to be considered.

Maddox and McCall (1964) suggest that gender differences in drinking may be partially attributed to cultural differences or expectations and to different levels of risk taking. Women are subjected to a double standard with regard to drinking (regardless of age), possibly because of the sexual connotations and consequences of alcohol use. In terms of varying cultural standards, a number of subjects in the Maddox and McCall study made comments to the effect that drinking by girls "just doesn't look right." In terms of risk taking differences, Maddox and McCall find that females who did report drinking were likely to do so in protected contexts at home or when parents or relatives are present.

Moral Development and Gender

Carol Gilligan (1982) asserts that since most social science research has tended to focus on males, male behavior has come to be accepted as the norm and female behavior (if different from male behavior) is regarded as deviant. When females do not conform to the dictates of social science, then it is concluded that women are in some way deficient. We would suggest that, while we generally agree with Gilligan's observations, within the study of crime and delinquency males are considered far more problematic than females (unfortunately, to the point that females were excluded until recently from most criminological studies).

Gilligan observes that the equation of individual development and autonomy with maturity translates into negative evaluations of women, whose other-directed or empathetic outlook makes them appear less mature and vulnerable. Lawrence Kohlberg (who has taught and collaborated with Gilligan) describes the development of moral judgment based only on observations of males. Females, Gilligan argues, will not reach the so-called higher stages of moral development in Kohlberg's scheme because women have a different sense of obligation and morality than males. Females are trapped in the third stage of Kohlberg's scheme, wherein morality is defined in terms of helping and pleasing others. The "higher" stages of moral development require that rules and universal principles take precedence over relationships. The differing conceptions of morality reflect the concerns expressed in the differing types of play activities by gender (Lever, 1976); males are concerned with abstract rights and rules, while females are concerned with relationships and nurturance.

In studies of moral judgment and decisions regarding abortion, Gilligan concludes that women attempt to resolve conflicts so that no one is harmed. Under Kohlberg's scheme of preconventional, conventional, and postconventional morality, the individual's moral development is tied to changing conceptions of the application of rules (from inability to share societal rules to creating universal principles that transcend societal rules). Gilligan observes that women's moral development is tied to changes in their conceptions of relationships and responsibility (rather than shifting conceptions of abstract rules). Among women there may be an initial stress on concern for the self and for survival, a selfish stage paralleling preconventional morality. A second stage focuses on nurturance of others with morality equated with maternal empathy. The third stage described by Gilligan attempts to eliminate the extreme self-sacrifice entailed in the second stage through recognition of the interrelationship or interdependence between self and others. There is a universal principle expressed in this third stage, but it is focused on relationships and responsibility; in the third stage, there is a universal proscription against harm and exploitation of both self and others. Empathy and activities of care will enhance the well being of both self and others. Morality in this third stage is judged on the basis of honest treatment of self and others, rather than mere conformity to societal expectations.

For women, Gilligan concludes that the moral imperative is to perceive and mitigate significant global problems. For men, the moral imperative is to protect the individual's right to freedom and self-fulfillment.

Both the conceptual and empirical work of Gilligan have been subjected to considerable criticism (Jackson and Griffiths, 1991). Some have argued that Gilligan tends to reinforce the stereotype that men are rational and women are emotional. Others have suggested that the primary research used by Gilligan fails to include a comparison group of male subjects; hence, it is conceivable that males might be as compassionate as females in evaluating moral dilemmas about abortion. However, more recent work by Gilligan and her associates (1988) has incorporated comparison groups of male subjects, and females are found to be much more likely than males to display a caring moral orientation.

Beutel and Marini (1995) also find substantial gender differences in values regarding compassion and materialism. In studies of high school seniors from 1977 to 1991, they report that females are more sympathetic to others and less profit oriented and competitive than males. Such gender differences in values persist over time and remain significant holding constant measures of religiosity and social support.

We believe that Gilligan's insightful analysis of gender differences in moral development may be very useful in studies of crime and delinquency. Gilligan's work should not be interpreted to imply that we cannot conduct research on males and females using common measures of values and indicators of behavior. Indeed, with respect to crime and delinquency, Gilligan observes that women in the first stage of moral development are quite comparable to males typified by adherence to preconventional morality. Both males and females in this stage of moral development may be characterized as selfish and instrumental, ignoring the rules of society and pursuing goals that primarily benefit themselves. It is precisely this category of people that the criminologist will be most interested in analyzing, for these people are the most likely to break the law.

Prior Research on Gender-Based Subcultures

Tanner (1988) examined the level of involvement in street culture and popular media culture in Edmonton junior and senior high schools. He found that gender, rather than social class, was a strong predictor of participation in the youth culture. Males were far more likely than females to be participants in both delinquent and popular youth cultures, regardless of social class.

Ball-Rokeach (1973) attempted to distinguish the value systems of male and female respondents with respect to a subculture of violence thesis. Although she reports a number of significant differences in the values of males and females (males place greater emphasis on excitement, family security, and pleasure than do females, while females place greater emphasis on being ambitious, imaginative, and self-controlled than do males), much of the evidence is interpreted as inconsistent with subcultural theory. For example, Ball-Rokeach states that only four of nineteen value differences by gender (including emphasis on an exciting life and being imaginative) correspond to those value differences that affect participation in interpersonal violence among males. Further, she observes that the values that distinguish participation in interpersonal violence among females (including emphasis on equality and freedom) tend to be quite distinct from the values which distinguish participation in interpersonal violence among males. However, these findings do suggest that there is some evidence consistent with a subcultural explanation of gender differences in criminal behavior.

An Exploratory Empirical Analysis

As a guide to further research on a subcultural explanation for the relationship between gender and crime and delinquency, we present a preliminary analysis of data to illustrate a test of subcultural theory. The data are taken from the Seattle Youth Study, which included interview and questionnaire responses from over one thousand subjects (Hindelang, Hirschi, and Weis, 1981). Our analysis is not intended to be read as an exhaustive study of subcultures, gender, and delinquency. Instead we encourage other researchers to develop and test the subcultural theory (using a similar general approach or logic) to determine how the theory might account for gender, age, and other group differences in rates of crime and delinquency.

In Table 5.1 we present a small correlation matrix of the variables of central concern to a test of subcultural theory. Besides gender and delinquency (as measured by a standard self-report index of theft, vandalism and fighting), we include measures of adherence to legal values and maternal supervision. You will recall that there is nearly universal agreement among theorists as diverse as Sutherland and Cressey, Turk, and Hirschi that parental supervision is a significant barrier to delinquent

Table 5.1 Zero Order Correlation Coefficients[a] Among Gender, Delinquency, Subcultural Values, and Maternal Supervision (Seattle Youth Study)

	Delinquency	Gender	Subcultural Values
Gender	−.27		
Subcultural Values	.27	−.10	
Maternal Supervision	−.18	.11	−.11

[a]All of the above coefficients are significant at the .05 level.

Source: Data from Michael Hindelang, Travis Hirschi, and Joseph Weis, 1981, *Measuring Delinquency* (Beverly Hills, CA: Sage).

behavior. Patterson and Dishion (1985) argue that parental monitoring or supervision is a key factor in accounting for delinquency. Hagan, Gillis, and Simpson, (1985) report that maternal supervision in particular is significantly correlated with self-reported delinquent behavior.

We constructed an index of maternal supervision based on the following items from the Seattle Youth Study: "When you're away from home, does your mother know where you are and who you're with?"; and "As far as my mother is concerned, I'm pretty much free to come and go as I please." Our measure of subcultural values is based on an index that describes the respondent's level of agreement with an instrumental ethic. Respondents were asked to agree or disagree with the following statements: "It's all right to get around the law if you can get away with it"; "Suckers deserve what they get"; and "To get ahead, you have to do some things that are not right." Control theorists such as Hirschi (1969) have used these and similarly worded items to measure the concept of belief or faith in conventional institutions.

In the next chapter, we will consider in much greater detail "latent structure analysis," a statistical method that may be used to create indices or measures such as delinquency, maternal supervision, and subcultural values. Brownfield and Sorenson (1987) found that the delinquency index including measures of theft, vandalism, and assault seems to be a valid measure for males in this sample. A separate latent structure analysis of the measures of theft, vandalism, and assault for females in the Seattle sample also suggests that the delinquency index is valid.

We next applied latent structure analysis to create indices of maternal supervision and subcultural values. The results suggest that both of these indices are valid measures for this sample. In Chapter 6, we will devote more attention to the specific procedures and the potential utility of latent structure analysis to help address a wide range of substantive issues.

The correlations in Table 5.1 follow a predictable pattern. These zero order correlations reveal that females are less likely to be delinquent than males ($r = -.27$), adolescents who are well supervised are less likely to be delinquent than poorly-supervised adolescents ($r = -.18$), and respondents who disagree with the instrumental ethic are less likely to be delinquent than those who agree with this ethic ($r = .27$). The correlation matrix also shows, as predicted, that females are better supervised than males by mothers ($r = .11$), and females are somewhat less likely to express an instrumental attitude toward the law than are males ($r = -.10$).

These simple correlations yield only part of the information needed to provide evidence consistent with a subcultural theory explanation for gender differences in delinquency. At a minimum, it must be shown that subcultural values account for the relationship between delinquency and gender (such that this correlation is reduced to nonsignificance). Further, we must show that controls for alternative, structural

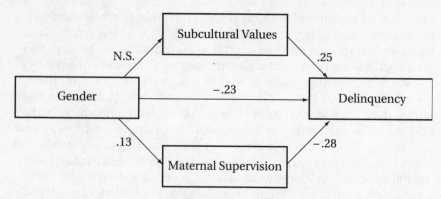

Figure 5.1 Parameter Estimates Based on Multivariate Model of Gender, Delinquency, Subcultural Values, and Maternal Supervision. Seattle Youth Study.

Source: Data from Michael Hindelang, Travis Hirschi, and Joseph Weis, 1981, *Measuring Delinquency* (Beverly Hills, CA: Sage).

factors, such as maternal supervision, do not eliminate the effects of subcultural variables.

In Figure 5.1 we present a diagram with parameter estimates based on a multivariate model of our measures of gender, delinquency, subcultural values, and maternal supervision. Again, this model is a simplification; we would include numerous other structural variables such as grade point average, peer influence, and additional measures of attachment, perceived risk, and subcultural values to make a more complete analysis of the effects of cultural and structural variables.

Based on the parameter estimates in Figure 5.1, we conclude that there is, at best, only partial support for a subcultural explanation of gender differences in delinquent behavior. Our measure of subcultural values remains significantly related to delinquency controlling for the effects of maternal supervision; in fact, this variable has a slightly stronger effect on delinquency than gender. However, maternal supervision also remains significantly related to delinquency, and to gender as well; note that the correlation between subcultural values and gender is reduced to nonsignificance after controlling for maternal supervision. Further, we find that gender continues to have a significant direct effect on delinquency controlling for both maternal supervision and subcultural values.

Conclusion

We would not conclude from our preliminary analysis that subcultural theory fails to explain the association between gender and delinquency.

A much more detailed analysis of a wider range of factors is still needed. We would also stress that gender is one of the most persistent correlates of delinquency, remaining a significant factor in several studies that have included an impressive array of variables (see Jensen and Eve, 1976; Steffensmeier, 1980; Hagan, Gillis, and Simpson, 1985).

We also return to the argument that both structural and cultural factors may cause crime and delinquency. In an eloquent examination of punishment, Garland (1990) emphasizes the interrelatedness of culture and structure. He describes penal institutions as cultural artifacts or as embodiments of cultural values, sensibilities, and meaning. A variety of cultural influences affect institutions of punishment, including changing conceptions of justice, feminist ideology, theology, and scientific developments in medicine, criminology, and psychology. Garland also depicts institutions of punishment as independent forces that affect culture, in particular by conveying meaning and value—not merely about what is condemned as criminal by society—but also about power, legitimacy, and morality.

Curtis (1975) and Bernard (1990) have suggested that structural and cultural explanations may be combined to account for criminal behavior. Structural conditions such as poverty or inequality may generate more occasions upon which an individual must demonstrate his masculinity or bravery. Luckenbill (1984:35) suggests that the number of "character contests" is increased under conditions of poverty or inequality. However, Luckenbill also states that subcultures of crime and violence need not be restricted to racial minorities and the lower class. Male and adolescent subcultures with an emphasis on risk taking and physical ability may foster crime and violence across race and class lines.

6

The Drugs and Crime Connection and Offense Specialization:

A Latent Variable Approach

David Brownfield

One of the most consistent findings in criminology has been that a wide range of deviant or criminal behaviors are positively correlated with one another (Akers, 1984; Donovan and Jessor, 1985; Brownfield and Sorenson, 1987; Osgood et al., 1988; Dembo et al., 1992; Harrison and Gfoerer, 1992; Nurco, Kinlock, and Balter, 1993; Hirschi and Gottfredson, 1994). Osgood et al. identify two reasons or possible explanations for these findings. First, we may hypothesize that involvement in one form of criminal or deviant activity causes or leads to involvement in another form of crime or deviance. The economist's theory of drug use and property crime is an example of this hypothesis, wherein the financial needs created by drug use and addiction cause the individual to commit property crimes to support the drug habit. A second hypothesis might state that different forms of crime and deviance are correlated because they have the same underlying causes. Gottfredson and Hirschi (1990) argue that all forms of crime are manifestations of a lack of self-control.

Osgood et al. (1988:81–82) observe that issues of generality and specificity are topics of interest to sociologists studying a variety of issues. For example, to what extent are income, education, and occupation indicators of a single, more general concept of social status? Duncan's socioeconomic scale is based on the premise that income, occupation, and education are indicators of a single underlying variable of status. Socioeconomic status is not observed directly by people, but it can be measured indirectly by creating unobserved or "latent" variables based on income, occupation, and education. Similarly, "social disorganization" is not observed directly but might be inferred from manifest or observed variables. Social disorganization may be conceived of as a latent variable and described by neighborhoods with high levels of unemployment, migration, and transition from residential to industrial zoning.

Most criminological theories (Osgood et al., 1988) predict that deviance will be a general phenomenon that does not require specific explanations for specific forms of criminal or deviant behavior. Control theorists predict that individuals will steal, commit acts of assault and vandalism, use drugs, and cheat on their income taxes if they lack

125

attachment to others and a stake in conformity. Cultural deviance theorists predict that members of subcultures will commit a similar variety of deviant behaviors if they are provided the normative support for such action. Strain theorists predict that crime will occur in a variety of forms for those who are denied the legitimate means to succeed.

Hirschi (1984) argues that the pattern of correlations among drug use and crime refutes Cloward and Ohlin's (1960) version of strain theory. Cloward and Ohlin in effect predicted the absence of a relationship between drug use and crime by arguing that access to illegitimate means is differentially distributed. Those who could neither succeed by conventional occupation nor even by profitable criminal behavior are labelled retreatists or "double failures." The retreatists are characterized by their use of drugs and alcohol. However, the positive correlation between drug use and crime refutes the conceptualization of differential access to illegitimate means of success. The form of criminal activity may depend only on the opportunities available for either relatively profitable involvement in illegal gambling, for example, or less profitable violent crime and drug use.

Causal homogeneity is thus predicted by most criminological theories. The causes or correlates of assault are generally the same as the causes or correlates of property crime or drug use. Empirical research has confirmed that certain factors are nearly universal correlates of all forms of crime. Peer influence, age, gender, educational achievement, and parental supervision are among the variables that are consistently found to be correlated with diverse forms of criminal behavior.

Donovan and Jessor (1985) argue that "problem behaviors" may be conceived of as a single syndrome measured by a latent variable of unconventionality. Hirschi and Gottfredson (1986) use the concept of "criminality," or the propensity to seek short term and immediate pleasures, to describe the general tendency to commit a wide range of crimes. If there is a general tendency to engage in crime or deviance, then there should be little specialization in criminal behavior. There should be no discernible pattern in the type of criminal behavior that is committed.

In this chapter we will describe two related controversies in criminology, the relationship between drug use and crime and the issue of specialization among offenders. Both of these issues continue to receive considerable attention in the research literature (see, e.g., Tonry and Wilson, 1990) and both have public policy implications. The assumed economic connection linking drug use and crime is used as a primary justification for the considerable effort expended in controlling drug trafficking. A reduction in drug use or consumption is often predicted to lead to a substantial decline in rates of property crime and robbery. Drug treatment programs typically focus on the individual's drug habit or addiction and may ignore other relevant tendencies or behavioral patterns.

Much of public policy dealing with efforts to control crime is based on implicit assumptions about specialization among offenders and patterns of progression. Career criminals supposedly show a patterned involvement of specialization and progressively more serious involvement in crime. Efforts to identify and then control career offenders presume that there are indeed specialists in certain types of crime or a clear pattern of progressively more serious involvement in crime. Research on career criminals has been supported by major funding initiatives in the past decade.

Police departments have for years adopted an implicit assumption about specialization among offenders, with specialized bureaus or units dealing separately with homicide cases, sexual assault, vice crimes, and robbery (cf. Gottfredson and Hirschi, 1990). This form of organization is based to a degree on the implicit assumption that offenders specialize in particular types of crime.

In this chapter, we will apply latent variable analysis as a technique to address the controversies of the drug-crime relationship and the issue of specialization. Latent variable analysis may allow us to take a somewhat different perspective on these controversies, and it may further help us to resolve some of the questions surrounding the debates. Latent variable analysis can help us to test whether a single general scale may be created to describe involvement in a variety of forms of illegal behavior.

We will therefore focus on the question of how general involvement in deviance may be. We will also examine to what extent there may be progressive involvement in either crime or drug use. Such analysis may help us to more systematically understand the causes and correlates of crime and to avoid a fragmented or piecemeal approach.

The Relationship Between Drug Use and Crime

Three kinds of information are required to infer a causal relationship in social science research (Hirschi and Selvin, 1967). First, the statistical association between the two variables or between cause and effect must be demonstrated. There is considerable evidence demonstrating the statistical association between drug use and crime. However, as a second requirement, we must demonstrate correct causal ordering among the variables. Does drug use precede criminal behavior, or does criminal behavior precede drug use? Third, we must demonstrate that other variables do not account for the association between drug use and crime. In traditional statistical analyses, we might attempt to eliminate the association between drug use and crime by holding constant such factors as age, family structure, gender, and race. In latent variable analyses, a "third" variable or unobserved construct is estimated to determine if the original association among the observed measures can be accounted for by the latent variable (McCutcheon, 1987).

The National Institute on Drug Abuse (NIDA) (1978) lists three conflicting hypotheses about the relationship between drug use and crime and presents some empirical support for each of the three hypotheses. The most popular hypothesis proposes that drug use leads to crime. This is the hypothesis most consistent with an economics model of drug use and crime. A second hypothesis contends that involvement in criminal behavior leads to drug use. A third hypothesis proposes that both drug use and crime are caused by some other set of factors or are manifestations of the same underlying latent variable (Hirschi, 1984).

We will assess the existing evidence on the drugs-crime relationship by reviewing some of the key studies on this issue. We begin with a summary of an influential report issued by the National Institute on Drug Abuse (1978).

The NIDA Report

Much of the research on drug use and crime tends to focus either on narcotics addicts or less serious drugs such as marijuana (NIDA, 1978). Little of this research has focused on other drugs such as cocaine, PCP, amphetamines, and barbiturates.

The literature on narcotics addiction and criminal behavior is relatively substantial. Use of addictive narcotics is strongly associated with criminal behavior. Heroin use in particular has been linked to income-generating or acquisitive crimes such as shoplifting and other forms of property crime. Narcotics use seems to be somewhat less correlated with violent crimes than is the use of alcohol or amphetamines and barbiturates. One study found that amphetamine use is correlated with a somewhat greater tendency to commit violent crimes than are users of other drugs in a sample of arrested individuals (NIDA, 1978). However, the NIDA concludes that amphetamine use does not seem to be a cause of violent crime in particular nor of any other form of crime. The evidence suggests that amphetamine users tend to have a record of arrests prior to their first use of amphetamines.

Fagan (1990) argues that the evidence on drug use and violence suggests that any causal relationship is at best contingent and variable. Cultural definitions or expectations as well as personality (or "set") factors and structural determinants (or "setting") may affect the relationship between drug use and violent behavior. For example, ethnographies summarized by Fagan (1990:270) show that drinking is not necessarily related to violence in some societies. Type of substance used may also affect the relationship between drug use and violence; for example, marijuana use seems to have little causal effect on violent behavior. Self-report data (based on interviews with drug users) and police statistics show that heroin users, in contrast to other drug users, are much more likely to be involved in robbery, breaking and entering, and shoplifting.

The NIDA examined how patterns of criminal behavior change as there are changes in patterns of drug use. Much of the early research focused only on an assumed simple sequence of initial drug use, initial crime or delinquency, and then increased criminal behavior following greater use of drugs. The assumption that drug use would only increase or that people would become addicted was an oversimplification. Some research has documented that drug use and even addiction are to some extent reversible and variable (Ball et al., 1981).

Given that drug use may be variable or episodic, it may be important to assess levels of criminal behavior before, during, and after episodes of drug use. We may examine to what extent the rates of property crime are sensitive to changes in the cost of narcotics use and changes in amounts of drugs used. Some studies suggest considerable price elasticity of demand for heroin, far greater than predicted by a simplistic economics model of the relationship between drug use and crime. For example, the NIDA concludes that there is considerable substitution of methadone for heroin when prices of heroin increase. Methadone has even been described as a preferred drug (when combined with alcohol, tranquilizers, or cocaine) over heroin in that it is perceived as providing "pleasurable highs" and helps to avoid the high cost, high risk activities associated with heroin (Smith and Watkins, 1976; Agar and Stephens, 1975).

The NIDA found that, as expected, rates of arrest for criminal behavior were substantially higher during episodes of narcotics use than during periods of abstention from narcotics. For policy purposes, we should take note of the increased level of crime associated with drug use. For purposes of etiological analysis, however, it is probably false to presume that drug use causes crime, particularly given some findings that show involvement in crime tends to precede drug use. Similarly, we may restrict sales of aerosol paint cans to reduce vandalism as a policy choice, but no one would seriously argue that the presence of spray paint causes vandalism (Gottfredson and Hirschi, 1987). The rate of criminal behavior during periods of narcotics use may be as much as five times the rate during periods of non-use of narcotics. Declines in use of narcotics were in many cases attributed to imprisonment of the addicts. While narcotics use may still continue in prison, the rate of use declines appreciably and the opportunity to commit further crimes also declines substantially (though many offenses may still be committed in prison). The NIDA reports that differences in level of criminal behavior during periods of narcotics use and periods of non-use may actually disappear when controlling for time spent in jail and prison. However, a recent study on opportunity or availability of drugs is not consistent with this finding. Bachman, Johnston, and O'Malley, (1990) argue that reported availability of marijuana and cocaine are not related to drug use patterns. Instead, they find that social disapproval and perceived risk of physical or other harms have reduced levels of drug use recently.

We turn now to a review of an important study by Anglin and Speckart (1988) on the drugs-crime relationship. Anglin and Speckart provide additional information and analysis on the relationship between narcotics use and criminal behavior.

Narcotics Addiction and Crime: The Anglin and Speckart Study

Anglin and Speckart (1988) argue that the samples employed in the research on the connection between drug use and crime have serious limitations. For example, many of the studies are based solely on addicts identified by criminal records. This may disproportionately represent only those with the greatest involvement in narcotics use or in criminal behavior, and such samples may ignore the vast majority of narcotics users.

Prior research has been criticized for a number of other methodological shortcomings (Anglin and Speckart, 1988). For example, rates of interview completion have been relatively low, as might be expected given the nature of studies of narcotics addicts. Many self-report or interview studies have focused almost exclusively on white adolescents. Very few studies have focused on minority groups such as Mexican-Americans, and comparatively little is known about such minority communities.

In their own study, Anglin and Speckart (1988:206–207) report that the majority of both Anglo and Mexican-American subjects (in an analysis of methadone maintenance patients) had been arrested *before* their first use of narcotics. Approximately one-fifth of their sample had been arrested for the first time at a point between first use of narcotics and addiction to narcotics (defined as daily use of narcotics). Only about 10 percent of the sample was arrested for the first time after addiction to narcotics was recorded.

Both Anglo and Mexican-American subjects in this study self-reported a higher prevalence rate of initial involvement in theft *before* the onset of addiction. In contrast, robbery and forgery arrests were more likely to occur after the onset of addiction. Anglin and Speckart (1988:226) conclude that drug use is not a "cause" of property crime in the sense that drug use *initiates* property crime, but drug use may be viewed as a "*multiplier* of existing criminologic predisposition."

Anglin and Speckart's findings are also consistent with prior research (Simpson and Sells, 1982; Nash, 1976) that documents a reduced level of criminal behavior while patients undergo methadone maintenance treatment. Unfortunately, following treatment there is also some increase in the discharged patient's involvement in criminal behavior. However, the effects of methadone maintenance in terms of reduced crime rates while patients are still in treatment are substantial. In fact, the effects of treatment through methadone maintenance are far stronger than the effects of legal supervision such as probation.

Prior to considering the common correlates of drug use and crime, we next briefly discuss the issue of "progression" in drug use. We will examine to what extent there is a clear developmental sequence of involvement in drugs from less serious substances such as marijuana to addictive substances such as narcotics.

Patterns of Progression in Drug Use

Several researchers (Akers, 1985; Clayton and Voss, 1981; Yamaguchi and Kandel, 1984; Marcos, Bahr, and Johnson, 1986) have suggested that there are ordered patterns of drug use ranging from commonly used substances such as alcohol and marijuana to more serious drugs such as cocaine and heroin. Marcos, Bahr, and Johnson, (1986), for example, describe drug use in terms of four ordered categories that imply a progression pattern. Separate categories are maintained for both alcohol and tobacco use. Marijuana use is described in yet a separate category that seems to be a precursor for the use of more serious substances. Amphetamine and depressant use characterizes the fourth and final category of the ordered typology described by Marcos, Bahr, and Johnson.

Despite the clear ordering of different types of drug use, this research does not support theories that such progression is inevitable. For example, there is little evidence to suggest that marijuana use is a necessary or sufficient factor leading to more serious forms of drug use such as narcotics.

Sorenson and Brownfield (1989) find that diverse measures of drug use (such as alcohol, marijuana, and cocaine) can be treated as a single scale or latent variable. They fit a three category latent variable model to a set of five measures of drug use (including alcohol, marijuana, amphetamines, and cocaine use). The three categories of drug use suggest ordered levels of involvement from relative conformity to moderate and extensive levels of drug use. Diversity of drug use, as well as seriousness of drug use, seemed to affect assignment of respondents to particular categories.

From patterns of progression in drug use, we now turn to an examination of common or shared correlates of drug use and crime. If drug use and crime are behavioral manifestations of the same underlying characteristic, we would expect considerable similarity in the correlates of both drug use and crime. In this next section, we draw primarily on Akers's (1984) review of the relationship between drug use and crime.

Common Correlates of Drug Use and Crime

A few studies have reported (Kandel, Kessler, and Marguiles, 1978; Johnston, 1973; Brook and Cohen, 1992) that the correlates of some forms of deviance or drug use are not identical. For example, parental influence may be more significant for deterring illicit drugs other than marijuana. However, most studies have found that the correlates of one form of deviance are very similar to the correlates of other forms of deviance. As mentioned before, peer influence, age, gender, educational achievement, and parental supervision are correlated with a variety of forms of deviance. Elliott, Huizinga, and Ageton, (1985; 1989) found that the variables that help to account for alcohol and drug use are very similar to the variables that help to account for delinquent behavior.

Akers (1984) points out that among adolescents drug use is by definition delinquent behavior. Even the use or purchase of alcohol by a teenager is a status offense in many jurisdictions. The use of other drugs such as narcotics or cocaine are also violations of the criminal law. Akers notes, however, that the legal similarity among these various actions denoted as "crime" or "delinquency" does not necessarily mean that these actions are behaviorally identical. It may therefore still be reasonable to study the interrelationships among different forms of law violations. Thus, an individual may commit an assault, shoplift from a store, and use illicit drugs. Although each of the actions is a crime, we may still pose questions about the relationships among these actions and determine whether any of these relationships is causal.

Longitudinal studies based on national samples (Johnston, O'Malley, and Eveland, 1978; Elliott and Huizinga, 1984) have consistently shown that shared correlates have the greatest effect on the relationship between crime and drug use, while the influence of one type of deviance on another is relatively minor. Osgood et al. (1988:88) report that marijuana use has a significant effect on other forms of illicit drug use, but this was the only instance of 20 such "cross-behavior" effects that was significant. Furthermore, they conclude (1988:91) that adding an effect of marijuana on other forms of illicit drug use yields only a marginal improvement in the fit of their model. Such cross-behavior effects are negligible relative to "the general finding that people who engage in one form of deviance are likely to engage in others as well" (Osgood et al., 1988:91).

The correlates of drug use and criminal behavior tend to be the same; correlates such as age, gender, education, family structure and relationships, and peer influence appear to be nearly identical for both drug use and crime (Akers, 1984). White, Pandina, and La Grange, (1987) also find general similarity of the correlates of drug use and delinquency (with the exception of "intrapsychic" factors such as self-esteem and impulsivity, which were correlated with drug use but not delinquency.)

Some interesting factors seem to condition or alter the correlation between drug use and crime. For example, there appear to be significant historical differences (Akers, 1985; NIDA, 1978) in the nature of drug addiction. There also appears to be some variation by gender in terms of the correlation between drug use and crime. Female addicts appear to have a wider variety of sources of income other than property crime by which to support a drug habit (Hser, Chou, and Anglin, 1990). In addition to property crime, female addicts often rely on prostitution to obtain money for drugs. Hunt (1990:193) reports that more than three-fourths of females who were found to be regular drug users also had been recently involved in prostitution. However, among female drug users involvement in prostitution is typically sporadic and may vary somewhat contingent on opportunities to make money by selling drugs. Both male and female addicts rely substantially on drug selling as a source of income for their habits, which removes much of the pressure to commit property crimes. Drug use may also, however, reduce legitimate job performance and stability, which may lead to an increased need to rely on property crime (see Kandel and Yamaguchi, 1987).

In the nineteenth and early twentieth centuries, drug addicts were typically white, from the South, and had become addicted to narcotics often through medical prescription of morphine. Many of the drug addicts were white middle-class females whose physicians had prescribed narcotics for their patients. Very few of these drug addicts had a record of criminal behavior in this early period.

Since the 1950s, however, the description of the typical narcotics addict has changed dramatically to become poor blacks living in urban areas. This new generation of narcotics addicts has been found to have extensive involvement in criminal behavior, both before and during periods of drug use.

National surveys (Johnston, O'Malley, and Eveland, 1978; Huizinga and Elliott, 1981; Elliot, Huizinga, and Menard, 1989) have examined the relationship between drug use and crime in longitudinal samples, with data collected during at least two different points in time. This research should help us to address the question of causal ordering between drug use and crime. However, these studies have not documented a clear causal ordering. For example, Johnston, O'Malley, and Eveland, report a weak correlation between drug use measured at time one and delinquent behavior measured at a later time. A similarly weak correlation was reported between delinquency measured at time one and drug use measured later. Elliott and his associates (Huizinga and Elliott, 1981) also have not found a consistent ordering between drug use and delinquency. The most frequent pattern they report was desistance from drug use or delinquency given involvement in either type of behavior earlier.

Nurco, Kinlock, and Balter (1993) conclude that patterns of involvement in both addiction and crime probably develop in a roughly parallel manner, rather than one type of deviance causing the other type of deviant behavior. In a study of young urban narcotics addicts, Nurco, Kinlock, and Balter find that crime severity is inversely related to the age of onset of addiction. Thus, younger addicts are also engaging in serious crimes at a relatively young age.

Hirschi (1984) concludes that research on the relationship between drug use and delinquency has satisfied only one of the three criteria necessary to demonstrate a causal relationship. Cross-sectional research has clearly demonstrated that drug use and delinquency are strongly correlated. However, in terms of a second criterion of causal ordering, the evidence is ambiguous as to whether drug use precedes crime or criminal behavior precedes drug use. Hirschi (1984:50) argues that there is no clear causal ordering because initial involvement in drug use or delinquency is a random process. It makes little sense to even ask whether the teenager first drank the bottle of beer or smoked a cigarette and then shoplifted. This implies that we should discontinue the causal analysis of the relationship between drug use and crime given no clear temporal ordering. However, because the two forms of behavior are correlated, this also implies that both drug use and crime may be caused by common factors.

We could then test the hypothesis that a set of third factors (such as age, gender, and peer influence) accounts for the relationship between drug use and crime. Statistical controls for this set of third factors could be entered in a multivariate analysis, but Hirschi predicts that drug use and delinquency would remain significantly associated controlling for the effects of social correlates such as age, gender, and family relationships. Hirschi argues that this is because drug use and delinquency are manifestations of the same thing, "criminality" (Hirschi and Gottfredson, 1986). Criminality refers to the tendency of the individual to seek short-term, immediate gratification and to disregard or have little concern for long term consequences of such behavior.

The use of drugs may easily be seen as a pursuit of immediate pleasure (or avoidance of pain). Taking things satisfies a desire for possessions without the demands of work, and assaulting others is the fastest form of revenge or self-help (Gottfredson and Hirschi, 1990; cf Black, 1983).

In the following discussion we will consider the related controversy over specialization among criminals. Researchers who test for a causal relationship between drug use and crime seem to implicitly assume that there may be offense specialization or that there are discrete categories of involvement in different types of crime and deviance.

Specialization or Diversity in Criminal Behavior

It is important to distinguish specialization and progression in offending. For example, there may be patterns of progression without a pattern of specialization, as the evidence on drug use seems to suggest. There might be progression patterns in criminal behavior that vary by age groups, but no research to our knowledge has established this. Loeber and LeBlanc (1990), utilizing a developmental psychology perspective, address the issue of specialization patterns that may increase with age. They argue that we should consider patterns of stability, progression, and regression in offending. There may be both escalation and deescalation in seriousness of crimes committed. Specialization should be considered a distinct issue from progression also because an offender may either escalate or deescalate while simultaneously specializing in certain crimes (LeBlanc, Cote, and Loeber, 1991).

Klein (1984) reviews several studies that have examined specialization among offenders and patterns of progression from less serious to more serious crimes. He first notes that there seems to be a consensus among criminologists that there is no clear pattern to most delinquent behavior. Yet, inconsistent with and ignoring this consensus, much of public policy is based on the assumption that there is specialization and clear patterns of progression. For example, as noted earlier, police departments have special units dealing with homicide or with sexual assault.

Enforcement of drug laws has been compartmentalized at the federal government level with specific agencies such as the Drug Enforcement Administration (DEA). Specific welfare programs or agencies have been established to deal with minor or status offenses such as truancy and running away. Alcohol treatment programs, for example, have been established that focus on a single form of drug use. All of these programs are based on assumptions that there is specialization in the types of offenses committed and that there is a clear pattern of progression. Special or separate treatment of status offenders, as in deinstitutionalization programs, presume that status offenders exist as a distinct type who may progress to more serious forms of criminal involvement.

Klein (1984) offers a number of reasons to account for the public policy presumptions that there is specialization and patterned progression among offenders. For example, common discourse has reified the conception of specialization by describing offenders as "addicts" or "rapists" or "thieves." A related reason for these presumptions has been the popularity of typologies in academic criminology, notably those advanced by Gibbons (1965). Klein also points to the influence of behaviorist theory in criminology, which tends to depict behavior as discrete or modular. Theory on delinquent gangs has also reinforced the presumption of specialization among offenders. Cloward and Ohlin (1960) describe specialized involvement in profitable organized crime in some contexts, violent gangs in disorganized neighborhoods, and drug use confined to retreatist gangs.

Klein notes that the presumptions about specialization among gangs persist despite research (e.g., Short and Strodtbeck, 1965) that finds little support for specialization among gang members. Klein describes this versatility as a "cafeteria-style" pattern of delinquency, in which a gang member may choose to steal on one occasion, engage in violent behavior on another, be truant, commit vandalism, and choose various other forms of deviant behavior.

In one of the earliest studies on offense specialization, Wolfgang, Figlio, and Sellin, (1972) report an analysis of involvement in nonindex offenses, injury, theft, vandalism, and a combined offense category. They found no evidence of specialization nor any pattern of progression from minor offense to more serious crimes.

Rojek and Erickson (1982) conclude that the subjects in their study showed considerable versatility in the types of offenses for which they were arrested. The single most likely offense to occur, not unexpectedly, appears to be property crime. Bursik (1980) reports that there is a somewhat greater than expected tendency for some specialization, particularly among property offenders. Bursik found a greater than chance level of repetition among those arrested for property crimes. This may be due to the sheer high volume of this type of offense. Nevertheless, Rojek and Erickson point out that the probability of this being the next offense committed in a "deviant career" is not exceptionally high.

Rojek and Erickson (1982) report that there is no evidence consistent with a progression pattern from less serious to more serious offenses. Overall there seems to be very little propensity for offenders to persist in committing a particular type of offense. Kempf (1987) cites more than a dozen studies that have examined the topic of specialization among offenders. All of these studies have concluded that versatility in offending is a more common pattern than specialization in a particular form of offense. However, Kempf notes that most studies have also found exceptions to the versatility pattern found in this body of research. For example, some specialization may be observed among particular crime categories, at certain stages in the deviant career, or among certain demographic groups (looking at, for example, differences by race and gender). Brennan, Mednick, and John, (1989) argue that the way in which specialization has been defined may account for any inconsistencies in the findings. They develop three definitions of specialization (probabilistic, sequential, and distributional) to attempt to refine previous research. Brennan, Mednick, and John (1989) report some evidence consistent with all three types of specialization. However, regardless of offense type or number of arrests, the patterns of specialization do not appear to be especially pronounced.

Klein (1984) reviews more than 30 additional studies that address the issue of specialization among offenders. These studies utilize a variety of statistical methods and types of data, including police and court records as well as self-report studies. Klein concludes that 21 of the 33 studies surveyed find strong support for the versatility hypothesis. Only four of the studies surveyed find support for the specialization hypothesis; the remaining eight studies yield mixed conclusions regarding the specialization issue.

Among the implications of the lack of specialization, Klein notes that use of a global variable of delinquency in criminological research seems well justified. Further, treatment based not on the instant offense but rather on the needs of the child in general is also supported. The purely legalistic response to grade punishment to the offense committed may be undermined somewhat by findings of a syndrome of behavior suggested by the versatility hypothesis.

To this point, we have confined our review of the evidence largely to juvenile delinquency, to common law crimes such as theft and assault, and to drug use. We next consider white collar crime as a separate category of criminal behavior. We briefly summarize Hirschi and Gottfredson's (1987; 1989) arguments that white collar crime is not a distinct or unique category of crime.

White Collar Crime as a Distinctive Category

Hirschi and Gottfredson (1987; 1989) argue that the concept of white collar crime as a distinctive category of criminal behavior has little scientific value. They assert that white collar crimes are like any other form of criminal activity in that they represent the pursuit of immediate gratification through relatively unsophisticated means. They conclude that most white collar crimes tend to be petty offenses and that white collar criminals will tend to commit other types of offenses as well. Thus, the social distribution of white collar crime will in fact be similar to the social distribution of other forms of crime such as assault and burglary.

Hirschi and Gottfredson (1987) test the hypothesis that the demographic correlates of white collar crime are the same as the correlates for other types of crimes, controlling for opportunity to commit white collar crimes (by calculating rates of crime per 100,000 white collar workers). Using arrest rates for fraud and embezzlement from the Uniform Crime Reports, they examine patterns of white collar crime by age, race, and sex in comparison with patterns of murder by age. Plots of the arrest rates of fraud (per 10,000) and embezzlement (per 1,000,000) by age reveal the same pattern found for nearly every other type of crime: rates peak in late adolescence and early adulthood and decline significantly throughout the age distribution. Rates of embezzlement and fraud are also found to be significantly higher for males than for females, and for blacks relative to whites. The gender and race differences for white collar crime are also consistent with differences for other offenses as recorded in the Uniform Crime Reports. Controlling for age, gender differences in rates of embezzlement remain significant. Controlling for opportunity (by standardizing embezzlement rates to the number of white collar workers in the labor force), the demographic correlates of white collar crime (gender, age, race) remain the same as the demographic correlates of other forms of crime.

The utility of "organized crime" as a distinct category may also be questioned (cf. Reuter, 1983). Contrary to a romanticized or inflated image, individuals associated with organized crime may often be involved in petty thefts, drug use, and acts of senseless violence. This pattern of petty and absurd illicit behavior is illustrated in the film *Goodfellas.*

Benson and Moore (1992) report some additional evidence consistent with Hirschi and Gottfredson's arguments. However, they also find that white collar offenders tend to commit somewhat fewer crimes and are somewhat more likely to specialize in white collar crimes than are so-called "common offenders." White collar offenders with a high rate of recidivism are very similar to common offenders in terms of deviant activities such as problem drinking. However, white collar offenders with less extensive prior records (and who constituted over 80 percent of the white collar offenders in the sample) are less likely to be involved in deviant activities such as drug use and problem drinking than the common offenders (Benson and Moore, 1992).

The conception of white collar crime as a trivial offense is clearly contrary to conventional wisdom on this subject. Croall (1989:158) states that, contrary to popular imagery, white collar crimes typically involve "lists of seemingly trivial and routine cases involving dirty milk bottles and mouldy food." Powerful corporations are rarely prosecuted, but this may reflect discrimination by the criminal justice system.

Hirschi and Gottfredson also cite the impressions of Wheeler et al. (1988), who describe anti-trust cases as typically "banal, mundane," and "requiring little sophistication." This characterization is based on an assessment of hundreds of presentencing reports in white collar crime cases in federal courts. If this is true of one of the supposedly most significant white collar crimes, anti-trust, then the characterization of other "lesser" forms of white collar crime as trivial or petty may also be reasonably accurate.

We have reviewed several studies on the interrelated issues of the drugs-crime relationship and specialization among offenders. Much of the research on the relationship between drug use and crime suggests that conceptualizing this relationship as causal may be misguided. While many assume that drug use causes involvement in criminal behavior, the evidence yields no clear causal or temporal ordering between drug use and crime. Similarly, much of public policy seems to be based on the assumption that offenders specialize in certain types of crime. Again, the evidence suggests that, contrary to this assumption, there is considerable diversity and variety in criminal activity.

Both the research on the drugs-crime relationship and on specialization point to the strong possibility that diverse manifestations of crime may be conceived as a single latent construct of deviant behavior. In the next part of this chapter, we explore this possibility through the use of a statistical technique called latent structure analysis.

Latent Structure Analysis of Drug Use and Delinquency

McCutcheon (1987) points out that many of the concepts in the social sciences may be thought of as latent variables. Anomie, egoism, self-control, differential association, and secondary deviance are concepts within criminology that are not observed directly. We do not directly observe Sutherland's concept of differential association. Instead, we must infer the characteristic of differential association by examining indirect measures of this concept. One strategy has been to analyze a series of items that indicate the subject's attitudes toward the law or toward the police, and attitudes that may characterize an instrumental ethic or a manipulative personality. Latent variable analyses have found that such measures may be considered a single factor interpreted as a measure of differential association (Matsueda, 1982).

The lack of self-control (Gottfredson and Hirschi, 1990) may be inferred by a pattern of responses to items assessing willingness to defer gratification, attachment to others, and cognitive ability. Attachment to others itself may be a latent variable, indicated by observed measures such as identification with others or intimacy of communication. In each case, the latent variable (whether it is self-control, attachment, or differential association) is hypothesized to be the cause of the observed measures. There should be a clear pattern of intercorrelation among the observed variables that we attempt to account for by creating a latent variable. The latent variable, according to McCutcheon (1987), can be thought of as explaining the relationships among the observed variables.

Factor analysis is the statistical technique used to describe the latent variable approach for continuous level observed and latent measures, such as income or socioeconomic status. Categorical variables, nominal or ordinal, require the use of latent class analysis. Categorical variables include gender, ethnicity, religious affiliation, and attitudinal items that require responses such as strongly agree to strongly disagree. Clogg (1979) notes that the majority of variables in social science data sets are categorical measures. The latent class technique does not assume that the variables are continuous level measures nor that the measures approximate a multivariate normal distribution.

Lazarsfeld developed much of the conceptual basis for latent variable analysis (Clogg, 1981). The method of latent structure analysis may be considered a generalization of the "elaboration" principle in sociological research. Under the elaboration process, an attempt is made to account for the association between two or more variables by controlling for the effects of other variables or "test factors." For example, we may attempt to account for an association between gender and delinquent behavior by controlling for other variables such as parental supervision or school performance. If we found that the effects of gender on delinquent behavior were accounted for by parental supervision, we should find no association between gender and delinquency for each level of the control variable or test factor. If there were two levels of parental supervision, high and low, we should then find no association between gender and delinquency in subtables including only those well supervised and including only those poorly supervised.

When the control variables are observed or manifest variables, then the above situation describes the standard elaboration technique. If, however, the control variable (or variables) is unobserved or a latent variable, then this situation describes latent structure analysis. Latent structure analysis then attempts to create a latent variable that will account for the association among observed variables. A latent variable of "deviant behavior" may account for the association among measures of theft, violence, vandalism, and drug use.

"Local independence" is the term Lazarsfeld and Henry (1968) use to describe a situation wherein one variable accounts for all of the association among a set of other variables. Within levels of the control variable, there should be no significant association among the other variables if local independence exists. Local independence is one criterion by which to assess latent variables. The latent variable should eliminate all the association among the observed measures that constitute manifest indicators of the latent variable, if local independence exists.

Although latent structure analysis seemed to be a promising method with wide scope addressing a variety of topics, the computer techniques for estimating models were not available for several years (Clogg, 1981). Some early programs discussed by Lazarsfeld and Henry (1968) failed to provide consistent results (and even absurd results such as probabilities in excess of 1.0). Algorithms and programs developed in the 1970s (e.g., Clogg, 1977), however, have begun to make latent structure analysis widely available with consistent, efficiently estimated models.

The method of latent structure analysis is also applicable to longitudinal problems (Clogg, 1981). For example, Lazarsfeld's 16-fold table on voting intentions and opinion of candidates in a two-panel study or at two points in time may be described by a latent structure model. This model might specify latent variables of voting intention and opinion. (Compare Duncan (1984) who specifies a Rasch model alternative to latent class models and Mare and Winship (1991) who discuss simultaneous effects models for such tables involving longitudinal data.)

Previous Applications of Latent Variable Analysis

Studies conducted by Sorenson and Brownfield (1989) have employed latent structure analysis to examine patterns of involvement in delinquent behavior and drug use. This research has attempted to construct latent variable measures of delinquency and drug use and to test for patterns of progression among drug users (from common and less serious forms of drug use such as alcohol and marijuana to less common but more serious forms of drug use such as cocaine). Klein (1984) concludes that there is no evidence documenting a pattern of progression among non-drug offenses such as theft and assault.

Britt (1994) conducts a latent structure analysis of four observed measures of delinquency among males from the Seattle Youth Study. These four items measured theft of items worth $2 or less, theft of items worth between $2 and $50, assault of a teacher, and fighting. Britt concludes that a single latent variable may be constructed to describe the relationships among the four observed measures. This implies that involvement in delinquency, whether property or violent offenses, is general.

Brownfield and Sorenson (1987) discuss previous strategies to develop a measure of delinquency. For example, an offense-specific approach has characterized the conceptual work of Gibbons (1965) and the empirical work of Elliott and Ageton (1980). Elliott and Ageton (1980) use a set of subscales of delinquency which provide separate measures of, for example, property crime, status offenses, and hard drug use. The use of separate subscales seems to imply that there is no single underlying latent variable of delinquency but rather distinct measures of delinquent behavior.

Sellin and Wolfgang (1964) created an index of seriousness of offenses based on ratings of diverse samples of respondents. Seriousness of offense has been a criteria used in many definitions of delinquency (e.g., Nye, 1958; Shannon, 1978). Other researchers, such as Hindelang, Hirschi, and Weis, (1981), have combined measures of involvement in delinquency into a single, unweighted scale regardless of type of offense or seriousness of offense. An unweighted scale sums the number of offenses committed, giving equal consideration to each act regardless of its seriousness; armed robbery would be counted the same as petty theft by an unweighted scale. Such a strategy presumes that there is a single underlying variable or latent construct of delinquency.

Brownfield and Sorenson (1987) point out that these diverse strategies all use manifest or observed measures of behavior to describe the latent variable of delinquency. Most theorists and researchers further conceive of the latent variable as a composite or scaled measure of *behavior* rather than as a latent personality trait. Conceptions of crime as a manifestation of criminality (Hirschi and Gottfredson, 1986) or as an absence of self-control (Gottfredson and Hirschi, 1990) imply that delinquency may be a manifestation of a personality trait or characteristic.

One potential advantage of latent structure analysis is that it may help researchers to increase the magnitude of associations among variables. This is desirable in a field in which we typically account for only about one-fourth of the variance in measures of delinquent behavior. (Compare Lieberson [1985] and Freedman [1991] who criticize the pursuit of increased explained variance.) Latent structure analysis may also provide an important statistical method by which to measure independent variables such as scales of attachment to others or measures of peer influence.

We noted earlier that we would expect the observed measures or variables to be significantly associated with one another if we hope to construct a single, latent variable. A standard justification for including diverse indicators of delinquency in a single scale has been to inspect correlation matrices (Hirschi, 1969). Observed measures should be positively and strongly interrelated to justify their inclusion in a single scale. (Face validity or the content of the items indicating a similar phenomenon, such as violations of the criminal law, has been used as a justification for creating a single scale of delinquency.)

Formal modeling techniques have also been used in the construction of scales of delinquency. Two of the most prominent techniques have been Guttman scaling and factor analysis.

Guttman scaling was one of the first techniques used to create latent variables or indices. A distinctive unidimensional pattern is specified by the Guttman scaling procedure in which a positive response to one item (the item having the lowest rate of positive response) implied a positive response to all other items in the scale. For example, if questions were posed about violent behavior, such as separate items about simple assault, aggravated assault, and assault with a weapon, we might be able to construct a Guttman scale from these items. Such a scale, for example, would require that all subjects with a positive response to the measure of assault with a weapon also had positive responses to items on simple and aggravated assault. Likewise, a positive response to the item on aggravated assault would also imply a positive response to the item on simple assault (but not necessarily requiring a positive response to the item on assault with a weapon).

Unfortunately, this unidimensional approach to scaling in the Guttman procedure has not worked well in most cases in criminology. For example, it is recommended in using the Guttman scaling procedure that items with a low positive response rate (below 20 percent) be excluded from the analysis (Hindelang, Hirschi, and Weis, 1981). Unfortunately, this would effectively eliminate from consideration several of the serious offenses in most samples because the rates for serious offenses such as armed robbery are rarely more than 5 percent.

There are additional problematic aspects of the Guttman scaling technique. For example, there is no acceptable method within Guttman scaling to deal with the modeling of respondent uncertainty or sampling variability. In any data set there are likely to be departures from a specified model pattern that reflect chance variation. Traditional Guttman scaling has generally failed to deal with this type of variation. Some have recommended image analysis or data transformations that eliminate any departures from the specified model pattern. However, this artificially creates a scaled pattern in the data before the Guttman scale is tested on a set of items. Such data transformations make it more likely that a Guttman scale will fit the set of items under consideration, but this confuses the original issue as to whether the Guttman scale would have fit the items in the first place. Data transformations such as image analysis may substantially alter patterns inherent among the items so that it is guaranteed that a Guttman scale will fit the data.

Guttman scaling has generally been successfully applied to only a limited range of problems. For example, such a procedure has a better chance of success in analyses of relatively few items that measure very similar behaviors. The Guttman scale may adequately describe a small set of items describing theft of various amounts of money (for example, under $10, between $10 and $25, and from $25 to $50).

A second and more popular technique of formal modeling in the construction of delinquency scales has been factor analysis. The logic and methods of factor analysis have been subsumed under the more recently developed LISREL technique. The LISREL technique may combine, among other things, factor analysis and multivariate regression into a single model approach. In factor analysis, items that are interrelated may be identified as a single factor or scale; the single factor seeks to account for the intercorrelation among the observed items.

The factor analysis procedure is derived from a linear model approach similar to a regression technique, with the observed variables determined by the latent or unobserved factors. Factor analysis, unlike the Guttman scale procedure, also includes an error term to allow for the possibility of departures from the specified model. Observed variables that tend to load on a single common factor may be regarded as a latent variable. However, the decision rules for selecting factors are not very clear, and a variety of criteria are recommended in selecting a certain factor structure (Kim and Mueller, 1978:45). The results of factor analysis are considered ambiguous in many situations. The substantive meaning of the results are also often ambiguous with subjective interpretation of the factors identified.

Latent structure analysis offers a significant improvement over factor analysis in that the decision rules for choosing a particular latent variable are more clear-cut. Models under latent structure analysis must provide an adequate fit to the data under standard chi-square tests of significance. (The chi-square distribution is used to help select models in a variety of statistical techniques, including LISREL, as well as latent structure analysis.) However, both latent structure analysis and factor analysis may yield ambiguous substantive results unless the analysis is guided by prior theory or specific hypotheses about the relationships among a set of observed items.

Latent structure analysis offers another important advantage over factor analysis in criminological research. The statistical assumptions of factor analysis require that the observed measures be continuous interval level variables that are distributed in a multivariate normal fashion (cf. Muthen, 1989). Researchers often employ dichotomous measures of involvement in crime and delinquency (for example, "yes" or "no" responses) or ordered categories such as "never, once or twice, three or more times." Such items are preferred to incidence measures which assess the total number of offenses committed because such frequency measures have been found to be less reliable than prevalence measures (Sampson, 1985; Hindelang, Hirschi, and Weis, 1981). Further, the assumption of multivariate normal distribution of factor analysis is questionable in the case of measures of deviant behavior that are often skewed variables that more closely approximate a Poisson distribution (Greenberg, 1979). The Poisson distribution helps to describe many variables that do not approximate a normal distribution.

Factor analysis also treats the resulting latent variables or factors as continuous level variables. Latent structure analysis does not presume that the latent variable of interest is a continuous level variable (nor does it preclude this possibility); latent structure analysis implies that the latent variable is qualitative or categorical, although the categories may be ordered.

Latent structure analysis may be conceived as the qualitative analogue to factor analysis. Both techniques attempt to attribute the intercorrelations among observed items to their common association with an unobserved or latent variable. The latent structure analysis technique posits that the relationship among a set of categorical variables is accounted for completely by their relationship with a latent variable X that has T categories. If we examined the relationship among theft, vandalism, and assault, we would attempt to create a single latent variable X (interpreted as a general measure of delinquency) that accounted for the association among the observed measures of behavior.

Some researchers (Dembo et al., 1992; White, 1992) observe that prior latent variable studies have failed to account for much of the variance among various measures of deviance. (Also, compare Hirschi's (1984) statement that delinquency and drug use would remain intercorrelated controlling for demographic factors such as age, gender, and race.) The criterion of local independence in latent structure analysis requires that *all* of the association among the observed measures be accounted for by creating a single latent variable.

Analysis and Findings

We extend the latent class analysis of items measuring delinquency and drug use separately by considering whether manifest variables of both delinquency and drug use can be considered indicators of a single latent variable. This analysis represents an attempt to help resolve the debates over the relationship between drug use and crime and the issue of specialization among offenders. If we can demonstrate that a set of measures of delinquent involvement and drug use can be described by a single latent variable, then questions regarding the causal ordering of drug use and crime in large measure become moot. If drug use and delinquency are manifest indicators of a single latent variable of deviance, then we should focus our casual analysis on factors antecedent to both involvement in drugs and delinquency. Disentangling causal relationships between drug use and crime becomes an unproductive and irrelevant effort in that both forms of behavior are manifestations of a single unobserved characteristic.

With regard to the issue of specialization among offenders, the creation of a single latent variable of deviance has even more apparent consequences. If there is a single unobserved variable that describes both drug use and delinquency, then this is evidence that there is little pattern of specialization among offenders. Such a finding would be consistent with most research on this topic that we summarized earlier.

Clogg (1981) outlines the basic process of creating the latent variable in three steps. First, we must estimate the relative frequency distribution for the latent variable or the percentage of the sample within each category of the latent variable. Second, we must estimate the relative frequency for each observed variable under consideration for each category of the latent variable. Finally, based on our estimates of the latent variable in the first two steps, we must develop a substantive definition of the newly created latent variable. For example, observed measures of instrumental attitudes toward the law may be manifest indicators of a single latent variable that we might label differential association.

We begin by considering a set of four observed measures of delinquency or drug use. Here we will analyze a relatively small set of items to simplify the analysis and presentation of results. A more systematic study of a latent construct of deviance incorporating drug use and delinquency would require analysis of a wider range of measures.

The four items to be considered are self-reported measures of theft, vandalism, assault, and cocaine use. Only white male respondents are included in this analysis given concerns about the validity of self-report data among black respondents (Hindelang, Hirschi, and Weis, 1981) and concerns about the comparability of delinquency measures—particularly measures of violent behavior—between male and female subjects (Smith and Davidson, 1986). Future latent variable research should consider replications across various social groups.

In Table 6.1, we present the percentage distribution of positive responses to the four self-report measures. The measure of assault includes instances of simple assault, which are relatively common among adolescent males. The measure of theft includes only those instances where property in excess of $50 was stolen; this measure likely includes

Table 6.1 Percentage Distribution of Positive Responses to Observed Measures of Delinquency and Drug Use (Seattle Youth Study)

	Percent
Assault	54.4
Vandalism	48.1
Theft	25.2
Cocaine Use	28.8

Source: Data from Michael Hindelang, Travis Hirschi, and Joseph Weis, 1981, *Measuring Delinquency* (Beverly Hills, CA: Sage).

Table 6.2 Cross-classification of Observed Measures of Deviant Behavior
(Seattle Youth Study)

			Cocaine Use	
Assault	*Vandalism*	*Theft*	*No*	*Yes*
No	No	No	187	21
		Yes	10	10
	Yes	No	84	30
		Yes	20	14
Yes	No	No	122	28
		Yes	24	26
	Yes	No	108	36
		Yes	29	75

Source: Data from Michael Hindelang, Travis Hirschi, and Joseph Weis, 1981, *Measuring Delinquency* (Beverly Hills, CA: Sage).

only relatively serious instances of theft and therefore has a comparatively low rate of positive response.

In Table 6.2, we present the cross-classification of the observed measures of delinquency and drug use. An inspection of the table reveals a few patterns, such as a concentration of respondents in the category of conformity or negative responses to all four items. There tends to be a lesser concentration of respondents in the category of involvement in all four types of behavior. The visual inspection of the data is not sufficient, however, to discern a pattern of a single latent variable that might account for the association among the observed measures. We must use the formal modeling technique of latent structure analysis to make that assessment.

As a first step in the latent structure analysis, we must specify how many classes or categories we believe there may be in the proposed latent variable. A useful beginning in this case would be to specify two latent classes, a first category describing conformity (or relative conformity) and the second category describing a deviant status. Such a dichotomous measure is parsimonious and has the virtue of facilitating analysis and description of patterns in the data. We must further specify estimates or "start values" of the proportions of the sample within each category of the proposed latent variable. We estimated that each category would describe 50 percent of the sample. (The computer program, MLLSA, adjusts these start values or estimates to fit the data more closely; thus the start values are indeed only initial estimates that begin the analysis of the latent variable.)

Start values must also be provided for "conditional probabilities" for each of the observed measures of delinquency and drug use. In this case, the conditional probabilities provide estimates of the proportions of positive and negative responses to the observed measures for each category of the latent variable.

For example, we estimated that the probability of a positive response to the measure of cocaine use in the first category of the latent variable would be relatively low. (Recall that the first category was intended to describe relative conformity or little involvement in deviance.) We estimate the conditional probability of cocaine use in this first category of the latent variable to be .25 (or one of four respondents). In contrast, we estimated the probability of a positive response to the measure of cocaine use for the second category (describing a deviant status) to be relatively high. A start value or initial estimate of .75 was provided for this conditional probability.

Since assault and vandalism are more common behaviors than cocaine use, we estimated that involvement in the former types of behavior would be more likely even in the first category of the latent variable. Start values of .40 estimating the probability of positive responses to assault and vandalism measures were provided for these conditional probabilities. Given the relatively low prevalence of involvement in theft of property worth more than $50, we estimated that the probability of a positive response to this item to be only .10 in the first category of the latent variable.

Prior to further consideration of latent structure models, we first examine the model of independence for the cross-classification of the four observed measures. Clogg (1981) describes the meaning of the model of independence in the context of latent structure analysis. The model of independence specifies that there is only a single latent class within the entire table. (The model of independence may also imply that there is no single latent variable describing the data.) If there is only a single latent class, the pattern of responses to the observed variables is predicted to be completely random. In Table 6.1, the model of independence would specify no association among theft, assault, vandalism, and cocaine use. In this case, not surprisingly, the model of independence provides a very poor fit to the data ($L^2 = 249.03$, p < .01, df = 11).

If the model of independence is rejected, then we may proceed to consider latent structure models. It is recommended that the most parsimonious model possible be selected. Such a model must adequately fit the data (as measured by chi-square tests), but a parsimonious model should specify the fewest number of classes possible in the latent variable. Interpretation of a two-class model is generally easier than interpretation of, for example, a five-class model.

Taylor (1983) points out that there may be complications in selecting a particular latent structure model. He points out that latent structure models are hierarchical (or may be compared) only to the model of independence but not formally to one another. We may find two latent structure models providing adequate fits to the data. However, one guideline in selecting a final model would be to choose the most parsimonious model or the model with the fewest classes in the latent variable. Ultimately we may have to rely on substantive arguments or intuitive judgments about which model best describes the data or provides the most meaningful result. Clogg (1981) recommends additional criteria for assessing the fit of latent structure models, including an index of dissimilarity and a lambda measure.

We proceeded to consider the fit of a two-class latent structure model. Such a model specifies that the four observed measures of delinquency and drug use are manifest indicators of a single latent variable with two categories. We find that the two-class model does provide a considerable improvement in fit relative to the model of independence ($L^2 = 21.88$, $p < .05$, $df = 6$); however, the two-class model fails to provide a significant fit exceeding the .05 probability level.

The lack of an adequate fit may imply that the observed measures cannot be described by a single latent variable. It may be necessary to consider separate latent variables describing delinquency and drug use (or offenses that are more or less common or frequent in occurrence). However, we should consider additional latent structure models before we dismiss the potential of a latent variable to account for the association among the observed measures. In particular, we will consider a three-class latent variable. Three-class latent structure models were found to provide adequate descriptions of the separate sets of measures of delinquency and drug use in the research of Sorenson and Brownfield (1987; 1989).

Before fitting a three-class model, we examined the standardized residuals for the two-class latent structure model to determine more precisely the source of the lack of fit of the latter model. The residuals provide a measure of the difference between observed frequencies and expected frequencies predicted by the model. A pattern may emerge among residuals that are substantial.

The standardized residuals for each cell frequency of the table are approximately normally distributed with a mean of zero and a standard deviation not larger than one. Standardized residuals in excess of 2.0 indicate an especially poor fit of the model to the data. In this case, none of the standardized residuals exceeds 2.0; however, two of the standardized residuals are noteworthy and comparatively high, indicating a poor fit to the data. One of these standardized residuals is for the cell representing respondents with only a positive response to the vandalism item (cell, 1, 1, 2, 1). The second standardized residual that is noteworthy is for the cell representing positive responses to the assault and vandalism items but negative responses to the theft and cocaine items (1, 1, 2, 2).

These residuals may indicate that there is a need to fit an intermediate category of involvement in deviance in the latent variable to describe those with a high probability of involvement in assault and vandalism, yet a low level of involvement in theft and cocaine use.

Start values for the three-class latent structure model were estimated as .30, .40, and .30. The conditional probabilities for the three-class model specify little likelihood of involvement in theft (.10) or cocaine (.25) for the first category of the latent variable, and a 50 percent chance of such behaviors in the second category of the latent variable. In contrast, we estimate the probabilities of a positive response to the vandalism and assault items to be .80 for both the second and third categories of the latent variable.

Each of the four observed measures of delinquency or drug use is part of a single latent variable, but these observed measures contribute differentially to the assignment of respondents to particular categories of the latent variable. For example, responses to the theft and cocaine use items appear to be more crucial than responses to the assault and vandalism items in assigning respondents to the third category of the latent variable. The latent variable is roughly similar or analogous to a weighted scale of items that differentially weights the significance of each constituent item of the scale.

We find that the three-class latent structure model provides an adequate fit to the data ($L^2 = 3.65$, $p > .05$, df = 1). Technically, a restricted model must be fit because the parameters of the model are not identified (see McCutcheon, 1987). Such a restricted model provides very similar results compared with the unrestricted model discussed here. An additional measure of goodness of fit based on the Pearson chi-square statistic indicates that the three-class model provides for a substantial reduction in unexplained variation relative to the model of independence. Based on the formula $X^2(H_O) - X^2(H^*)/X^2(H_O)$, where $X^2(H_O)$ represents the Pearson's chi-square statistic for the model of independence and $X^2(H^*)$ represents the Pearson's chi-square statistic for the alternative model, we find that nearly all of the unexplained variation (.99) is reduced by specifying the three-class model.

The three-class model may be interpreted as describing three categories of relative conformity, moderate involvement in deviance, and extensive involvement in deviance. Hirschi (1969) has employed a similar measure of delinquency, an additive scale including categories of 0 delinquent acts, 1 delinquent act, and 2 or more delinquent acts.

Describing the Latent Variable

We may proceed to derive and describe more precisely the nature of the latent structure variable specified by the three-class model. The latent structure analysis program (MLLSA) assigns respondents in particular

Table 6.3 Observed and Expected Frequencies, Latent Class Assignments, and Probability of Error for Four Observed Measures of Deviant Behavior (Seattle Youth Study)

Frequency					
Observed	Expected	Latent Class	Probability or error	Score Pattern $(i,j,k,l)^*$	Recoded Cell Value
187	186.34	1	.22	(1,1,1,1)	0
21	21.86	2	.22	(2,1,1,1)	8
10	12.88	2	.03	(1,2,1,1)	4
10	7.66	2	.32	(2,2,1,1)	12
84	86.62	2	.29	(1,1,2,1)	2
30	26.13	2	.03	(2,1,2,1)	10
20	18.97	2	.02	(1,2,2,1)	6
14	15.55	3	.49	(2,2,2,1)	14
122	123.43	2	.49	(1,1,1,2)	1
28	28.23	2	.08	(2,1,1,2)	9
24	20.25	2	.05	(1,2,1,2)	5
26	27.35	3	.29	(2,2,1,2)	13
108	104.02	2	.10	(1,1,2,2)	3
36	39.38	2	.02	(2,1,2,2)	11
29	31.50	2	.10	(1,2,2,2)	7
75	73.84	3	.16	(2,2,2,2)	15

*i = cocaine use, j = theft, k = vandalism, l = assault

Source: Data from Michael Hindelang, Travis Hirschi, and Joseph Weis, 1981 *Measuring Delinquency* (Beverly Hills, CA: Sage).

cells to a particular class or category of the latent variable. In addition, the program provides an estimate of the probability that an individual will be assigned to a particular latent class given a pattern of responses to the observed measures of delinquency.

In Table 6.3 we present latent class assignments for each cell of the observed cross-classification of theft by cocaine use, assault, and vandalism. The probability of an incorrect assignment to a latent class is also provided in the table. This is estimated by simply subtracting the probability that an individual will be assigned to a particular latent class from 1.0 ($e_{ijkl} = 1.0 - \pi^{ABCD}$). In the first cell of Table 6.3, the probability of assigning an individual to latent class 1 is .78; the probability of an incorrect assignment is $1.0 - .78$ or .22. The probability of an incorrect assignment in most cases or for most cells is less than .25. In no instance is the probability of an incorrect assignment greater than .50.

Approximately four-fifths (78.2 percent) of the sample were correctly assigned to a latent class under the three-class model.

The score patterns in Table 6.3 provide a useful way to determine which respondents are assigned to a particular latent class. Those who are assigned to the first latent class include only those who had negative responses to all four measures. The first category of the latent variable, therefore, describes an absolute conformist pattern, at least in terms of the measures of theft, cocaine use, vandalism, and assault.

The second class or category of the latent variable appears to be a more diverse group of respondents. In most cases, respondents in the second class have only one or two positive responses to the observed measures of deviant behavior. However, there are two exceptions to this pattern including those with positive responses to the theft, assault, and vandalism items (1, 2, 2, 2) and those with positive responses to the cocaine use, vandalism, and assault items (2, 1, 2, 2). These respondents thus had positive responses to three of the four observed measures of deviance.

The third class or category of the latent variable is limited to only three cells in the table. This class includes 14 respondents who had positive responses to the theft, cocaine use, and vandalism items (2, 2, 2, 1) and the 26 respondents who had positive responses to the theft, cocaine use, and assault items (2, 2, 1, 2). The third latent class also includes the 75 respondents who confess to involvement in all four types of deviant behavior. A common pattern among the respondents in the third latent class is that they all have positive responses to the theft and cocaine use items, the least common and arguably the most serious offenses among the four items. Further, all respondents in the third class have confessed to a minimum of three types of offenses. However, as noted earlier, several respondents in the second class also had confessed to three types of offenses.

In Table 6.4 we present the final latent class probabilities under the three-class model. The probabilities are the final estimates based on the starting values for conditional probabilities for each of the observed measures of delinquency and drug use discussed earlier. The response distributions summarized in Table 6.4 provide a more precise description of the nature of the three-classes of the latent variable.

In the first latent class, the probability of a positive response is relatively low for all four variables. The chances of a positive response to the cocaine use and theft items are extremely small in the first category of the latent variable. Respondents assigned to the first latent variable category are also unlikely to self-report either vandalism (.15) or assault (.29). In contrast, respondents assigned to the second latent variable category are more likely than not to self-report involvement in vandalism and assault (.60). Approximately one-fourth of the respondents

Table 6.4 Response Distributions to Four Observed Measures by Latent Class Under the Three Class Model (Seattle Youth Study)

		Latent Class		
		I	*II*	*III*
Cocaine Use	No	.97	.71	.05
	Yes	.03	.29	.95
Theft	No	.99	.77	.01
	Yes	.01	.23	.99
Vandalism	No	.85	.40	.24
	Yes	.15	.60	.76
Assault	No	.71	.40	.11
	Yes	.29	.60	.89

Source: Data from Michael Hindelang, Travis Hirschi, and Joseph Weis, 1981, *Measuring Delinquency* (Beverly Hills, CA: Sage).

assigned to this second or intermediate category of deviant behavior self-report cocaine use (.29) or theft (.23). For all four observed measures of delinquency and drug use, the probability of involvement increases in the third category of the latent variable. More than three-fourths of the respondents assigned to this category self-report vandalism (.76) or assault (.89). Nearly all of the respondents in the third category of the latent variable self-report involvement in theft (.99) and cocaine (.95).

The four observed measures of delinquency and drug use have been found to form a single latent variable of deviant behavior with three categories. We have described in some detail the nature of these three categories. Our findings suggest that instead of conceiving of drug use and crime as causing one another, it might be more accurate to conceive of drug use and delinquency as manifestations of the same underlying variable or characteristic. Instead of specialization among offenders, there appears to be considerable diversity or involvement in a variety of types of deviant behavior. Involvement in one form of deviance, whether it is assault, vandalism, theft, or drug use, is correlated with involvement in other types of deviance.

External Validity of the Latent Variable

As an alternative to a latent structure analysis of deviant behavior, we might construct a simple unweighted additive scale wherein the number of positive responses to the observed measures is merely summed. This strategy is employed by a number of researchers (Hirschi, 1969;

Hagan, Gillis, and Simpson, 1985; Messner and Krohn, 1990). The additive scale approach also assumes that the observed variables are manifest indicators of a single latent variable.

We may assess the "external validity" of our latent class measure of deviant behavior by examining patterns of association with known correlates (or variables external to the latent variable) of delinquency. The magnitude of the associations between the latent structure variable and these external variables should approximately equal (or perhaps exceed) the magnitude of associations between an additive scale of delinquency and the same external variables or known correlates if the latent structure measure is to be deemed valid. We select the same set of external or exogenous variables used by Brownfield and Sorenson (1987) in their analysis of delinquency measures.

The first of these measures is officially recorded delinquency, defined as recorded instances of police contact. Self-report measures are often compared with official measures of delinquency, with the expectation of a strong positive association between the two variables (Hindelang, Hirschi, and Weis, 1981; Nettler, 1984). Three additional external measures are used in our validity check of the latent structure variable. Each of these three variables has been employed as a central construct in prominent theories of delinquency, such as social learning theory and social control theory. Attachment to others is considered a significant dimension in explaining deviance in most versions of control theory. We use as an indicator of attachment the following item: "Would you like to be the kind of person your mother is?" The remaining two measures used as tests of external validity are central to social learning theory. Peer delinquency and instrumental attitudes toward the law (measured by the item "it's all right to get around the law if you can get away with it.") have been found to be consistently and strongly associated with deviant behavior.

We use a three category additive scale (0 offenses, 1 offense, and 2 or more offenses) for purposes of comparability with the three-class latent structure variable. This is consistent with previous treatment of such additive scales. To construct the measure of the three-class latent structure variable, we must first assign unique coding scores to each cell of the original cross-classification in Table 6.2. Recall that each cell is assigned to a particular latent variable category; we recode a positive response to each of the four observed measures to create a unique score for each cell of the table. Here we recoded positive responses to the four observed measures in the following manner: assault = 1, vandalism = 2, theft = 4, cocaine use = 8. These recodes produced the cell values in the last column of Table 6.3. (Thus, for the ten respondents who had positive responses to the items of theft and cocaine use, their recoded cell value would be 8 + 4 = 12.) Respondents with a recoded cell value of 0

Table 6.5 Measures of Association (Somers's d) for Addictive and Latent Class Measures of Deviant Behavior (Seattle Youth Study)

Exogenous Variable	Additive Scale	Latent Class Scale
Official Delinquency	.27	.28
Attachment	.12	.12
Peer Delinquency	.42	.38
Instrumental Attitudes	−.28	−.25

Source: Data from Michael Hindelang, Travis Hirschi, and Joseph Weis, 1981, *Measuring Delinquency* (Beverly Hills, CA: Sage).

are assigned to latent class 1; respondents with recoded cell values of 1 through 12 are assigned to latent class 2; respondents with recoded cell values of 13 through 15 are assigned to latent class 3.

In Table 6.5 we present measures of the association between the latent structure variable and the exogenous variables and between the additive scale and the exogenous variables. In general, we find little difference in the magnitude of the association between the measure of deviant behavior and the exogenous variable, regardless of whether we employ an additive scale or the latent class scale. Although we would have hoped for increases in the level of association with these known correlates, the relatively stable pattern of coefficients is also reassuring. Such a stable pattern allows us to conclude that the latent class measure seems to be valid when assessed in conjunction with these external variables and in comparison with an additive scale.

Conclusion

The findings of our latent structure analysis suggest that involvement in drug use, theft, vandalism, and assault can be reasonably understood as manifest indicators of a single latent variable. We might conveniently refer to this latent variable as "deviant behavior."

The implications of such findings are significant for the debates over the causal relationship between drug use and crime and the issue of specialization among offenders. Consistent with most prior research, we believe that there is little specialization among offenders and considerable diversity or variety in the kinds of crime committed. The construction of a single latent variable of deviant behavior also renders meaningless to a large degree the issue of the causal relationship between drug use and crime. Indeed, the studies (Johnston, O'Malley, and Eveland, 1978; Osgood et al., 1988; Elliott, Huizinga, and Menard, 1989) that have examined this issue have not reached a consistent conclusion about the causal relationship between drug use and crime.

More effort should be expended on the explanation of deviant behavior in general rather than particular manifestations of deviant behavior, such as drug use, homicide, white collar crime, or shoplifting. One such recent effort (Gottfredson and Hirschi, 1990) attempts to account for involvement in a wide spectrum of deviant behavior by delineating the concept of self-control. Self-control is defined as the ability to defer gratification, tolerate frustration, and to develop long term commitments and attachments to others. Such a concept is itself an unobserved characteristic that may be usefully measured by latent structure analysis.

Epilogue:
Toward a Science of Crime

The preceding chapters do not constitute final decisions about the criminological controversies on which they focus. Rather, these chapters outline the central issues in the debates, and try to give conceptual and methodological foci for further empirical investigation and analysis.

Class

The first chapter of this book addresses what is probably the most controversial of the questions facing students of crime over the ages: whether adverse class conditions cause crime. Common sense may say yes, but many modern criminologists say no. To some social scientists this very question has seemed a mean-spirited provocation, implying that the poor are not only destitute, but also criminal. Critics worry that contemporary discussions of the "underclass" are too much concerned about a presumed poverty-induced threat of rising crime, which in this sense is little different from historical discussions of the dangerous classes. This preoccupation with the criminal threat from poor people may be less fact than a fiction, an ideology justifying and enabling the political domination of the poor. There is a similar concern that discussions of the underclass reflect the self-consciousness of a privileged class who are concerned first and foremost with maintaining their privileges.

However, there are also more scientific reasons to be worried about the concept of the underclass. Most notably, this concept can be faulted for being more of a description than a useful step toward the explanation of crime. The problem may be that the idea of an underclass simply mixes together depictions of poverty and crime, in a tautologous fashion, rather than articulating the processes that actually connect class to crime. More is needed to build a theoretical explanation.

These concerns are further encouraged by a research tradition in modern criminology that asks adolescents to self-report in paper and pencil surveys how often they have committed various kinds of crimes. Too often these surveys are done among youth attending school and are focused on children of mostly employed parents who report relatively minor misdeeds. When economically challenged parents and adolescents

157

are considered in terms of their more severe deprivations (i.e., lack of housing, food, and work), more crime and delinquency is revealed.

But this is not the end of the class and crime controversy, for there is also confusion about the levels of analysis at which this problem should be addressed. Studies focused on city blocks, census tracts, and neighborhoods have nearly always found substantial relationships between class and crime, leading to the conclusion that often it is the larger environment in which economic deprivation and connected problems are encountered that causes crime, rather than the personalized experience with economic deprivation alone. To focus so narrowly on personal rather than social processes may be an individualistic fallacy that we should try to avoid.

Ethnographic studies of impoverished communities sometimes add explanatory dimension to the conceptualization of an underclass, documenting problems of weak or nonexistent job networks and role models that may make delinquent and criminal solutions more common among youth who have few opportunities to pursue legitimate occupational careers. Increasingly these studies describe community settings and individual lives in which young people follow a life course that leads from delinquency to crime to unemployment and related problems. These studies underline the importance of articulating causal processes that lead through a set of intervening and interacting links to criminal outcomes. As these studies do so, they begin to raise a simple concern with the underclass or distressed communities to a more informative level that leads to theoretical explanation.

Gender

In the second chapter of this book we present an example of the way in which a causal theory of crime can be developed and tested. The theory presented is known as power-control theory and is used to explain the strong correlation that is observed in much crime research between gender and delinquency. This theory has generated controversy because it postulates that patriarchal families play an important role in creating the conditions under which boys become more delinquent than girls.

In patriarchal families power-control theory suggests fathers use the power they derive from authority positions in work outside the home to assign mothers primary responsibility for child care. As mothers assume this responsibility there is a tendency to reproduce the gender roles of the patriarchal family by controlling daughters more than sons. This inclines daughters in patriarchal families to be more risk averse and sons to be risk seekers. In turn, this risk seeking makes delinquency more common among boys, and exposes boys to a greater likelihood than girls of police contact.

Most of the second chapter is devoted to demonstrating the ways in which tabular and regression techniques can be used to test power-control theory. In undertaking this demonstration, we are less concerned with establishing the validity of this theory than with documenting the ways in which a propositional theory can be explored and tested. One of the tests of the theory we undertake involves extending the theory to the explanation of teenage smoking behavior that in recent years has become more common among girls. By extending attention beyond delinquency per se, we begin to make the point that this theory has a wide ranging application. Taken more broadly, power-control theory can be used to explain prosocial as well as neutral or antisocial forms of risk-taking. For example, the theory implies that in less patriarchal or egalitarian kinds of families, girls are encouraged to take the kinds of risks that lead to nontraditional occupations, career changes and efforts at career advancement, competitive forms of athletics and leisure activities, and risk-oriented forms of financial activity and investment.

Meanwhile, power-control theory also has implications for male involvement in some specific kinds of delinquency, including violent and assaultive behavior. We are able to show that patriarchal attitudes held by adolescents can play a role in accounting for the greater involvement of boys in fighting and assaultive behavior. These attitudes are more inclined to develop among boys in families that leave them freer than girls from parental control. Again, this is not to say that power-control theory is a fully developed or a proven explanation of gender differences in delinquency. However, the theory does stimulate predictions that are open to test in a manner that we suggest is the hallmark of a scientific criminology.

Urbanization

Chapter 3 focuses on the relationship between urbanization and crime. The American experience has given rise to a number of arguments that provide different reasons for expecting urbanization to generate an increasing rate of serious crime. Chief among these is the idea that the growth in number and especially the size of cities impairs the development and operation of community and associated institutions of formal and informal control. Recent explanations have suggested that suburbanization and the associated erosion of human and economic capital from central cities may account for their social disorganization and high rates of criminal activity.

On the other side, if civil society in modern American cities is declining because of the dispersion of their capital, this may mean that at other times, and in other locations, the concentration and accumulation of capital in urban areas depressed crime. An analysis of data from nineteenth-century France is consistent with this view. Between the middle of the nineteenth century and the beginning of World War I, urbanization was a negative predictor of the rate of serious crime in France.

The idea that there is a direct relationship between urbanization and crime is not controversial among students of cities and crime in the United States. Few social scientists would take issue with the proposition. It is only with a broader perspective, less limited in time and space, that the relationship loses its inevitability. In fact, the late twentieth-century U.S. may be a unique circumstance, making generalizations from its range of experience a very risky undertaking. U.S. cities are not even representative of the urban scene in North America, let alone the rest of the industrialized world. Canadian cities, even when they are large, show few signs of the decay and danger found in U.S. centers (Gillis, 1994a).

The bad news for those who live in them is that urban areas in the United States are more dangerous than rural areas. This may be one of the reasons why so many Americans continue to vote with their feet for life in the suburbs. However, before they give up on cities as inherently crime-ridden, sociologists and criminologists need to extend their analyses of urban life beyond the U.S. in the late twentieth century. Confining research in time and space jeopardizes social science because it prevents scientific generalization. Attempts to generalize the findings of analyses beyond the boundaries of time and space from which the data were drawn is not only without foundation, but also arrogant: ethnocentricity with social scientific trappings. This is why the question of the impact of urbanization may be more controversial outside the United States than it is within. In any case, the good news is that cities can be livable, perhaps even in the United States.

Police

Chapter 4 examines whether police produce or reduce crime. This controversy has raged among students of crime for decades, and the debate is unresolved. Deterrence theory suggests that if the severity, swiftness, and certainty of punishment outweigh the probability of a pleasurable payoff, crime rates will fall. The certainty of punishment is not only increased, but signaled by the presence of uniformed purveyors of state-sanctioned violence; therefore, the growth of policing should have produced a decline in criminal behavior.

On the other hand, a reaction perspective suggests a very different outcome. If one assumes a more or less constant amount of crime, any variations in rates reflect differences in the detection and processing of offenders. Increasing the capacity of the state to do this will result in an increase rather than a decrease in rates of officially recorded crime, especially in minor offenses, where officers have greater discretion in deciding to arrest and charge offenders.

These two perspectives predict opposite effects of policing on crime: one inflationary and the other deflationary. Pure logic and normal social scientific expectations would imply that these are mutually exclusive possibilities. However, an analysis of data taken from the place where state policing began, in nineteenth-century France, shows how policing both increased and decreased rates of crime. Increasing surveillance, reflected by the growth of the police force, is directly related to spiraling crime rates. This is the case whether one examines major or minor offenses, or crimes against persons or property. It is unlikely that an increasing crime rate could result in a growth in the state police force within the same budget year. So unless a third factor simultaneously increased rates of crime and policing, reaction rather than deterrence describes the impact of policing on crime in nineteenth-century France.

Detecting crime and laying charges most likely follows quickly after the criminal event occurs (if charges are to be laid at all). However, a general deterrence effect which would reduce criminal behavior in the wider population probably takes more time. With this in mind, a time-series analysis with lagged variables examined the possibility that increased policing might have had a deterrent effect at later in time. The data suggest that this may have indeed occurred. Several years after an increase in the size of the police force most crime rates showed a decline. This was most evident in the case of serious crime and was persistent in the case of major property offenses. Further, in the case of these crimes, the subsequent decline associated with policing outweighed the initial increase, giving overall support to the deterrence argument.

Whether the reaction viewpoint or deterrence theory receives empirical support not only depends on whether one seeks to explain changes in rates of major or minor crimes, but whether one examines immediate or long-run effects. Thus, quantitative analyses gives support to both sides. This will not satisfy polemicists or true believers. But provision of this satisfaction is not the goal of research in the social sciences.

Subcultures

The subcultural theories of crime and delinquency have been ignored or dismissed by many criminologists. This may be because support is at best limited for the propositions derived from this type of explanation. Much of the empirical research in this area has focused on class-based subcultures, and the correlation between class and crime has not

proven to be consistently strong or robust either, as noted in the open-
ing chapter of this volume.

We have argued that subcultural theories deserve further attention
on both empirical and conceptual levels. The combined influence of
structural and cultural effects on crime and delinquency needs to be
reassessed not so much as competing philosophies but as mutually
reinforcing explanations. Class-based subcultures, for example, might
be discovered by using measures of membership in an underclass rather
than continuing to focus on traditional socioeconomic indicators of
income, education, and occupation. There is some reason to believe
that subcultures may be found among the chronically unemployed and
those who exist on welfare for extended periods of time.

The values and behaviors of those in working class families are
probably not significantly different from the values and behaviors in
middle and upper class families, particularly in terms of crime and
delinquency. In contrast, families that are characterized by chronic
unemployment and welfare dependency may have a greater tendency to
endorse values that encourage crime and delinquency. At the other end
of the class distribution, white collar crime may be fostered by values
that promote deceptive business practices and an instrumental ethic.

As noted before, we must demonstrate that the values that encourage crime and delinquency are linked to an identifiable group in order
to establish the existence of a subculture. Kornhauser (1978) rightly
questions the notion that the entire lower class can be accurately
depicted as a close-knit group. Instead, members of the lower class
might be better described as belonging to a collectivity or aggregate with
little opportunity to interact directly with one another. In contrast, the
underclass in ghettos and public housing projects may have much
greater opportunity and reason to interact and socialize one another as
members of a subculture that serves to protect as well as deflect members toward illegal activities. The corporate boardroom (and the country
club) might be another setting providing ample opportunity to promote
subcultural values leading to white collar crime.

Subcultures based on region, gender, and age may also seem more
plausible than subcultures within broad collectivities such as the lower
class. People probably identify and interact with one another more on
the basis of shared regional affiliation, being of the same gender, or being
in the same stage of the life cycle than they do on shared social class.

Regional subcultures have been hypothesized to affect crime rates,
particularly in the American South. The South has a shared history as
well as a distinctive religious heritage that may have contributed to a
defensive attitude. This defensive attitude may in turn lead to the more
ready or even an obligatory use of violence in response to affronts to
honor. An "external locus of control" wherein personal frustrations are
blamed on outside forces may contribute to both high homicide and low

suicide rates in the South. However, such regional differences seem to be diminishing over time in more recent or younger cohorts.

Many of our society's institutions remain differentiated on the basis of age and gender, notably in school and families. Boys and girls in schools often pursue very different interests in both academic subjects and extracurricular activities such as sports; social activities and peer groups remain segregated by age and gender to a large extent. Husbands and wives continue to report a substantial division of labor in the household based on relatively traditional gender roles. It is improbable that differences in age and gender have no effect on human behavior and values. In view of this, if there is indeed a subculture that fosters crime and delinquency, it will most likely be found among young males.

Drugs and Crime Specialists

Criminologists continue to debate the nature of the connection between drug use and crime and the related issue of specialization among offenders. An economics theory of drug use and property crime suggests that the financial needs created by drug use and addiction cause the offender to commit property crimes in order to support the drug habit. This theory implies that there is a clear causal or time ordering between drug use and crime, with drug use preceding other forms of crime. The research on this issue has not yielded any clear picture of the causal sequence of the relationship between drug use and property crime. However, researchers have consistently documented a strong correlation between drug use and other forms of criminal behavior. This finding suggests that involvement in deviance is general or is not specialized. Official records and self-report studies show that offenders will tend to commit a wide variety of crimes, rather than limit themselves to, for example, only certain types of property crime or violent crime. It seems somewhat implausible that an offender willing to violate one law or social norm would be very reluctant to break another law or social norm. Imagine an offender, contemplating some form of crime that he had not yet committed, saying to himself, "I can't do that! It's against the law!" This is not only implausible, it is inconsistent with most of the data on crime and deviance.

Some films on organized crime have depicted the bosses as being opposed to selling narcotics on moral grounds. The depiction of eclectic involvement in petty property offenses, violence, and drug use among organized criminals in the film *Wiseguys* seems to be more accurate. In *Chinatown*, John Huston portrays a very versatile offender, involved in incest and murder, as well as white collar crime. Huston's character says, "Most people don't have to face the fact that at the right time, in the right place, they're capable of *anything*" [emphasis in the original].

It may be more productive to consider the diverse forms of crime and deviance to be manifestations of the same underlying or latent variable. We have assessed a seemingly diverse set of offenses, including assault, vandalism, theft, and cocaine use, utilizing the statistical method of latent structure analysis. The latent structure analysis allowed us to conclude that these offenses are indicators of a single underlying factor. In line with the findings of prior research, this latent variable consists of three categories that reflect relative conformity, moderate involvement in deviance, and extensive involvement in deviance. These results are only tentative and should be subjected to further analysis with a wider range of measures of deviance, and other data sets should also be examined before more definitive conclusions can be drawn.

The latent variable analysis technique may be applied to a wide range of substantive issues in criminology. For example, several central theoretical constructs in criminology may be conceived of as latent variables. Differential association, secondary deviance in labeling theory, "self-control" in Gottfredson and Hirschi's (1990) general theory of crime, anomie, and social disorganization may all be measured or assessed as latent variables which are not directly observed.

The relationship between drugs and crime and the degree of specialization among offenders are not merely "academic" issues. As we discussed earlier, much of public policy on law enforcement seems to make assumptions about these issues. Considerable sums of money are spent on drug interdiction programs and drug treatment programs, and these programs seem to make implicit assumptions about the causal relationship between drug use and crime and patterns of offense specialization. Police departments have specialized bureaus dealing with homicide cases, sexual assault, drug offenses, and robbery. Criminal investigations occasionally make use of so-called "offender profiles" based on social scientific research. Criminologists should provide the best possible information regarding such profiles, and some of the techniques described here may help us to do so.

A Science of Crime

The approaches, variables, levels, and methods of analysis differ across the chapters of this book. This reflects the different interests, analytic techniques, abilities, and, regrettably, the disabilities of the authors. Implicitly or explicitly, each chapter deals with a cause of crime and the controversy surrounding it. But this is only part of the unifying theme of our work. The more important connection is a shared commitment to the application of social scientific techniques, especially quantitative analysis, to the study of crime and delinquency.

Like qualitative research, quantitative approaches rarely give the final word on a research issue. More often, both types of research illustrate that situations are far more complex than was initially expected, and that conditions and contexts play an important part in shaping the relationships between variables. We want life to be simple and manageable, but most often it is not. Pretending that it is and disregarding social science is tempting for politicians, activists, and other meliorists who are trying to find quick fixes for complicated problems. Indefinite fence sitting by scientists in ivory towers may err by failing to act at all, but mindless action, even if well intentioned, will in the long run create at least as much pain as it will alleviate. Even a short time listening to their professors will convince most students that it would be foolhardy to give social scientists the keys of government. However, it is equally dangerous for governments to ignore the results of our research.

References

Abbot, Andrew. 1983. "Sequences of Social Events: Concepts and Methods for the Analysis of Order in Social Processes." *Historical Methods* 16(4):129–47.

Agar, M., and R. Stephens. 1975. "The Methadone Street Scene." *Psychiatry* 38:383.

Agnew, Robert. 1985. "A Revised Strain Theory of Delinquency." *Social Forces* 64:151–67.

Akers, Ronald L. 1984. "Delinquent Behavior, Drugs, and Alcohol: What is the Relationship?" *Today's Delinquent* 3:19–47.

———. 1985. *Deviant Behavior: A Social Learning Approach.* (3rd ed.) Belmont, CA: Wadsworth.

Alschuler, Albert. 1979. "Plea Bargaining and its History." *Law and Society Review* 13:211–45.

Alwin, Duane F., and Robert M. Hauser. 1975. "The Decomposition of Effects in Path Analysis." *American Sociological Review* 40:37–47.

Aminzade, Ronald. 1992. "Historical Sociology and Time." *Sociological Methods and Research* 20: 456–80.

Amir, Menachem. 1971. *Patterns in Forcible Rape.* Chicago: University of Chicago Press.

Anderson, Elijah. 1978. *A Place on the Corner.* Chicago: University of Chicago Press.

———. 1990. *Streetwise: Race, Class, and Change in an Urban Community.* Chicago: University of Chicago Press.

Anglin, M. Douglas, and George Speckart. 1988. "Narcotics Use and Crime: A Multisample, Multimethod Analysis." *Criminology* 26:197–233.

Archer, Dane, and Rosemary Gartner. 1976. "Violent Acts and Violent Times: A Comparative Approach to Postwar Homicide Rates." *American Sociological Review* 41:937–963.

———. 1984. *Violence and Crime in Cross-National Perspective.* New Haven: Yale University Press.

Auletta, Ken. 1982. *The Underclass.* New York: Random House.

Bachman, Jerald, Patrick O'Malley, and Jerome Johnston. 1978. *Youth in Transition, Volume VI, Adolescence to Adulthood—Change and Stability in the Lives of Young Men.* Ann Arbor, MI: Institute for Social Research, University of Michigan.

Bachman, Jerald, Lloyd Johnston, and Patrick O'Malley. 1990. "Explaining the Recent Decline in Cocaine Use among Young Adults." *Journal of Health and Social Behavior* 31:173–184.

Bailey, William C., J. David Martin, and Louis N. Gray. 1972. "On Punishment and Crime (Chiricos and Waldo 1970): Some Methodological Commentary." *Social Problems* 19(Fall):280–289.

Ball, John, Lawrence Rosen, John Flueck, and David Nurco. 1981. "The Criminality of Heroin Addicts." In J. Inciardi (ed.), *The Drugs-Crime Connection*, 39–65. Beverly Hills CA: Sage.

Ball-Rokeach, Sandra. 1973. "Values and Violence: A Test of the Subculture of Violence Thesis." *American Sociological Review* 38:736–749.

Banfield, Edward C. 1968. *The Unheavenly City.* Boston: Little, Brown.

———. 1970. *The Unheavenly City: The Nature and Future of Our Urban Crisis.* Boston: Little, Brown.

———. 1974. *The Unheavenly City Revisited.* Boston: Little, Brown.

Bayley, David H. 1975. "The Police and Political Development in Europe." In Charles Tilly (ed.) *The Formation of National States in Western Europe*, 328–379. Princeton, NJ: Princeton University Press.

———. 1985. *Patterns of Policing: A Comparative International Analysis.* New Brunswick, NJ: Rutgers University Press.

———. 1986. *Social Control and Political Change.* Princeton, NJ: Princeton University Press.

Beattie, J. M. 1986. *Crime and the Courts in England, 1660–1800.* Princeton, NJ: Princeton University Press.

———. 1992. "Crime, Gender and Inequality in the 18th Century England." Paper presented at the American Society of Criminology Meetings, San Francisco.

Becker, Gary. 1964. *Human Capital: A Theoretical and Empirical Analysis, with Special Reference to Education.* New York: National Bureau of Economic Research.

Becker, Howard. 1953. "Becoming a Marijuana User." *American Journal of Sociology* 59:235–42.

Becker, Marvin B. 1988. *Civility and Society in Western Europe, 1300–1600.* Bloomington: Indiana University Press.

Beirne, Piers. 1987. "Adolphe Quetelet and the Origins of Positivist Criminology." *American Journal of Sociology* 92(5):1140–1169.

Benson, Michael L., and Elizabeth Moore. 1992. "Are White Collar and Common Offenders the Same?" *Journal of Research in Crime and Delinquency* 29:251–272.

Berelson, Bernard, and Gary A. Steiner. 1964. *Human Behavior: An Inventory of Scientific Findings.* New York: Harcourt, Brace & World.

Berger, Bennett M. 1963. "Adolescence and Beyond." *Social Problems* 10:394–408.

Berman, Harold J. 1983. *Law and Revolution: The Formation of the Western Legal Tradition.* Cambridge, MA: Harvard University Press.

Bernard, Thomas. 1990. "Angry Aggression among the 'Truly Disadvantaged'." *Criminology* 28(1):73–96.

Bernstein, Ilene Nagel, William R. Kelly, and Patricia A. Doyle. 1977. "Societal Reaction to Deviants: The Case of Criminal Defendants." *American Sociological Review* 42:743–55.

Bertaux, D. 1982. "The Life Course Approach as a Challenge to the Social Sciences." In Tamara K. Hareven and Kathleen J. Adams (eds.), *Ageing and Life Course Transitions: An Interdisciplinary Perspective*, 127–50. New York: Guilford.

Beutel, Ann, and Margaret Mooney Marini. 1995. "Gender and Values." *American Sociological Review* 60:436–448.

Biderman, A. D. et al. 1967. *Report of a Pilot Study in the District of Columbia on Victimization and Attitudes Toward Law Enforcement*. Washington, DC: U.S. Government Printing Office.

Billingsley, Andrew. 1992. *Climbing Jacob's Ladder: The Enduring Legacy of African-American Families*. New York: Simon and Shuster.

Black, Donald. 1976. *The Behavior of Law*. New York: Academic Press.

———. 1983. "Crime as Social Control." *American Sociological Review* 48:34–45.

Blalock, Hubert. 1964. *Causal Inferences in Nonexperimental Research*. Chapel Hill: University of North Carolina Press.

Blau, Judith, and Peter Blau. 1982. "The Cost of Inequality: Metropolitan Structure and Violent Crime." *American Sociological Review* 47:114–129.

Blau, Peter. 1977. *Inequality and Heterogeneity: A Primitive Theory of Social Structure*. New York: Free Press.

Bloch, Marc. 1964. *Feudal Society*, Vols. 1 and 2. Chicago: The University of Chicago Press.

Blum, R. 1976. "Mind-Altering Drugs and Dangerous Behavior." The President's Commission on Law Enforcement and Administration of Justice, Task Force Report: Narcotics and Drug Abuse. Washington, DC: U.S. Government Printing Office.

Blumenthal, Monica, Robert Kahn, Frank Andrews, and Kendra Head. 1972. *Justifying Violence: Attitudes of American Men*. Ann Arbor, MI: Institute for Social Research, University of Michigan.

Blumstein, Alfred, J. Cohen, and D. Nagin. 1978. *Deterrence and Incapacitation: Estimating the Effects of Criminal Sanctions on Crime Rates*. Washington, DC: National Academy of Sciences.

Boritch, Helen, and John Hagan. 1987. "Crime and the Changing Forms of Class and Crime Control: Policing Public Order in 'Toronto the Good': 1859–1955." *Social Forces* 66:307–35.

———. 1990. "A Century of Crime in Toronto: Gender, Class and Patterns of Social Control, 1859 to 1955." *Criminology* 28:567–99.

Bourdieu, Pierre. 1977. *Outline of a Theory of Practice*. Cambridge, MA: Cambridge University Press.

———. 1980. "Le capital sociale: Notre provisaires." *Actes de la Recherche en Sciences Sociales* 3:2–3.

———. 1984. *Distinction: A Social Critique of the Judgement of Taste*. Cambridge, MA: Harvard University Press.

———. 1986. "The Forms of Capital." In J.G. Richardson (ed.), *Handbook of Theory and Research for the Sociology of Education*. New York: Greenwood Press.

Boutel, Ann, and Margaret Mooney Marini. 1995. "Gender and Values." *American Sociological Review* 60:436–448.

Brace, Charles. 1872. *The Dangerous Classes of New York*. New York: Wynkoop.

Bradshaw, York H., and L. Radbill. 1987. "Method and Substance in the Use of Ratio Variables." *American Sociological Review* 52:132–35.

Braithwaite, John. 1989. *Crime, Shame and Reintegration*. Cambridge, MA: Cambridge University Press.

Braudel, Fernand. 1986. *L'Identiti de la France*. Paris: Arthaud – Flammarion.

———. 1988. *The Identity of France: History and Environment*. London: Collins.

———. 1989. *The Identity of France: People and Production*. London: Fontana Press.

Brehm, Jack, and Arthur Cohen. 1962. *Explorations in Cognitive Dissonance*. New York: Wiley.

Brennan, Patricia, Sarnoff Mednick, and Richard John. 1989. "Specialization in Violence: Evidence of a Criminal Subgroup." *Criminology* 27:437–453.

Britt, Chester. 1994. "Versatility." In Travis Hirschi and Michael Gottfredson (eds.), *The Generality of Deviance*, 173–192. New Brunswick, NJ: Transaction.

Brook, Judith, and Patricia Cohen. 1992. "A Developmental Perspective on Drug Use and Delinquency." In J. McCord (ed.), *Facts, Frameworks, and Forecasts: Advances in Criminological Theory*, Vol. 3. New Brunswick, NJ: Transaction.

Brown, R., J. Durbin, and J. Evans. 1975. "Techniques for Testing the Constancy of Regression Relations over Time." *Journal of the Royal Statistical Society* 37: 149–92.

Brownfield, David. 1986. "Social Class and Violent Behavior." *Criminology* 24:421–38.

———. 1987. "A Reassessment of Cultural Deviance Theory: The Use of Underclass Measures." *Deviant Behavior* 8:343–359.

Brownfield, David, and Ann Marie Sorenson. 1987. "A Latent Structure Analysis of Delinquency." *Journal of Quantitative Criminology* 3:103–124.

Bruce, Charles Loring. 1872. *The Dangerous Classes of New York, and Twenty Years' Work Among Them*. New York: Wynkoop.

Bryant, Joseph M. 1994. "Evidence on Explanation in History and Sociology: Critical Reflections on Goldthorpe's Critique of Historical Sociology." *British Journal of Sociology*. 45:3–19.

Burgess, Robert L., and Ronald L. Akers. 1966. "A Differential Association-Reinforcement Theory of Criminal Behavior." *Social Problems* 14:128–146.

Bursik, Robert. 1980. "The Dynamics of Specialization in Juvenile Offenses." *Social Forces* 58:851–864.

———. 1988. "Social Disorganization and Theories of Crime and Delinquency: Problems and Prospects." *Criminology* 26(4):519–51.

Cameron, Iain A. 1977. "The Police of Eighteenth-Century France." *European Studies Review* 7: 47–75.

———. 1981. *Crime and Repression in the Auvergne and the Guyenne, 1720–1790*. Cambridge, MA: Cambridge University Press.

Campbell, Anne. 1986. "The Streets and Violence." In Anne Campbell and John J. Gibbs (eds.), *Violent Transactions: The Limits of Personality*, 115–132. Oxford: Blackwell.

Centerwall, Brandon S. 1984. "Race, Socioeconomic Status and Domestic Homicide, Atlanta, 1971–2." *American Journal of Public Health* 74:813–15.

Chambliss, William J. 1964. "A Sociological Analysis of the Law of Vagrancy." *Social Problems* 12:67–77.

———. 1973. "The Saints and the Roughnecks." *Society* 11(1):24–31.

Chesnais, Jean-Claude. 1975. *Les Morts Violentes en France Depuis 1826*. Paris: Presses Universitaires de France.

———. 1981. *Histoire de la Violence en Occident de 1800 à nos jours*. Paris: R. Lafont.

Chevalier, Louis. 1973. *Laboring Classes and Dangerous Classes in Paris During the First Half of the Nineteenth Century.* Translated by Frank Jellinek. Princeton: Princeton University Press.

Chilton, Roland J. 1964. "Continuity in Delinquency Area Research: A Comparison of Studies for Baltimore, Detroit and Indianapolis." *American Sociological Review* 29:71–83.

Chiricos, Theodore G. 1987. "Rates of Crime and Unemployment: An Analysis of Aggregate Research Evidence." *Social Problems* 34:187–212.

Chiricos, Theodore G., and Gordon P. Waldo. 1970. "Punishment and Crime: An Examination of Some Empirical Evidence." *Social Problems* 18(Fall):200–217.

Chirot, Daniel. 1985. "The Rise of the West." *American Sociological Review* 50(2):181–95.

Chodorow, Nancy. 1974. "Family Structure and Feminine Personality." In Michelle Z. Rosaldo and Louise Lamphere (eds.), *Woman, Culture and Society,* 43–66. Stanford, Stanford University Press.

Cicourel, Aaron. 1968. *The Social Organization of Juvenile Justice.* New York: John Wiley.

Clark, John P., and Richard E. Sykes. 1974. "Some Determinants of Police Organization and Practice in a Modern Industrial Democracy." In Daniel Glaser (ed.), *Handbook of Criminology,* 455–494. Chicago: Rand McNally College Publishing Company.

Clayton, Richard, and Harwin Voss. 1981. *Young Men and Drugs in Manhattan.* Washington, D.C.: U.S. Government Printing Office.

Clogg, Clifford. 1977. "Unrestricted and Restricted Maximum Likelihood Latent Structure Analysis: A Manual for Users," Working Paper No. 1977–09, Pennsylvania State University, University Park.

———. 1979. "Some Latent Structure Models for the Analysis of Likert-Type Data." *Social Science Research* 8:287–301.

———. 1981. "New Developments in Latent Structure Analysis." In D. Jackson and Edgar Borgatta (eds.). *Factor Analysis and Measurement in Social Research: A Multi-dimensional Perspective,* 215–246. Beverly Hills, CA: Sage.

Cloward, Richard and Lloyd E. Ohlin. 1960. *Delinquency and Opportunity: A Theory of Delinquent Gangs.* New York: Free Press of Glencoe.

———. 1963. *Delinquency and Opportunity: A Theory of Delinquent Gangs.* Glencoe, IL: Free Press.

Cobban, Alfred. 1961. *A History of Modern France. Volume 2: 1799–1871.* London: Penguin Books.

———. 1965. *A History of Modern France. Volume 3: 1871–1962.* New York: Penguin.

Cohen, Albert K. 1955. *Delinquent Boys: The Culture of the Gang.* Glencoe, IL: Free Press.

Cohen, David, and Eric A. Johnson. 1982. "French Criminality: Urban-Rural Differences in the Nineteenth Century." *Journal of Interdisciplinary History* XII(3):477–501.

Cohen, Lawrence E., and Marcus Felson. 1979. "Social Change and Crime Rate Trends: A Routine Activity Approach." *American Sociological Review* 44:588–608.

Cohen, Richard, and Lloyd Ohlin. 1960. *Delinquency and Opportunity.* Glencoe, IL: Free Press.

Coleman, James S. 1961. *The Adolescent Society: The Social Life of the Teenager and its Impact on Education.* New York: The Free Press of Glencoe.

———. 1987. "Norms as Social Capital." In Gerard Radnitzky and Peter Bernholz (eds.), *Economic Imperialism: The Economic Approach Applied Outside the Field of Economics*, 133–55. New York: Paragon House Publishers.

———. 1988a. "Social Capital in the Creation of Human Capital." *American Journal of Sociology* 94(Supplement):S95-S120.

———. 1988b. "The Family's Move from the Center to Periphery, and its Implications for Schooling." In Liah Greenfield and Michael Martin (eds.), *Center Ideas and Institutions*, 173–185. Chicago: University of Chicago Press.

———. 1990. *Foundations of Social Theory.* Cambridge, MA: Harvard University Press.

Coleman, James W. 1989. *The Criminal Elite: The Sociology of White Collar Crime.* New York: St. Martin's Press.

Collins, James. 1981. *Drinking and Crime.* New York: Guilford Press.

Colvin, Mark, and John Pauly. 1983. "A Critique of Criminology: Toward an Integrated Structural-Marxist Theory of Delinquency Production." *American Journal of Sociology* 89:513–551.

Corsaro, William A., and Thomas A. Rizzo. 1990. "An Interpretive Approach to Childhood Socialization." *American Sociological Review* 55:466–468.

Coser, R. 1985. "Power Lost and Status Gained." Paper presented at the meeting of the American Sociological Association, Washington, DC.

Croall, Hazel. 1989. "Who is the White-Collar Criminal?" *British Journal of Criminology* 29:157–174.

Cullen, Francis T., Martha Todd Larson, and Richard A. Mathers. 1985. "Having Money and Delinquency Involvement: The Neglect of Power in Delinquency Theory." *Criminal Justice and Behavior* 12:171–92.

Curtis, Lynn. 1975. *Violence, Race, and Culture.* Lexington, MA: Lexington Books.

Davis, Natalie. 1975. *Society and Culture in Early Modern France.* Stanford: Stanford University Press.

Davidovitch, Andre. 1961. "Criminalité et répression en France depuis un siècle: 1851–1952." *Review Francaise de Sociologie* II:30–49.

Davis, Natalie. 1975. *Society and Culture in Early Modern France.* Stanford: Stanford University Press.

Defoe, Daniel. 1730. *An Effectual Scheme for the Immediate Prevention of Street Robberies and Suppressing of All Other Disorders of the Night.* London.

Dembo, Richard, Linda Williams, Werner Wothke, James Schmeidler, Alan Getreu, Estrellita Berry, and Eric Wish. 1992. "The Generality of Deviance: Replication of a Structural Model Among High Risk Youths." *Journal of Research in Crime and Delinquency* 29:200–216.

Dhrymes, Phoebus J. 1971. *Distributed Lags: Problems of Estimation and Formulation.* San Francisco: Holden-Day.

DiMaggio, Paul. 1987. "Classification in Art." *American Sociological Review* 52:440–55.

DiMaggio, Paul, and John Mohr. 1985. "Cultural Capital, Educational Attainment, and Marital Selection." *American Journal of Sociology* 90(6):1231–61.

Dixon, Jo, and Alan Lizotte. 1987. "Gun Ownership and the 'Southern Subculture of Violence'." *American Journal of Sociology* 93:383–405.

Donovan, James. 1981. "Justice Unblind: The Juries and the Criminal Classes in France, 1825–1914." *Journal of Social History* 15(1):89–107.

Donovan, John E., and Richard Jessor. 1985. "Structure of Problem Behavior in Adolescence and Young Adulthood." *Journal of Consulting and Clinical Psychology* 53:890–904.

Duncan, Otis Dudley. 1975. *Introduction to Structural Equation Models*. New York: Academic Press.

———. 1984. "Measurement and Structure: Strategies for Design and Analysis of Subjective Survey Data." In Charles Turner and Elizabeth Martin (eds.), *Surveying Subjective Phenomena*, 1: 179–230. New York: Russell Sage.

Durkheim, Émile. (1893) 1964. *The Division of Labor in Society*. New York: The Free Press of Glencoe.

Eco, Umberto. 1983. *The Name of the Rose*. San Diego: Harcourt Brace Jovanovich.

Elias, Norbert. (1939) 1978. *The Civilizing Process: The History of Manners*. New York: Pantheon Books.

———. (1939) 1982. *The Civilizing Process: Power and Civility*. New York: Pantheon Books.

———. (1969) 1983. *The Court Society*. Oxford: B. Blackwell.

Elliott, Delbert S., and Suzanne S. Ageton. 1980. "Reconciling Race and Class Differences in Self-Reported and Official Estimates of Delinquency." *American Sociological Review* 45:95–110.

Elliott, Delbert, and David Huizinga. 1984. *The Relationship Between Delinquent Behavior and ADM Problems*. Boulder, CO: Behavioral Research Institute.

Elliott, Delbert, David Huizinga, and Suzanne Ageton. 1985. *Explaining Delinquency and Drug Use*. Beverly Hills, CA: Sage.

Elliott, Delbert, David Huizinga, and Scott Menard. 1989. *Multiple Problem Youth: Delinquency, Substance Use, and Mental Health Problems*. New York: Springer-Verlag.

Ellison, Christopher. 1991. "An Eye for an Eye? A Note on the Southern Subculture of Violence Thesis." *Social Forces* 69(4):1223–1239.

Ellsworth, P.C. 1988. "Unpleasant Facts: The Supreme Court's Response to Empirical Research on Capital Punishment." In K.C. Haas and I. Inciardi, eds., *Challenging Capital Punishment*. Newbury Park, CA: Sage.

Empey, LaMar Taylor. 1982. *American Delinquency, Its Meaning and Construction*. Homewood, IL: Dorsey Press.

Emsley, Clive. 1983. *Policing and Its Context, 1750–1870*. London: Macmillan.

England, Ralph. 1960. "A Theory of Middle Class Juvenile Delinquency." *Journal of Criminal Law, Criminology, and Police Science* 50:535–540.

Erlanger, Howard S. 1974. "The Empirical Status of the Subculture of Violence Thesis." *Social Problems* 22:280–292.

———. 1975. "Is There a 'Subculture of Violence' in the South?" *The Journal of Criminal Law & Criminology* 66(4):483–490.

Etzioni, Amitai. 1975. *A Comparative Analysis of Complex Organizations: On Power, Involvement, and Their Correlation*. New York: The Free Press.

Fagan, Jeffrey. 1990. "Intoxication and Aggression." 241–320 In *Drugs and Crime*, Michael Tonry and James Q. Wilson (eds.). Chicago: University of Chicago Press.

Fanning, D.M. 1967. "Families and Flats." *British Medical Journal* 18:382–6.

Farnworth, Margaret, Terence Thornberry, Marvin Krohn, and Alan Lizotte. 1994. "Measurement in the Study of Class and Delinquency: Integrating Theory and Research." *Journal of Research in Crime and Delinquency* 31:32–61.

Farrington, David. 1979. "Longitudinal Research on Crime and Delinquency." In Norval Morris and Michael Tonry (eds.). *Crime and Justice: An Annual Review of Research.* 1: 289–348. Chicago: University of Chicago Press.

Farrington, David, Bernard Gallagher, Lynda Morley, Raymond St. Ledger, and Donald J. West. 1986. "Unemployment, School Leaving and Crime." *British Journal of Criminology* 26:335–56.

Feeley, Malcolm. 1979. *The Process is the Punishment.* New York: Russell Sage.

Feeley, Malcolm, and Deborah Little. 1991. "The Vanishing Females: The Decline of Women in the Criminal Process, 1687–1912." *Law & Society Review* 25:719–757.

Felson, Richard, Allen Liska, Scott South, and Thomas McNulty. 1994. "The Subculture of Violence and Delinquency: Individual vs. School Context Effects." *Social Forces* 73:155–173.

Ferdinand, Theodore N. 1967. "The Criminal Patterns of Boston Since 1849." *American Journal of Sociology* 73:84–99.

Firebaugh, Glenn, and Jack P. Gibbs. 1985. "User's Guide to Ratio Variables." *American Sociological Review* 50:713–722.

———. 1987. "Defensible and Indefensible Commentaries." *American Sociological Review* 52:136–141.

Fischer, Claude S. 1975. "Toward a Subcultural Theory of Urbanism." *American Journal of Sociology* 80:1319–1341.

———. 1976. *The Urban Experience.* San Diego: Harcourt Brace & Jovanovich.

———. 1980. "The Spread of Violent Crime from City to Countryside, 1955 to 1975." *Rural Sociology* 45:416–434.

———. 1984. *The Urban Experience* (2d ed.). San Diego: Harcourt Brace Jovanovich.

Foucault, Michel. 1973. *Moi, Pierre Rivière, Ayant Égorgé ma Mère, ma Soeur et mon Frère* Paris: Gallimard.

———. 1975. *Surveiller et Punir: Naissance de la Prison.* Paris: Gallimard.

France, Ministère de l'économie nationale. *Annuaire Statistique.* Paris: L'Imprimerie nationale.

France, Ministère de la Justice. *Compte général de l'administration de la justice criminelle en France, 1853–1913.* Paris: L'Imprimerie nationale.

France, Ministère de la Justice. *Compte général de l'administration de la justice criminelle en France, 1865–1913.* Paris: L'Imprimerie nationale.

Freedman, David. 1991. "Statistical Models and Shoe Leather." In Peter Marsden (ed.), *Sociological Methodology*, 291–313. Oxford: Blackwell.

Freeman, Richard B. 1987. "The Relation of Criminal Activity to Black Youth Employment." *The Review of Black Political Economy.* 16:99–107.

———. 1991. "Crime and the Economic Status of Disadvantaged Young Men." Paper presented to Conference on Urban Labor Markets and Labor Mobility. Airlie House, Virginia.

Freeman, Richard, and Harry Holzer. 1991. "The Deterioration of Employment and Earnings Opportunities for Less Educated Young Americans: A Review of

Evidence." Paper prepared for National Academy of Sciences Panel on High Risk Youth.

Frégier, H. A. 1840. *Des Classes Dangereuses de la Population dans des Grandes Villes, et des Moyens de les Rendre Meilleurs.* (2 vols.) Paris: Baillière.

Friedman, Lawrence. 1979. "Plea Bargaining in Historical Perspective." *Law and Society Review* 13:247–59.

Gans, Herbert. 1990. "Deconstructing the Under-Class: The Term's Danger as a Planning Concept." *Journal of the American Planning Association* 56(Summer):271–7.

Garland, David. 1990. *Punishment and Modern Society: A Study in Social Theory.* Oxford: Clarendon Press.

Garofalo, James. 1977. "Time: A Neglected Sociological Dimension." In Robert Meier (ed.), *Theory in Criminology*, 93–116. Beverly Hills, CA: Sage.

Gastil, Raymond. 1971. "Homicide and a Regional Culture of Violence." *American Sociological Review* 36:412–427.

Gatrell, V.A.C. 1980. "The Decline of Theft and Violence in Victorian and Edwardian England." In V.A.C. Gatrell, B. Lenman and G. Parker (eds.). *Crime and the Law: History of Crime and the Law in Western Europe since 1500.* London: Europa Publications.

Gaylord, Mark, and John Galliher. 1988. *The Criminology of Edwin Sutherland.* New Brunswick, NJ: Transaction Books.

Gibbons, Don. 1965. *Changing the Lawbreaker: The Treatment of Delinquents and Criminals.* Englewood Cliffs, NJ: Prentice-Hall.

Gibbs, Jack P. 1978. "Deterrence, Penal Policy, and the Sociology of Law." *Research in Law and Sociology* 1:101–114.

———. 1989. *Control: Sociology's Central Notion.* Urbana: University of Illinois Press.

Gibbs, Jack, and Maynard Erickson. 1976. "Crime Rates of American Cities in an Ecological Context." *American Journal of Sociology* 82:605–620.

Giddens, Anthony. 1981a. *A Contemporary Critique of Historical Materialism, Volume 1.* London: Macmillan.

———. 1982. *Sociology: A Brief But Critical Introduction.* New York: Harcourt Brace Jovanovich.

———. 1981b. *The Nation-State and Violence. Volume 2 of A Contemporary Critique of Historical Materialism.* Cambridge, MA: Polity Press.

———. 1985. *The Nation-State and Violence.* Cambridge, MA: Polity Press.

Gilligan, Carol. 1982. *In a Different Voice.* Cambridge, MA: Harvard University Press.

Gilligan, Carol, Janie Ward, Jill Taylor, and Betty Bardige. 1988. *Mapping the Moral Domain.* Cambridge, MA: Harvard University Press.

Gillis, A.R. 1977. "High-Rise Housing and Psychological Strain." *Journal of Health and Social Behavior* 18(4):418–31.

———. 1987. "Crime, Punishment, and Historical Perspectives." *Sociological Forum* 2(3):602–9.

———. 1989. "Crime and State Surveillance in 19th-Century France." *American Journal of Sociology* 95(2):307–41.

———. 1994a. "Urbanization and Urbanism." In Robert Hagedorn (ed.), *Sociology* (5th ed.), pp. 465–540. Toronto: Harcourt Brace.

———. 1994b. "Literacy and the Civilization of Violence in 19th-Century France." *Sociological Forum* 9(3):371–401.

Gillis, A.R., and John Hagan. 1982. "Density, Delinquency, and Design: Formal and Informal Control and the Built Environment." *Criminology* 19(4):514–29.

———. 1990. "Delinquent Samaritans: Network Structure, Social Conflict, and the Willingness to Intervene." *Journal of Research in Crime and Delinquency* 27(1):30–51.

Given, James B. 1977. *Society and Homicide in Thirteenth-Century England*. Stanford, CA: Stanford University Press.

Glueck, Sheldon, and Eleanor Glueck. 1950. *Unraveling Juvenile Delinquency*. New York: Commonwealth Fund.

———. 1968. *Delinquents and Nondelinquents in Perspective*. Cambridge, MA: Harvard University Press.

Goody, Jack. 1977. *The Domestication of the Savage Mind*. Cambridge, MA: Cambridge University Press.

Gordon, Milton M. 1947. "The Concept of the Subculture and its Application." *Social Forces* 26:40–42.

Gottfredson, Michael R., and Travis Hirschi. 1987. "The Methodological Adequacy of Longitudinal Research on Crime." *Criminology* 25:581–614.

———. 1990. *A General Theory of Crime*. Stanford: Stanford University Press.

Granovetter, Mark. 1985. "Economic Action and Social Structure: The Problem of Embeddedness." *American Journal of Sociology* 91:481–510.

Grasmick, Harold, John Hagan, Brenda Sims Blackwell, and Bruce Arnekiev. 1996. "Risk Preferences and Patriarchy: Extending Power-Control Theory." *Social Forces*, Forthcoming.

Greenberg, David F. 1979. *Mathematical Criminology*. New Brunswick, NJ: Rutgers University Press.

———. 1985. "Age, Crime and Social Explanation." *American Journal of Sociology* 91:1–21.

Greenberg, Stephanie, and Freda Adler. 1974. "Crime and Addiction: An Empirical Analysis of the Literature, 1920–1973." *Contemporary Drug Problems* 3:221–269.

Griffin, Larry J. 1992. "Temporality, Events, and Explanation in Historical Sociology: An Introduction." *Sociological Methods and Research* 20(4):403–27.

———. 1993. "Narrative, Event-Structure Analysis, and Causal Interpretation in Historical Sociology." *American Journal of Sociology* 98(5):1094–1133.

Griffin, Larry J., and Larry W. Isaac. 1992. "Recursive Regression and the Historical Use of 'Time' in Time-Series Analyses of Historical Processes." *Historical Methods* 25(4): 166–179.

Grogger, Jeff. 1991. "The Effect of Arrest on the Employment Outcomes of Young Men." Unpublished Manuscript, University of California at Santa Barbara.

Gurr, Ted Robert. 1976. *Rogues, Rebels, and Reformers: A Political History of Urban Crime and Conflict*. Beverly Hills, CA: Sage.

———. 1979. "On the History of Violent Crime in Europe and America." In D. Graham and T.R. Gurr (eds.), *Violence in America: Historical and Comparative Perspectives*, 353–74. Beverly Hills, CA: Sage.

———. 1981. "Historical Trends in Violent Crime: a Critical Review of the Evidence." *Crime and Justice: An Annual Review of Research* 3:295–353.

———. 1989. "Historical Trends in Violent Crime: Europe and the United States." In Ted Robert Gurr (ed.), *Violence in America: The History of Crime*, 21–54. Newbury Park, CA: Sage.

Gurr, Ted Robert, Peter N. Grabosky, and Richard C. Hula. 1977. *The Politics of Crime and Conflict: A Comparative History of Four Cities*. Beverly Hills, CA: Sage.

Hackney, Sheldon. 1969. "Southern Violence." *American Historical Review* 74:906–925.

Hagan, John. 1985. *Modern Criminology: Crime, Criminal Behavior, and its Control*. New York: McGraw-Hill.

———. 1989. *Structural Criminology*. New Brunswick, NJ: Rutgers University Press.

———. 1991a. *The Disreputable Pleasures: Crime and Deviance in Canada*. (3rd ed.). Toronto: McGraw-Hill.

———. 1991b. "Destiny and Drift: Subcultural Preferences, Status Attainments, and the Risks and Rewards of Youth." *American Sociological Review* 56:567–582.

———. 1993. "The Social Embeddedness of Crime and Unemployment." *Criminology* 31:465–91.

Hagan, John, and Celesta Albonetti. 1982. "Race, Class and the Perception of Criminal Injustice in America." *American Journal of Sociology* 88:329–55.

Hagan, John, and Kristin Bumiller. 1983. "Making Sense of Sentencing: A Review and Critique of Sentencing Research." In Alfred Blumstein, Jacqueline Cohen, Susan E. Martin, and Michael H. Tonry (eds.). *Research on Sentencing: The Search for Reform*. 2: 1–54. Washington, DC: National Academy Press.

Hagan, John, and Fiona Kay. 1990. "Gender and Delinquency in White-Collar Families: A Power-Control Perspective." *Crime and Delinquency* 36:391–407.

Hagan, John, and Bill McCarthy. 1992. "Streetlife and Delinquency: The Significance of a Missing Population." *British Journal of Sociology* 43:533–61.

Hagan, John, and Alberto Palloni. 1990. "The Social Reproduction of a Criminal Class in Working Class London, Circa 1950–80." *American Journal of Sociology* 96:265–99.

Hagan, John, and Patricia Parker. 1985. "White Collar Crime and Punishment: The Class Structure and Legal Sanctioning of Securities Violations." *American Sociological Review* 50:302–16.

Hagan, John, A.R. Gillis, and Janet Chan. 1978. "Explaining Official Delinquency: A Spatial Study of Class, Conflict, and Control." *Sociological Quarterly* 19:386–98.

Hagan, John, A.R. Gillis, and John Simpson. 1985. "The Class Structure of Gender and Delinquency: Toward a Power-Control Theory of Common Delinquent Behavior." *American Journal of Sociology* 90:1151–78.

———. 1987. "Class in the Household: A Power-Control Theory of Gender and Delinquency." *American Journal of Sociology* 92:788–816.

———. 1990. "Clarifying and Extending Power-Control Theory." *American Journal of Sociology* 95:1024–37.

Hagan, John, Edward Silva, and John Simpson. 1977. "Conflict and Consensus in the Designation of Deviance." *Social Forces* 56:320–340.

Hagan, John, John Simpson, and A.R Gillis. 1979. "The Sexual Stratification of Social Control: A Gender-Based Perspective on Crime and Delinquency." *British Journal of Sociology* 30(1):25–38.

Hagedorn, John. 1988. *People and Folks: Gangs, Crime and the Underclass in a Rust-belt City*. Chicago: Lake View Press.

Haller, Mark. 1970. "Urban Crime and Criminal Justice: The Chicago Case." *Journal of American History* 57:619–35.

Hannan, Michael. 1971. *Aggregation and Disaggregation in Sociology*. Lexington, MA: Lexington Books.

Hannerz, Ulf. 1969. "Roots of Black Manhood." *Transaction* 6:112–121.

Harrison, Lana, and Joseph Gfroerer. 1992. "The Intersection of Drug Use and Criminal Behavior: Results from the National Household Survey on Drug Abuse." *Crime and Delinquency* 38:422–443.

Hay, Douglas. 1975. "Property, Authority and the Criminal Law." In Douglas Hay et al. (eds.) *Albion's Fatal Tree: Crime and Society in Eighteenth-Century England*, 17–64. New York: Pantheon Books.

Hebdige, Dick. 1976. "The Meaning of Mod." In Stuart Hall and Tony Jefferson (eds.). *Resistance Through Rituals: Youth Subcultures in Post-War Britain*, 87–96. London: Hutchinson.

Henry, Andrew, and James Short. 1954. *Suicide and Homicide: Some Economic, Sociological and Psychological aspects of Aggression*. Glencoe, IL: Free Press.

Henslin, James, and Larry Reynolds. 1979. *Social Problems in American Society*. Boston: Allyn and Bacon.

Heumann, Milton. 1975. "A Note on Plea Bargaining and Case Pressure." *Law and Society Review* 9:515–28.

Heuser, J. 1979. *Are Status Offenders Really Different?* Salem, OR: Oregon Law Enforcement Council.

Higgins, Paul, and Gary Albrecht. 1981. "Cars and Kids: A Self-Report Study of Juvenile Auto Theft and Traffic Violations." *Sociology and Social Research* 66:29–41.

Hindelang, Michael J. 1971. "Age, Sex, and the Versatility of Delinquent Involvements." *Social Problems* 18:522–535.

Hindelang, Michael, Travis Hirschi, and Joseph Weis. 1981. *Measuring Delinquency*. Beverly Hills, CA: Sage.

Hirschi, Travis. 1969. *Causes of Delinquency*. Berkeley: University of California Press.

———. 1972. "Social Class and Crime." In Gerald W. Thielbar and Saul D. Feldman (eds.), *Issues in Social Inequality*, 503–20. Boston: Little, Brown.

———. 1984. "A Brief Commentary on Akers' 'Delinquent Behavior, Drugs, and Alcohol: What is the Relationship?'." *Today's Delinquent* 3:49–52.

Hirschi, Travis, and Michael Gottfredson. 1983. "Age and the Explanation of Crime." *American Journal of Sociology* 89:552–584.

———. 1986. "The Distinction Between Crime and Criminality." In Timothy Hartnagel and Robert Silverman (eds.). *Critique and Explanation: Essays in Honor of Gwynn Nettler*, 55–69. New Brunswick, NJ: Transaction.

———. 1987. "Causes of White Collar Crime." *Criminology* 25:949–974.

———. 1989. "The Significance of White-Collar Crime for a General Theory of Crime." *Criminology* 27:359–371.

———, (eds.) 1994. *The Generality of Deviance*. New Brunswick, NJ: Transaction.

Hirschi, Travis, and Hanan Selvin. 1967. *Delinquency Research: An Appraisal of Analytic Methods*. New York: Free Press.

Hirschman, Albert O. 1977. *The Passions and the Interests: Political Arguments for Capitalism Before its Triumph*. Princeton, NJ: Princeton University Press.

Hobsbawm, Eric J. 1975. *The Age of Capital, 1848–1875*. London: Weidenfeld & Nicolson.

Hohenberg, Paul M., and Lynn Hollen Lees. 1985. *The Making of Urban Europe, 1000–1950*. Cambridge, MA: Harvard University Press.

Howell, Joseph T. 1973. *Hard Living on Clay Street: Portraits of Blue Collar Families*. Garden City, NY: Anchor Press.

Hser, Yih-Ing, Chih-Ping Chou, and M. Douglas Anglin. 1990. "The Criminality of Female Narcotics Addicts: A Causal Modeling Approach." *Journal of Quantitative Criminology* 6:207–228.

Huff-Corzine, Lin, Jay Corzine, and David Moore. 1991. "Deadly Connections: Culture, Poverty, and the Direction of Lethal Violence." *Social Forces* 69(3):715–732.

Huizinga, David, and Delbert Elliott. 1981. *A Longitudinal Study of Drug Use and Delinquency in a National Sample of Youth: An Assessment of Causal Order*. Boulder, CO: Behavioral Research Institute.

Huizinga, Johan. 1924. *The Waning of the Middle Ages*. London: E. Arnold.

Hull, N.E.H. 1987. *Female Felons: Women and Serious Crime in Colonial Massachusetts*. Urbana, IL: University of Illinois Press.

Hunt, Dana. 1990. "Drugs and Consensual Crimes: Drug Dealing and Prostitution." 159–202 In *Drugs and Crime*, Michael Tonry and James Q. Wilson (eds.). Chicago: University of Chicago Press.

Ignatieff, Michael A. 1978. *A Just Measure of Pain: The Penitentiary in the Industrial Revolution, 1750–1850*. New York: Pantheon Books.

Irwin, John. 1985. *The Jail: Managing the Underclass in American Society*. Berkeley: University of California Press.

Isaac, Larry W., and L.J. Griffin. 1989. "Ahistoricism in Time-series Analyses of Historical Processes: Critique, Redirection, and Illustrations from U.S. Labor History." *American Sociological Review* 54: 873–890.

Jackson, Margaret A., and Curt T. Griffiths. 1991. *Canadian Criminology: Perspectives on Crime and Criminality*. Toronto: Harcourt Brace Jovanovich.

Jacobs, Jane. 1961. *The Death and Life of Great American Cities*. New York: Random House.

Jencks, Christopher, and Susan E. Mayer. 1990. "The Social Consequences of Growing Up in a Poor Neighborhood." In Laurence Lynn and Michael McGeary (eds.), *Inner-City Poverty in the United States*, 111–186. Washington, DC: National Academy Press.

Jensen, Gary F., and Raymond Eve. 1976. "Sex Differences in Delinquency." *Criminology* 13:427–448.

Jensen, Gary, and Dean Rojek. 1980. *Delinquency: A Sociological View*. Lexington, MA: DC Heath.

Jensen, Gary, and Kevin Thompson. 1990. "What's Class Got To Do With It? A Further Examination of Power-Control Theory." *American Journal of Sociology* 95:1009–1023.

Jessor, Richard, John Donovan, and Frances Costa. 1991. *Beyond Adolescence: Problem Behavior and Young Adult Development.* New York: Cambridge University Press.

Johnson, R.E. 1980. "Social Class and Delinquent Behavior: A New Test." *Criminology* 18:86–93.

Johnston, John. 1984. *Econometric Methods* (3rd ed.). New York: McGraw-Hill.

Johnston, Lloyd. 1973. *Drugs and American Youth: A Report from the Youth in Transition Project.* Ann Arbor, MI: Institute for Social Research, University of Michigan.

Johnston, Lloyd, Patrick O'Malley, and Leslie Eveland. 1978. "Drugs and Delinquency: A Search for Causal Connection." In Denise Kandel (ed.), *Longitudinal Research on Drug Use: Empirical Findings and Methodological Issues*, 137–156. Washington, DC: Hemisphere.

Joreskog, Karl G., and Dag Sorbom. 1984. *LISREL VI: Analysis of Linear Structural Relationships by Maximum Likelihood, Instrumental Variables, and Least Squares Methods.* 3rd Edition. Uppsala, Sweden: University of Uppsala.

Kandel, Denise, and R. Faust. 1975. "Sequences and Stages in Patterns of Adolescent Drug Use." *Archives of General Psychiatry* 32:923–932.

Kandel, Denise, and Kazuo Yamaguchi. 1987. "Job Mobility and Drug Use: An Event History Analysis." *American Journal of Sociology* 92(4):836–878.

Kandel, Denise, Ronald Kessler, and Rebecca Marguiles. 1978. "Antecedents of Adolescent Initiation into Stages of Drug Use: A Developmental Analysis." In Denise Kandel (ed.) *Longitudinal Research on Drug Use*, 73–100. Washington DC: Hemisphere.

Katz, Jack. 1988. *The Seductions of Crime: Moral and Sensual Attractions in Doing Evil.* New York: Basic Books.

Keane, C., A.R. Gillis, and John Hagan. 1989. "Deterrence and Amplification of Juvenile Delinquency by Police Contact: The Importance of Gender and Risk-orientation." *British Journal of Criminology* 29(4): 336–52.

Keen, Maurice H. 1990. *English Society in the Later Middle Ages, 1348–1500.* London: Penguin.

Kempf, Kimberly. 1987. "Specialization and the Criminal Career." *Criminology* 25:399–420.

Kennedy, Leslie, and Stephen Baron. 1995. "Routine Activities and a Subculture of Violence." In James Creechan and Robert Silverman, (eds.), *Canadian Delinquency*, 209–225. Scarborough, Canada: Prentice-Hall.

Kim, Jae-on, and Charles Mueller. 1978. *Factor Analysis: Statistical Methods and Practical Issues.* Beverly Hills, CA: Sage.

Kiser, Edgar, and Michael Hechter. 1991. "The Role of General Theory in Comparative-Historical Sociology." *American Journal of Sociology* 97(1):1–30.

Kleck, Gary, and Karen McElrath. 1991. "The Effects of Weaponry on Human Violence." *Social Forces* 69(3): 669–692.

Klein, Malcolm. 1971. *Street Gangs and Street Workers.* Englewood Cliffs, NJ: Prentice-Hall.

———. 1979. *American Juvenile Justice: Trends, Assumptions and Data.* Los Angeles: Regional Institute in Law and Mental Health.

———. 1984. "Offense Specialization and Versatility among Juveniles." *British Journal of Criminology* 24:185–194.

Kmenta, Jan. 1971. *Elements of Econometrics*. New York: Macmillan.

———. 1986. *Elements of Econometrics* (2nd ed.). New York: Macmillan.

Kornhauser, Ruth R. 1978. *Social Sources of Delinquency: An Appraisal of Analytic Models*. Chicago: University of Chicago Press.

Kraft, Manfred. 1987. "On 'User's Guide to Ratio Variables'." *American Sociological Review* 52:135–141.

Krohn, Marvin, William Skinner, James Massey, and Michelle Naughton. 1986. "Adolescent Cigarette Use." *Advances in Adolescent Mental Health* 1:147–94.

Lane, Roger. 1967. *Policing the City: Boston 1822–1885*. Cambridge, MA: Harvard University Press.

———. 1974. "Crime and the Industrial Revolution: British and American Views." *Journal of Social History* 287–303.

———. 1979. *Violent Death in the City: Suicide, Accident and Murder in Nineteenth-Century Philadelphia*. Cambridge, MA: Harvard University Press.

———. 1980. "Urban Homicide in the Nineteenth Century: Some Lessons for the Twentieth." In James A. Inciardi and Charles E. Faupel (eds.), *History and Crime: Implications for Criminal Justice Policy*, 91–109. Beverly Hills, CA: Sage.

———. 1989. "On the Social Meaning of Homicide Trends in America." In Ted Robert Gurr (ed.), *Violence in America: The History of Crime*, 55–79 . Newbury Park, CA: Sage.

Langbein, John. 1983. "Shaping the Eighteenth-Century Criminal Trial: A View from the Ryder Sources." *University of Chicago Law Review* 50:1–136.

Lauritsen, Janet, Robert Sampson, and John Laub. 1991. "The Link Between Offending and Victimization Among Adolescents." *Criminology* 29:265–292.

Lazarsfeld, Paul F., and Neil Henry. 1968. *Latent Structure Analysis*. Boston: Houghton Mifflin.

Lebigre, Arlette. 1979. "La naissance de la police en France." *L'histoire* 5–12.

LeBlanc, Marc, Gilles Cote, and Rolf Loeber. 1991. "Temporal Paths in Delinquency: Stability, Regression, and Progression Analyzed with Panel Data from an Adolescent and a Delinquent Male Sample." *Canadian Journal of Criminology* 33:23–44.

LeGoff, T.J.A., and D.M.G. Sutherland. 1974. "The Revolution and the Rural Community in Eighteenth Century Brittany." *Past and Present* 62:96–119.

Lemann, N. 1986. "The Origins of the Underclass." *The Atlantic* Part 1 June: 31–55, Part 2 July: 54–68.

Lerman, Paul. 1968. "Individual Values, Peer Values and Subcultural Delinquency." *American Sociological Review* 33:219–235.

Lever, Janet. 1976. "Sex Differences in the Games Children Play." *Social Problems* 23:478–487.

Lewis, Oscar. 1966. *La Vida: A Puerto Rican Family in the Culture of Poverty*. New York: Random House.

Lieberson, Stanley. 1980. *A Piece of the Pie: Black and White Immigrants Since 1880*. Berkeley: University of California Press.

———. 1985. *Making it Count: The Improvement of Social Research and Theory*. Berkeley: University of California Press.

Liebow, Elliot. 1967. *Tally's Corner: A Study of Negro Street-Corner Men*. Boston: Little, Brown and Company.

Liska, Allen. 1973. "Causal Structures Underlying the Relationship Between Delinquent Involvement and Delinquent Peers." *Sociology and Social Research* 58:23–26.

Lodhi, Abdul Q., and Charles Tilly. 1973. "Urbanization, Crime and Collective Violence in 19th Century France." *American Journal of Sociology* 79:296–318.

Loeber, Rolf, and Marc LeBlanc. 1990. "Toward a Developmental Criminology." In Michael Tonry and Norval Morris (eds.) *Crime and Justice: An Annual Review of Research*. 12: 375–473. Chicago: University of Chicago Press.

Loftin, Colin, and Robert Hill. 1974. "Regional Subculture and Homicide: An Examination of the Gastil-Hackney Thesis." *American Sociological Review* 39:714–724.

Loftin, Colin, and David McDowall. 1982. "The Police, Crime and Economic Theory: An Assessment." *American Sociological Review* 47:393–401.

Lowry, Philip, Susan Hassig, Robert Gunn, and Joyce Mathison. 1988. "Homicide Victims in New Orleans: Recent Trends." *American Journal of Epidemiology* 128:1130–36.

Luckenbill, David. 1984. "Murder and Assault." 19–45 in *Major Forms of Crime*, Robert Meier (ed.). Beverly Hills: Sage.

Lyman, J.L. 1964. "The Metropolitan Police Act of 1829." *Journal of Criminal Law, Criminology and Police Science* 55:141–154.

MacAulay, Stewart. 1963. "Non-Contractual Relations in Business: A Preliminary Study." *American Sociological Review* 28:55–67.

Maddox, George L., and B. McCall. 1964. *Drinking Among Teenagers*. New Brunswick, NJ: Rutgers Center of Alcohol Studies.

Magraw, Roger. 1983. *France 1814–1915: the Bourgeois Century*. London: Fontana.

Makkai, Toni, and John Braithwaite. 1991. "Criminological Theories and Regulatory Compliance." *Criminology* 29:191–220.

Marcos, Anastasios, Stephen Bahr, and Richard Johnson. 1986. "Test of a Bonding/Association Theory of Adolescent Drug Use." *Social Forces* 65:135–161.

Mare, Robert D., and Christopher Winship. 1991. "Loglinear Models for Reciprocal and Other Simultaneous Effects." 199–234 in *Sociological Methodology*, Peter Marsden (ed.). Oxford: Blackwell.

Marks, Carole. 1991. "The Urban Underclass." *Annual Review of Sociology* 17:445–66.

Marx, Karl. [1867–95] 1965. *Capital: A Critical Analysis of Capitalist Production*. New York: International.

Masaryk, Thomas G. [1881] 1970. *Suicide and the Meaning of Civilization*. Chicago: University of Chicago Press.

Matsueda, Ross. 1982. "Testing Control Theory and Differential Association: A Causal Modeling Approach." *American Sociological Review* 47:489–504.

———. 1989. "The Dynamics of Moral Beliefs and Minor Deviance." *Social Forces* 68(2):428–457.

Matsueda, Ross, and Karen Heimer. 1987. "Race, Family Structure and Delinquency: A Test of Differential Association and Social Control Theories." *American Sociological Review* 52:826–40.

Matza, David. 1964. *Delinquency and Drift.* New York: Wiley.

———. 1966. "The Disreputable Poor." In Reinhard Bendix and Seymour M. Lipset (eds.), *Class, Status and Power*, pp. 289–302. New York: Free Press.

———. 1969. *Becoming Deviant.* Englewood Cliffs, NJ: Prentice-Hall.

McBride, Duane C., and Clyde B. McCoy. 1981. "Crime and Drug-Using Behavior." *Criminology* 19:281–302.

McCleary, Richard, Barbara C. Nienstedt, and James M. Erven. 1982. "Uniform Crime Reports as Organizational Outcomes: Three Time Series Experiments." *Social Problems* 29(4):361–372.

McCleary, Robert, and R.A. Hay, Jr. 1980. *Applied Time Series Analysis for the Social Sciences.* Beverly Hills, CA: Sage.

McCutcheon, Allan L. 1987. *Latent Class Analysis.* Beverly Hills, CA: Sage.

McEvedy, Colin. 1988. "The Bubonic Plague." *Scientific American* 258(2): 118–23.

McGlothlin, William, M. Douglas Anglin, and Bruce Wilson. 1978. "Narcotic Addiction and Crime." *Criminology* 16:293–315.

McNally, Raymond T., and Radu Florescu. 1972. *In Search of Dracula: A True History of Dracula and Vampire Legends.* Greenwich, CN: New York Graphics Society.

McNeill, William H. 1976. *Plagues and Peoples.* Garden City, NY: Anchor Press.

McQuillan, Kevin. 1984. "Modes of Production and Demographic Patterns in Nineteenth-Century France." *American Journal of Sociology* 89(6): 1324–46.

Merton, Robert K. 1938. "Social Structure and Anomie." *American Sociological Review* 3:672–82.

Messner, Steven. 1983. "Regional and Racial Effects on the Urban Homicide Rate: The Subculture of Violence Revisited." *American Journal of Sociology* 88(5): 997–1007.

Messner, Steven, and Judith R. Blau. 1987. "Routine Leisure Activities and Rates of Crime: A Macro-level Analysis." *Social Forces* 65:1035–1052.

Messner, Steven, and Marvin Krohn. 1990. "Class, Compliance Structures, and Delinquency: Assessing Integrated Structural-Marxist Theory." *American Journal of Sociology* 96:300–328.

Milgram, S. 1970. "The Experience of Living in Cities." *Science* 167(3924): 1461–1468.

Miller, Walter B. 1958. "Lower Class Culture as a Generating Milieu of Gang Delinquency." *Journal of Social Issues* 14(3): 5–19.

Mills, C. Wright. 1942. "The Professional Ideology of Social Pathologists." *American Journal of Sociology* 49:165–80.

Mitchell, R.E. 1971. "Some Social Implications of High Density Housing." *American Sociological Review* 36:18–29.

Mizruchi, Ephraim H., and Robert Perrucci. 1962. "Norm Qualities and Differential Effects of Deviant Behavior: An Exploratory Analysis." *American Sociological Review* 27:391–399.

Moch, Leslie Page. 1983. *Paths to the City: Regional Migration in Nineteenth-Century France.* Beverly Hills, CA: Sage.

Monkkonen, Eric H. 1975. *The Dangerous Class: Crime and Poverty in Columbus, Ohio, 1860–1885.* Cambridge, MA: Harvard University Press.

———. 1981. *Police in Urban America, 1860–1920*. New York: Cambridge University Press.

———. 1988. *America Becomes Urban: The Development of U.S. Cities and Towns, 1780–1980*. Berkely: University of California Press.

———. 1989. "Diverging Homicide Rates: England and the United States, 1850–1875." In Ted Robert Gurr (ed.), *Violence in America: The History of Crime*, 80–191. Newbury Park, CA: Sage.

Monroe, Sylvester, and Peter Goldman. 1988. *Brothers: Black and Poor—A True Story of Courage and Survival*. New York: Morrow.

Moore, Joan W. 1991. *Going Down to the Barrio: Homeboys and Homegirls in Change*. Philadelphia: Temple University Press.

Morash, Merry, and Meda Chesney-Lind. 1991. "A Reformulation and Partial Test of the Power-Control Theory of Delinquency." *Justice Quarterly*. 8:347–377.

Mumford, Lewis. 1961. *The City in History: Its Origin, Its Transformation, and Its Prospects*. New York: Harcourt, Brace, and World.

———. 1970. *The Myth of the Machine: The Pentagon of Power*. New York: Harcourt Brace Jovanovich.

Munford, R.S., Ross Kazev, Roger Feldman, and Robert Stivers. 1976. "Homicide Trends in Atlanta." *Criminology* 14:213–32.

Muthen, Bengt. 1989. "Dichotomous Factor Analysis of Symptom Data." *Sociological Methods and Research* 18:19–65.

Myrdal, Gunnar. 1963. *Challenge to Affluence*. New York: Pantheon Books.

Naffine, Ngaire. 1987. *Female Crime: The Construction of Women in Criminology*. Sydney, Australia: Allen and Unwin.

Nash, George. 1976. "An Analysis of Twelve Studies of the Impact of Drug Abuse Treatment Upon Criminality." Appendix PB–259 167. Springfield, VA: National Information Service.

National Institute on Drug Abuse. 1978. "Drug Use and Crime." In Leonard Savitz and Norman Johnston (eds.), *Crime in Society*, 693–715. New York: Wiley.

Nettler, Gwynn. 1970. *Explanations*. New York: McGraw-Hill.

———. 1982. *Killing One Another*. Cincinnati, OH: Anderson.

———. 1984. *Explaining Crime* (3rd ed.). New York: McGraw-Hill.

Newman, Oscar. 1972. *Defensible Space*. New York: Macmillan.

Nurco, David, Timothy Kinlock, and Mitchell Balter. 1993. "The Severity of Preaddiction Criminal Behavior Among Urban, Male Narcotic Addicts and Two Nonaddicted Control Groups." *Journal of Research in Crime and Delinquency* 30:293–316.

Nye, Francis Ivan. 1958. *Family Relationships and Delinquent Behavior*. New York: Wiley.

Nye, F. Ivan, and James F. Short. 1957. "Scaling Delinquent Behavior." *American Sociological Review* 22:326–31.

O'Brien, Patricia. 1978. "Crime and Punishment as Historical Problem. "*Journal of Social History*. 11(June):508:520.

———. 1982. *The Promise of Punishment: Prisons in 19th-Century France*. Princeton, NJ: Princeton University Press.

Osgood, D. Wayne, Lloyd Johnston, Patrick, O'Malley, and Jerald Bachman. 1988. "The Generality of Deviance in Late Adolescence and Early Adulthood." *American Sociological Review* 53:81–93.

Ostrom, Charles W., Jr. 1978. *Time Series Analysis: Regression Techniques*. Beverly Hills, CA: Sage.

———. 1990. *Time Series Analysis: Regression Techniques* (2nd edition). Beverly Hills, CA: Sage.

Padilla, Felix M. 1992. *The Gang as an American Enterprise*. New Brunswick, NJ: Rutgers University Press.

Patterson, Gerald, and Thomas Dishion. 1985. "Contributions of Families and Peers to Delinquency." *Criminology* 23:63–79.

Paulos, John Allen. 1988. *Innumeracy: Mathematical Illiteracy and its Consequences*. New York: Hill and Wang.

Perrot, Michelle. 1975. "Délinquance et système pénitentaire en France au XIXe siècle." *Annales*, XXX:67–92.

Philips, David. 1977. *Crime and Authority in Victorian England: The Black Country 1835–1860*. London: Croom Helm.

Piliavin, Irving, and Scott Briar. 1964. "Police Encounters with Juveniles." *American Journal of Sociology* 70:206–14.

Polanyi, Karl. 1944. *The Great Transformation*. New York: Farrar & Rinehart.

Priestly, M.B. 1988. *Non-Linear and Non-Stationary Time Series Analysis*. London: Academic Press.

Prinsky, Lorraine, and Jill Rosenbaum. 1987. "'Leer-ics' or Lyrics: Teenage Impressions of Rock 'n Roll." *Youth and Society* 18:384–397.

Quetelet, Adolphe. (1842) 1969. *A Treatise on Man and the Development of his Faculties*. A facsimile reproduction by Solomon Diamond. Gainesvile, FL: Scholars' Facsimiles and Reports.

Rachal, J.V., J.R. Williams, M.L. Brehm, B. Cavanaugh, R.P. Moore, and W.C. Eckerman. 1975. *A National Study of Adolescent Behavior, Attitudes and Correlates*. Final Report to the National Institute on Alcohol Abuse and Alcoholism.

Rainwater, Lee. 1966. "Work and Identity in the Lower Class." In Sam Bass Warner (ed.) *Planning for a Nation of Cities*, 105–123. Cambridge, MA: MIT Press.

Reckless, Walter C. 1967. *The Crime Problem*. New York: Appleton-Century Crofts.

Reed, John Shelton. 1972. *The Enduring South: Subcultural Persistence in Mass Society*. Lexington, MA: Lexington.

———. 1982. *One South: An Ethnic Approach to Regional Culture*. Baton Rouge: Louisiana State University Press.

Reuter, Peter. 1983. *Disorganized Crime: The Economics of the Visible Hand*. Cambridge, MA: MIT Press.

Riesman, David. 1964. *Abundance for What?: And Other Essays*. Garden City, NY: Doubleday.

Robins, Lee. 1966. *Deviant Children Grown Up*. Baltimore: Williams and Wilkins.

Robinson, W.S. 1950. "Ecological Correlations and the Behavior of Individuals." *American Sociological Review* 15:351–7.

Rodman, Hyman. 1963. "The Lower Class Value Stretch." *Social Forces* 42:205–215.

Rojek, Dean, and Maynard Erickson. 1982. "Delinquent Careers: A Test of the Career Escalation Model." *Criminology* 20:5–28.

Rose, Dan. 1987. *Black American Street Life: South Philadelphia, 1969–1971.* Philadelphia: University of Pennsylvania Press.

Rosen, Lawrence. 1969. "Matriarchy and Lower Class Negro Male Delinquency." *Social Problems* 17:175–189.

Ross, H. Laurence. 1986. "Implications of Drinking-and-Driving Law Studies for Deterrence Theory." In Timothy F. Hartnagel and Robert A. Silverman (eds.), *Critique and Explanation: Essays in Honor on Gwynne Nettler*, 159–169. New Brunswick, NJ: Transaction.

Rossi, Peter H., Emily Waite, Christine E. Bose, and Richard E. Berk. 1974. "The Seriousness of Crimes: Normative Structure and Individual Differences." *American Sociological Review* 39:224–237.

Rudé, George F. 1964. *The Crowd in History: A Study of Popular Disturbances In France and England, 1730–1848.* New York: Wiley.

Russell, William Felton, as told to William McSweeny. 1966. *Go Up to Glory.* New York: Coward-McCann Inc.

Sampson, Robert J. 1985. "Sex Differences in Self-Reported Delinquency and Official Records: A Multiple-Group Structural Modeling Approach." *Journal of Quantitative Criminology* 1:345–367.

———. 1987. "Urban Black Violence: The Effect of Male Joblessness and Family Disruption." *American Journal of Sociology* 93:348–82.

———. 1988. "Local Friendship Ties and Community Attachment in Mass Society: A Multi-Level Systemic Model." *American Sociological Review* 53(5):766–79.

Sampson, Robert J., and W. Byron Groves. 1989. "Community Structure and Crime: Testing Social Disorganization Theory." *American Journal of Sociology* 94:774–802.

Sampson, Robert J., and John H. Laub. 1990. "Crime and Deviance over the Life Course: The Salience of Adult Social Bonds." *American Sociological Review* 55:609–27.

Sampson, Robert J., and William J. Wilson. 1995. "Toward a Theory of Race, Crime and Urban Inequality." In John Hagan and Ruth D. Peterson, (eds.), *Crime and Inequality.* Stanford, CA: Stanford University Press.

Schwartz, Richard D. and Jerome H. Skolnick. 1964. "Two Studies of Legal Stigma." In Howard Becker (ed.), *The Other Side: Perspectives on Deviance*, 103–117. New York: Free Press.

Schwendinger, Herman, and Julia Schwendinger. 1985. *Adolescent Subcultures and Delinquency.* New York: Praeger.

Sellin, Thorsten J. 1938. *Culture Conflict and Crime.* New York: Social Science Research Council.

Sellin, Thorsten, and Marvin Wolfgang. 1964. *The Measurement of Delinquency.* New York: Wiley.

———. 1969. *Delinquency: Selected Studies.* New York: Wiley.

Shannon, Lyle. 1978. "A Longitudinal Study of Delinquency and Crime." In Charles Wellford (ed.). *Quantitative Studies in Criminology*, 121–146. Beverly Hills, CA: Sage.

Sharpe, J.A. 1984. *Crime in Early Modern England 1550–1750.* London: Longman.

Shaw, Clifford R., and Henry D. MacKay. 1931. *Social Factors in Juvenile Delinquency.* Washington, DC: U.S. Government Printing Office.

———. 1942. *Juvenile Delinquency and Urban Areas.* Chicago: University of Chicago Press.

Shelley, Louise I. 1981. *Crime and Modernization: The Impact of Industrialization and Urbanization on Crime.* Carbondale, IL: Southern Illinois University Press.

Sherman, Lawrence W. 1993. "Defiance, deterrence and irrelevance: A theory of the criminal sanction." *Journal of Research in Crime and Delinquency* 30:445–73.

Short, James, Jr., and Fred Strodtbeck. 1965. *Group Process and Gang Delinquency.* Chicago: University of Chicago Press.

Shover, Neal. 1985. *Aging Criminals.* Beverly Hills, CA: Sage.

Silver, Allan. 1967. "The Demand for Order in Civil Society: A Review of Some Themes in the History of Urban Crime, Police and Riot." In David Joseph Bordua (ed.), *The Police: Six Sociological Essays,* 1–24. New York: Wiley.

Simmel, G. 1970. "The Metropolis and Mental Life." In Robert Guttman and David Popenoe (eds.), *Neighborhood, City, and Metropolis,* 777–88. New York: Random House.

Simpson, D. Dwayne, and Saul Sells. 1982. "Effectiveness of Treatment of Drug Abuse." In *Advances in Alcohol and Substance Abuse,* Vol 2. New York: Haworth.

Singer, Simon, and Murray Levine. 1988. "Power-Control Theory, Gender and Delinquency." *Criminology* 26:627–47.

Sjoberg, Gideon. 1970. "The Preindustrial City." In Robert Gutman and David Popenoe (eds.), *Neighborhood, City, and Metropolis,* 167–76. New York: Random House.

Skocpol, Theda, and Kenneth Finegold. 1982. "State Capacity and Economic Intervention in the Early New Deal." *Political Science Quarterly* 97(2): 255–278.

Skogan, W. 1989. "Social Change and the Future of Violent Crime." In Ted Robert Gurr (ed.), *Violence in America: The History of Crime,* 235–50. Newbury Park, CA: Sage.

Slovak, Jeffrey S. 1986. *Styles of Urban Policing: Organization, Environment,and Police Styles in Selected American Cities.* New York: New York University Press.

Smith, Douglas A., and Laura Davidson. 1986. "Interfacing Indicators and Constructs in Criminological Research: A Note on the Comparability of Self-Report Violence Data for Race and Sex Groups." *Criminology* 24:473–488.

Smith, Douglas A., and Christy A. Visher. 1981. "Street Level Justice: Situational Determinants of Police Arrest Decisions." *Social Problems* 29:167–77.

Smith, M. Dwayne, and Robert N. Parker. 1980. "Type of Homicide and Variation in Regional Rates." *Social Forces* 59:136–147.

Smith, R., and T. Watkins. 1976. "A Study of Addicts' Career Experiences with Methadone." *American Journal of Drug and Alcohol Abuse* 3:264.

Sorenson, Ann Marie, and David Brownfield. 1989. "Patterns of Adolescent Drug Use: Inferences from Latent Structure Analysis." *Social Science Research* 18:271–290.

Spergel, Irving. 1964. *Racketville, Slumtown, Haulburg: An Exploratory Study of Delinquent Subcultures.* Chicago: University of Chicago Press.

Stander, Julian, David Farrington, Gillian Hill, and Patricia Altham. 1989. "Markov Chain Analysis and Specialization in Criminal Careers." *British Journal of Criminology* 29:317–335.

Staples, Robert. 1981. *The World of Black Singles.* Westport, CN: Greenwood Press.

Stark, Rodney. 1979. "Whose Status Counts?" *American Sociological Review* 44:668–669.

Stead, Philip John. 1983. *The Police of France.* New York: Macmillan.

Steffensmeier, Darrell. 1980. "Sex Differences in Patterns of Adult Crimes, 1965–77: A Review and Assessment." *Social Forces* 58:1080–1108.

Stephan, G.E. and D.R. McMullin. 1982. "Tolerance of Sexual Non Conformity: City Size as a Situational and Early Learning Determinant." *American Sociological Review* 47:411–15.

Stewart, Jon. 1984. *Understanding Econometrics.* London: Hutchinson.

Stinchcombe, Arthur L. 1963. "Institutions of Privacy in the Determination of Police Administrative Practice." *American Journal of Sociology* 69:150–60.

Stone, Lawrence. 1967. *The Crisis of the Aristocracy, 1558–1641.* Abridged Education. London: Oxford University Press.

———. 1969. "Literacy and Education in England, 1640–1900." *Past and Present* 42:69–139.

———. 1977. *The Family, Sex and Marriage in England, 1500–1800.* New York: Harper & Row.

———. 1983. "Interpersonal Violence in English Society, 1300–1980." *Past and Present* 101:22–33.

Sullivan, Mercer L. 1989. "*Getting Paid: Youth Crime and Work in the Inner City.*" Ithaca, NY: Cornell University Press.

Sutherland, Edwin. 1937. *The Professional Thief.* Chicago: University of Chicago Press.

———. 1949. *White Collar Crime.* New York: Dryden.

Sutherland, Edwin, and Donald Cressey. 1978. *Principles of Criminology.* Philadelphia: Lippincott.

Suttles, Gerald D. 1968. *The Social Order of the Slum: Ethnicity and Territory in the Inner City.* Chicago: University of Chicago Press.

———. 1972. *The Social Construction of Communities.* Chicago: University of Chicago Press.

Sykes, Gresham, and David Matza. 1957. "Techniques of Neutralization: A Theory of Delinquency." *American Sociological Review* 22:664–670.

———. 1961. "Juvenile Delinquency and Subterranean Values." *American Sociological Review* 26:712–19.

Tanner, Julian. 1988. "Youthful Deviance." In Vincent Sacco (ed.), *Deviance: Conformity and Control in Canadian Society*, 323–359. Scarborough: Prentice-Hall.

Tanner, Julian, and Harvey Krahn. 1991. "Part-Time Work and Deviance Among High School Seniors." *Canadian Journal of Sociology* 16:281–302.

Taylor, D. Garth. 1983. "Analyzing Qualitative Data." 547–612 in *Handbook of Survey Research*, Peter Rossi, James Wright, and Andy Anderson (eds.). New York: Academic Press.

Taylor, Ian R., Paul Walton, and Jack Young. 1973. *The New Criminology: For a Social Theory of Deviance*. London: Routledge and Kegan Paul.

Thompson, Hunter. 1967. *Hell's Angels*. New York: Ballantine.

Thornberry, Terrence P., and R.L. Christenson. 1984. "Unemployment and Criminal Involvement: An Investigation of Reciprocal Causal Structures." *American Sociological Review* 49(3): 398–411.

Thrasher, Frederick M. 1927. *The Gang*. Chicago: University of Chicago Press.

Tilly, Charles. 1985. "Warmaking and Statemaking as Organized Crime." In Peter Evans, D. Rueschemeyer, T. Skocpol (eds.), *Bringing the State Back In*. Cambridge, MA: Cambridge University Press.

———. 1986. *The Contentious French*. Cambridge, MA: Belknap.

———. 1987. *How War Made States and Vice Versa*. CSSC Working Paper No. 42, Center for Studies of Social Change, New School of Social Research, New York.

———. 1990. *Coercion, Capital, and European States, A.D. 990–1990*. New York: Basil Blackwell.

Tilly, C., A. Levett, A.Q. Lodhi, and F. Menger. 1975. *How Policing Affected the Visibility of Crime in Nineteenth-Century Europe and America*. CRSO Working Paper No. 115, Center for Research on Social Organization, University of Michigan, Ann Arbor.

Tittle, Charles R. 1969. "Crime Rates and Legal Sanctions." *Social Problems* 16(Spring): 409–423.

———. 1980. *Sanctions and Social Deviance: The Question of Deterrence*. New York: Praeger.

———. 1989. "Urbaneness and Unconventional Behavior: A Partial Test of Claude Fischer's Subcultural Theory." *Criminology* 27:273–306.

Tittle, Charles R., and Robert Meier. 1990. "Specifying the SES/Delinquency Relationship." *Criminology* 28:271–99.

Tittle, Charles R., Wayne J. Villemez, and Douglas A. Smith. 1977. "The Myth of Social Class and Criminality: An Empirical Assessment of the Empirical Evidence." *American Sociological Review* 43:643–656.

Toby, Jackson. 1950. "Comment on the Jonassen-Shaw and McKay Controversy." *American Sociological Review* 15:107–108.

Todd, Emmanuel, and Hervi Le Bras. 1981. *L'Invention de la France: Atlas Anthropologique et Politique*. Paris: Livre de Poche.

Tombs, Robert. 1980. "Crime and the Security of the State: The 'Dangerous Classes' and the Insurrection in Nineteenth-Century Paris." In V.A.C. Gartrell, Bruce Lenman and Geoffrey Noel Parker (eds.), *Crime and the Law: The Social History of Crime in Western Europe since 1500*, 214–37. London: Europa Publications.

Tönnies, Ferdinand. (1887) 1957. *Community and Society*. New York: Harper Torch.

Tonry, Michael, and James Q. Wilson. 1990. *Drugs and Crime*. Chicago: University of Chicago Press.

Tuch, Steven A. 1987. "Urbanism, Region and Tolerance Revisited: The Case of Racial Prejudice." *American Sociological Review* 52:504–510.

Tufte, Edward R. 1983. *The Visual Display of Quantitative Information.* Cheshire, CN: Graphics Press.

Turk, Austin. 1969. *Criminality and the Legal Order.* Chicago: Rand McNally.

———. 1982. *Political Criminality: The Defiance and Defence of Authority.* Beverly Hills, CA: Sage.

Valentine, Charles A. 1968. *Culture and Poverty: Critique and Counter Proposals.* Chicago: University of Chicago Press.

Van de Walle, Etienne. 1974. *The Female Population of France in the Nineteenth Century: A Reconstruction of 82 Départments.* Princeton, NJ: Princeton University Press.

Vaz, Edmund. 1965. "Middle Class Adolescents: Self-Reported Delinquency and Youth Culture Activities." *Canadian Review of Sociology and Anthropology* 2(1): 52–70.

Viscusi, W. Kip. 1986. "Market Incentives for Criminal Behavior." In Richard Freeman and Harry Holzer (eds.), *The Black Youth Employment Crisis,* 301–351. Chicago: University of Chicago Press.

Voss, Harwin, and Richard Stephens. 1973. "Criminality History of Narcotic Addicts." *Drug Forum* 2:191–202.

Walker, Henry A., and Bernard P. Cohen. 1985. "Scope Statements: Imperatives for Evaluating Theory." *American Sociological Review.* 50:288–301.

Warr, Mark. 1991. "Public Perceptions of Crime and Punishment." In Joseph Sheley (ed.), *Criminology.* New York: Wadsworth.

Webber, Melvin. 1963. "Order in diversity: Community without propinquity." In Lowdon Wingo, Jr. (ed.), *Cities and Space: The Future Use of Urban Land.* Baltimore, MD: Johns Hopkins University Press.

Weber, Eugen J. 1976. *Peasants into Frenchmen: The Modernization of Rural France, 1870–1914.* Stanford, CA: Stanford University Press.

———. 1986. *France: Fin de Siècle.* Cambridge, MA: Belknap.

———. 1991. *My France: Politics, Culture, Myth.* Cambridge, MA: Belknap Press.

Weber, Max. 1947. *The Theory of Social and Economic Organization.* Glencoe, IL: Free Press.

———. [1904–05] 1958. *The Protestant Ethic and the Spirit of Capitalism.* New York: Charles Scribner's Sons.

———. (1921) 1958. *The City.* Glencoe, IL: Free Press.

———. (1922) 1968. *Economy and Society: An Outline of Interpretive Sociology.* New York: Bedminster Press.

Weis, Joseph G. 1987. "Social Class and Crime." In Michael Gottfredson and Travis (eds.), *Positive Criminology,* 71–90. Newbury Park, CA: Sage.

Wellman, Barry. 1979. "The Community Question: The Intimate Network of East Yorkers." *American Journal of Sociology* 84(5): 201–31.

Welter, Barbara. 1966. "The Cult of True Womanhood, 1820–1860." *American Quarterly* 18:151–74.

Westley, William A., and Frederick Elkin. 1957. "The Protective Environment and Adolescent Socialization." *Social Forces* 35:243–249.

Wheeler, Stanton, and Mitchell Lewis Rothman. 1982. "The Organization as Weapon in White-Collar Crime." *Michigan Law Review* 80(7): 1403–26.

Wheeler, Stanton, David Weisburd, Erin Waring, and Nancy Bode. 1988. "White Collar Crime and Criminals." *American Criminal Law Review* 25:331–357.

White, Helene. 1992. "Early Problem Behavior and Later Drug Problems." *Journal of Research in Crime and Delinquency* 29:412–429.

White, Helene Raskin, Robert Pandina, and Randy LaGrange. 1987. "Longitudinal Predictors of Serious Substance Use and Delinquency." *Criminology* 25:715–740.

White, Morton G. and Lucinda White. 1962. *The Intellectual versus the City.* Cambridge, MA: Harvard University Press.

Whyte, William Foote. 1943. *Street Corner Society: The Social Structure of an Italian Slum* Chicago: University of Chicago Press.

———. 1955. *Street Corner Society.* Chicago: University of Chicago Press.

Wiatrowski, Michael, Stephen Hansell, Charles Massey, and David Wilson. 1982. "Curriculum Tracking and Delinquency." *American Sociological Review* 47:151–160.

Wilbanks, W. 1986. "Criminal Homicide Offenders in the U.S.: Black vs. White." In D. Hawkins, (ed.), *Homicide Among Black Americans*, 43–56. Lanham, MD: University Press of America.

———. 1987. *The Myth of a Racist Criminal Justice System.* Monterey, CA: Brooks/Cole.

Wilson, James Q. 1968. *Varieties of Police Behavior.* Cambridge: Harvard University Press.

Wilson, James Q., and Richard J. Herrnstein. 1985. *Crime and Human Nature.* New York: Simon and Schuster.

Wilson, T.C. 1985. "Urbanism and Tolerance: A Test of Some Hypotheses Drawn from Wirth and Stouffer." *American Sociological Review* 50(1): 117–23.

Wilson, William J. 1968. *Varieties of Police Behavior.* Cambridge: Harvard University Press.

———. 1978. *The Declining Significance of Race.* Chicago: University of Chicago Press.

———. 1987. *The Truly Disadvantaged: The Inner City, the Underclass, and Public Policy.* Chicago: University of Chicago Press.

———. 1991. "Studying Inner-City Social Dislocations: The Challenge of Public Agenda Research." *American Sociological Review* 56:1–14.

Wirth, Louis. 1938. "Urbanism as a Way of Life." *American Journal of Sociology* 44:3–24.

Wolfgang, Marvin. 1958. *Patterns in Criminal Homicide.* Philadelphia: University of Pennsylvania Press.

Wolfgang, Marvin, and Franco Ferracuti. 1967. *The Subculture of Violence.* London: Tavistock.

———. 1982. *The Subculture of Violence.* Beverly Hills CA: Sage.

Wolfgang, Marvin, Robert Figlio, and Thorsten Sellin. 1972. *Delinquency in a Birth Cohort.* Chicago: University of Chicago Press.

Wright, Erik Olin. 1985. *Classes.* London: Verso.

Wright, Gordon. 1981. *France in Modern Times* (3rd ed.). New York: W.W. Norton.

———. 1983. *Between the Guillotine and Liberty: Two Centuries of the Crime Problem in France.* New York: Oxford University Press.

Wrong, Dennis H. 1961. "The Oversocialized Conception of Man in Modern Sociology." *American Sociological Review* 26:183–193.

———. 1994. *The Problem of Order.* New York: The Free Press.

Yablonsky, Lewis. 1959. "The Delinquent Gang as a Near Group." *Social Problems* 7:108–117.

Yamaguchi, Kazuo, and Denise Kandel. 1984. "Patterns of Drug Use from Adolescence to Young Adulthood. 3. Predictors of Progression." *American Journal of Public Health* 74:673–681.

Yinger, J. Milton. 1960. "Contraculture and Subculture." *American Sociological Review* 25:625–635.

Zatz, Marjorie. 1987. "The Changing Forms of Racial/Ethnic Biases in Sentencing." *Journal of Research in Crime and Delinquency* 24:69–92.

Zatz, Marjorie, and John Hagan. 1984. "Crime, Time and Punishment." In James Fox (ed.), *Criminological Research*. New York: Plenum.

Zehr, Howard. 1975. "The Modernization of Crime in Germany and France, 1830–1913." *Journal of Social History* 8:117–141.

Zinsser, Hans. 1963. *Rats, Lice, and History.* Boston: Little Brown.

About the Book and Authors

A lucid text addressed to students and scholars, this book explores some of the key controversies that have stimulated the scientific study of crime: disputes about the connections between gender, class, and crime; policing; the criminality of our cities; the role of subcultures in causing crime; and links between drugs and crime.

In pursuing the resolution of key controversies surrounding these and other issues, the authors introduce students to the fundamental methods of research and analysis. The book matches the methods of the field with important theoretical and empirical issues, providing students with a direct experience in criminological research and conveying the process and excitement of generating satisfying insights into important questions about crime.

John Hagan, professor of sociology and law at the University of North Carolina at Chapel Hill and at the University of Toronto, is the author of *Structural Criminology.* **A. R. Gillis** and **David Brownfield** hold appointments in the Sociology Department at the University of Toronto.

Index

Gratification delay, 106, 156
Guttman scaling, 142–143, 144

Hamlet (Shakespeare), 48–49
Hedonism, 112
Hell's Angels, 99
Henry VII, King, 79
Heroin, 128, 129, 131
Hidden crime, xiv, 84
Hispanics, 11–12, 13
Homicide
  class and, 10, 106–107
  in South, 110–111, 162–163
Human capital, 54–55, 74, 100

Image analysis, 143
Imprisonment, xv, 129–130
Independent variables
  in gender-crime connection, 17,
    18–19, 26–28, 29–34
  in policing-crime connection, 75,
    85, 88–89, 91
  in urbanization-crime connection,
    49, 59, 64, 65
Index of Southerness, 111
Indirect effects, of gender, 29, 32–33,
    42
Individualistic fallacy, 10, 15
Industrialization, 63
  crime opportunities produced by,
    95
  factors associated with, 59, 68–69
  gender roles and, 35–36
Instrumental attitudes, 104, 121, 146
Instrumental controls, 24, 40–42, 44
Interaction effects, 34–37, 40, 46
Interaction terms, 38–40
Intercept, 26, 62
Internal locus of control, 111
Intervening variables
  in gender-crime connection, 19,
    34, 46
  in policing-crime connection, 75,
    82
  in urbanization-crime connection,
    72

Justice de paix, 58

Labeling theory, 164
Latent structure analysis, 121,
    139–156, 164
  description of latent variable in,
    150–153
  external validity of latent variable
    in, 153–154
  three-class model in, 149–153
  two-class model in, 149
Latent variable analysis, 125, 131,
    139–156, 164. *See also* Latent
    structure analysis
  of offense specialization, 145–146
  previous applications of, 141–145
Law, origins of, 108
Line of least squares, 62–63
LISREL, 40–42, 144
Local independence, 140
London, 8
Longitudinal research
  on drug-crime connection, 132,
    133
  on policing-crime connection, 77
  on urbanization-crime connec-
    tion, 58
Los Angeles, California, 13, 14

McKay, Henry D., 47, 51
Macro-level research, 9–10, 14, 15
Major crimes
  policing and, 84–85, 86, 88, 90–93,
    94–95, 96
  urbanization and, 58–59, 60–61, 63,
    65–66, 67 (table), 69–70, 73
Maréchaussée, 87
Marijuana, 128, 129, 130, 131,
    132–133, 141
Marx, Karl, 76
Marxist theory, 83, 108
Materialism, gender and, 119
Maternal supervision, 17–24, 25,
    120–122, 158
  instrumental controls in, 24, 40–42,
    44
  in path analysis, 29–34
  relational controls in, 24, 44
  smoking and, 40–42
Medieval times. *See* Middle Ages